C. J. Shorrock
Parkwood Hospital
London.
July 18ᵗ 1979.

For Christopher my very
best wishes and hope
that Geriatrics will
continue to be a
rewarding interest for you

Ronald Cape

AGING:
ITS COMPLEX
MANAGEMENT

Stone figures in the Vigeland Sculpture Grounds, Frogner Park, Oslo, Norway

AGING: ITS COMPLEX MANAGEMENT

Ronald Cape

M.D., F.R.C.P. (Edin.), F.R.C.P. (Can.), F.A.C.P. Professor and Co-ordinator of Geriatric Medicine, Department of Medicine, University of Western Ontario, London, Ontario, Canada

Medical Department
Harper & Row, Publishers
Hagerstown, Maryland
New York, San Francisco, London

The author and publisher have exerted every effort to ensure that drug selection and dosage set forth in this text are in accord with current recommendations and practice at the time of publication. However, in view of ongoing research, changes in government regulations, and the constant flow of information relating to drug therapy and drug reactions, the reader is urged to check the package insert for each drug for any change in indications and dosage and for added warnings and precautions. This is particularly important when the recommended agent is a new and/or infrequently employed drug.

78 79 80 81 82 83   10 9 8 7 6 5 4 3 2 1

Library of Congress Cataloging in Publication Data

Cape, Ronald, 1921–
  Aging : its complex
management.

  Bibliography: p.
  Includes index.
  I. Geriatrics. 2. Aging. I.
Title. [DNLM: 1. Aging. 2.
Geriatrics. WT104.3 C237a]
RC952.C358   618.9'7
    78–15548
ISBN 0–06–140622–8

CONTENTS

PREFACE

I came to Canada in June, 1975, and was warmly welcomed by the President of the Medical Staff of the Continuing Care Hospital with which I was to be associated. I was, however, caught off-balance when he asked "By the way, what sort of case do I send to a geriatrician?" In England, the geriatrician is a well-established member of the hospital team and I had never fielded such a question. The query deserved a fuller answer than the one I was able to give at the time. Now, inter alia, I can provide a more detailed reply.

This book represents one man's attempt to focus attention on the clinical problems peculiar to the very old: it is intended as a clinical guide to the internal medicine of old age, and to delineate a coherent, unique area of knowledge and expertise which can be recognized as geriatric medicine. It is hoped that it will be useful to internists and family physicians in their daily practice, valuable to medical students in providing a basis for understanding the development of senescent changes and the clinical syndromes of old age, and a reference book in continuing care institutions.

Certain diseases which occur frequently in the elderly (such as diabetes mellitus or arteriosclerotic heart disease) illustrate obvious links between morbidity and advancing age. Endocrinologists and cardiologists have, therefore, developed their own particular interest in geriatric medicine (2) and those in other specialties have followed suit. But these specialized approaches have increased fragmentation of care for persons whose greatest need is for whole-person medicine.

There are certain problems that specially pertain to elderly patients but which do not fall neatly into one specialist area; at times these stray beyond the normal field of the internist into that of psychiatry and surgery. The early studies of large samples of old people (3, 5) emphasized this. My own experience (Tables 4–2 and 4–3) serves as an example. Such common disorders as loss of mobility, confusion, and incontinence pose diagnostic, therapeutic, and continuing-care problems and represent a large part of the geriatricians's clinical load. It seems to me that there must be a unifying element in the syndromes of extreme old age. If there is, it would be logical to look for it in the physical changes associated with aging and in the steadily advancing associated field of biologic gerontology. The crucial role of cerebral function stands out again and again, and the more that knowledge accumulates, the truer seems the probability that the time-clock of aging is linked to the neuroendocrine center of operations in the brain. Concentrating effort in this direction has meant discarding discussions of psychiatric, psychologic, and sociologic matters of great importance and relevance to the elderly. As a physician, I can only refer the reader to the works of others such as Post (3), Bromley (1) or Shanas (4).

In the opening chapters, aging changes and gerontologic knowledge are briefly described; this is a prelude to the more detailed comment presented in the chapters on "cerebral function as we grow older." This sequence provides the scientific base for a close examination of the interrelated complex of syndromes characteristic of the senescent years. As in all fields of internal medicine, the management of the complex depends on thoughtful systematic diagnosis and discriminating therapeutics.

I would be the first to agree that this book is only a modest beginning to a major task. I hope, however, that it will stimulate others to push forward to new and exciting knowledge that will help us to reduce morbidity and increase the independence of the elderly.

Ronald Cape
London, Ontario
1978

REFERENCES

1. Bromley D: The Psychology of Human Ageing. Middlesex, Penguin Books Ltd, 1974
2. Harris R: The Management of Geriatric Cardiovascular Disease. Philadelphia, Lippincott, 1970
3. Post F: The Clinical Psychiatry of Late Life. London, Pergamon Press, 1965
4. Shanas E: The Health of Older People: A Social Survey, Cambridge (MA), Harvard University Press, 1962
5. Sheldon JH: The Social Medicine of Old Age. London, Oxford University Press, 1948

ACKNOWLEDGMENTS

The experience which is distilled in this book has been gained from association with many people. I acknowledge my debt to medical and nursing colleagues at Selly Oak, Sheldon and Moseley Hall Hospitals in Birmingham, England, and at Parkwood and Victoria Hospitals in London, Ontario. Particular thanks are due to my elderly patients in both countries for teaching me so much.

My sincere thanks to Harper and Row for publishing the book, and particularly to those members of their staff who aided, prompted, and suffered my inadequacies throughout. I am very grateful to Ron Foster, who devoted much time and care to drawing and redrawing the diagrams, and to Peter Martin who not only completed the laborious task of typing and retyping the manuscript but spent many hours checking references. Philip Henschke and Bob Tripp read the proofs; Pat Cape found quotations, read and reread, listened, discussed, and cheerfully accepted a spouseless social life while maintaining contact with our friends.

Ronald Cape
London, 1978

AGING:
ITS COMPLEX
MANAGEMENT

Chapter 1

STRICKEN IN YEARS

BEAUTIFUL OLD AGE

It ought to be lovely to be old
to be full of peace that comes of experience
and wrinkled ripe fulfilment.

The wrinkled smile of completeness that follows a life
lived undaunted and unsoured with accepted lies.
If people lived without accepting lies
they would ripen like apples, and be scented like pippins
in their old age.

Soothing, old people should be, like apples
when one is tired of love.
Fragrant like yellow leaves, and dim with the soft
stillness and satisfaction of autumn.

And a girl should say:
It must be wonderful to live and grow old
Look at my mother, how rich and still she is!

And a young man should think: By Jove
my father has faced all weathers, but it's been a life!

D. H. Lawrence

BEING OLD

There is little glamour or excitement associated with being old; the popular concept is of physical and mental disabilities and a struggle to maintain independence and self-reliance to the end. This view is based partly on observation of the elderly among us and partly on our literary heritage. Cicero (4) offered four reasons why old age was regarded in his day as an unhappy time. "First, because it takes us away from active work; secondly, because it weakens the body; thirdly, because it deprives us of practically all physical pleasures and, fourthly, because it is not far from death." He expressed the view that "age has to be fought against." His advice for a "fixed regime" was good: "exercise in moderation, enough food and drink to strengthen, yet not enough to overburden." Shakespeare's (9) sixth and seventh ages, which end up in "second childishness and mere oblivion, sans teeth, sans eyes, sans taste, sans everything," maintain the gloomy picture. In the twentieth century, Dylan Thomas echoes the Ciceronian sentiments of struggling against senescence.

Do not go gentle into that good night,
Old age should burn and rave at close of day;
Rage, rage against the dying of the light.

Curiously, the one civilization to adopt a different attitude has been that of China, perhaps the most ancient of all. Lin Yutang (12) commented in 1939 that Eastern and Western cultures, although having much in common, differed in their attitude to age. "In China," he stated, "the first question a person asks the other on an official call, after the name and surname, is what is your glorious age?" To the young person, the response is "you have still a glorious future"; to the old, the response is more enthusiastic and reverent. Whether this attitude is maintained in modern China, I have been unable to discover.

Human nature has a penchant for excluding unpleasant things, and for this reason old age is something which tends to be discussed briefly as a problem best put on one side. Death is even more unmentionable, the final obscenity.

FACING FACTS

Old age and death, however, are inevitable parts of life. One worrying feature of our time is that many people refuse to believe that they will grow old and die. Women begin in middle age disguising their appearance trying to make themselves look younger, often going to extremes. Every woman in her 50s should do her best to look as attractive as ever she did—and many will and do look splendid—but they should not, perhaps, go to the lengths of surgery in an effort to disguise age. They would do better to stand before the looking glass and say "these lines are my legend," realizing that the lines make them, in reality, much more interesting people.

Our modern environment does not encourage us to face facts. We are surrounded by image creators of all kinds, politicians, public relations experts, advertisers and salesmen, who do not wish us to look at the truth but only at their version of it. We are encouraged to keep up appearances at all costs, and the mass media are highly developed technical aids for the image makers. Advertisers concentrate their efforts on the young and mature (up to age 40) rather than the old because of commercial market needs. To them the old have little appeal, but to the politician aware that the old constitute a fast growing group, they are important. The Canadian Conference on Aging held in Toronto in 1966 and the National Institute of Aging founded in 1976 in the United States are responses to this awareness.

ELDERLY POPULATION EXPLOSION

It is well known that both the absolute number of individuals over the age of 65 and the proportion of the total population which they represent has increased dramatically in recent decades. In England and Wales, between 1931 and 1971, the elderly (aged 65 and over) doubled their number from about 3 million to well over 6 million, and the very old (aged 75 and over) have trebled, from 800,000 to 2,400,000. During this 40-year span, the total population of the area to which these figures apply rose by one-fifth—from 40 million in 1931 to 48.6 million in 1971. This means that the proportion of elderly persons in the community increased from 7.5% to 11.7%. One hundred years ago, there were 22.7 million inhabitants in England and Wales, and only 1.1 million were old, less than 5% of the whole. A similar statistical picture has developed in all the old Western democracies of Europe.

In the New World, there is a difference. Taking Canada in 1973 (11) as the prototype, the proportion of the old is less, 8.3%. This must be due, at least partly, to an immigration policy which allowed an average of 126,422 between 1920–1929, 25,206 between 1930–1939 and an average of 149,000 per year since 1945. Over 4 million immigrants, the great majority of whom would be young, will maintain the proportion of old people in the country at a lower level than it would have been without immigration. The same factor of immigration will affect other countries with similar policies such as Australia, New Zealand, and the United States. If the proportions of elderly in the population are not as high in these countries as in Europe, the actual numbers of the old and, particularly, the very old will increase substantially as time goes by.

In many countries, a whole new industry has grown up over the past 25 years to provide residential accommodation, home help, meals on wheels, and a wide variety of other services to sustain this potentially dependent group. Welfare programs have swung, a little unevenly perhaps, into action. No one must be allowed to live in squalor or need. More institutional beds and more community services are being set up. Volunteer workers are encouraged to join in and help the professionals. The old are, to some extent, being cosseted as never before and are, at times, smothered by advice and help. Is this, however, what individual old people want? Margery Fry (8), at the age of 80, said to the International Association of Gerontology in 1954: "There is no one point upon which stress needs to be more constantly laid than this, that the external stigmata of old age must not be allowed to obscure lasting divergences of character: individuality must be respected." Overzealous health and social workers can destroy individuality very quickly! We should ask ourselves not how can we cope with the problem of all these old things about the place but what do old people want? What do we look forward to in our own old age? Let's face it—everyone grows old!

Why is a negative attitude toward old age so prevalent? No one complains about a granny who babysits for nothing or shops or cooks or even does all three. When she falls ill and becomes less able to contribute her efforts to the family routine, however, the situation begins to change. It is not old age, *per se,* that evokes unfortunate images but rather the disabilities with which it is associated. The breakdown in health is the critical happening.

BALANCE OF HEALTH AND ENVIRONMENT

Health is difficult to define in precise terms. When the sun shines, you have money in your pocket, you're young and fancy-free, and you feel marvelous, you exude confidence in yourself and the environment—this is good health! We've all felt that—at times. Equally, there are gray days towards the end of the week or month when you've quarreled with your spouse and your boss is unreasonable, when you have a puncture in a blizzard or run out of gas miles from a service station. Perhaps Verwoerdt (10) has the best definition of health when he describes the healthy person as one who is able to cope with any stress life has to offer. A state of well-being is not synonymous with health, but the healthy person enjoys the sense of well-being while it lasts and rides the stresses with determination and confidence. Morbidity develops when the individual's coping mechanism breaks down either from pure physical assault, such as in an acute bacterial infection, or from a combination of factors, such as in a coronary thrombosis. The effect of the former depends on the strength of the individual's resistance on the one hand and the virulence of the infection on the other. The individual and the environment are both involved. Similarly, factors causing coronary thrombosis arise in both the individual and the environment. It follows that by altering the environment we may be able to modify morbidity.

There is good evidence to support this suggestion; look again at the example of coronary thrombosis. The overweight tycoon who is driven from high pressure conference to business lunch and back again, who takes a few Kissinger-type jet trips, who puffs cigarettes incessantly, whose exercise is limited to feverish bursts of extravagant activity on the squash court, whose whole life-style is an endless saga of frantic competition, will almost certainly succumb to a myocardial infarction in his 40s or 50s. If we transformed his environment by removing the Cadillac, placing his house 1 mile from the factory, persuading him to walk to and from it daily and throw away his cigarettes, his life expectancy would be greatly increased.

There is a third factor in this hypothetical equation of morbidity and health, and that is what Verwoerdt calls ego, the driving force or personality of the individual. It is a common experience for a geriatrician to see old folk with no apparent mortal disease quietly but firmly turning their faces to the wall and dying; equally, we note the reverse when an individual with severe loss of brain tissue from a stroke or suffering from a fulminating pneumonia achieves an almost miraculous return to independence.

The state of health can thus be imagined as a set of scales with the person on one side and the environment on the other (Fig. 1–1). Stresses from physical or mental illness may cause tilting downwards on the person side, which may be corrected by a change in environment, *e.g.,* removal to a hospital. In the young person environmental deficiencies can be compensated by the presence of great

Fig. 1–1. State of health scales.

reserves of function, the whole controlled by the personality bestride the scales, the ego. These rather fanciful life scales are my interpretation of Verwoerdt's concept of dynamic equilibrium. They emphasize the need to look at the whole life of the individual and not solely at parts of it.

Can the effect of aging be represented on the life scales? Yes. The main characteristics of biologic aging are loss of nonmitotic or irreproducible cells on the one hand and of reserve function on the other. The behavior of striated or voluntary muscle illustrates the former situation. Man reaches his full size and strength about the middle 20s; allowing for individual variations due to lifestyle, environment, and heredity, most people maintain their muscle bulk and strength until the end of the fifth decade—and some for a good deal longer. In the sixth and later decades, however, there is a slow weakening process coinciding with the remorseless fall-out of muscle cells which are never replaced (see Ch. 2, Physical Aspects of Aging). There is a similar cell loss from the brain and, as with muscle, this loss in the sixth and later decades can result in reduced muscular dexterity, impaired sensory capability, and a tendency for thinking processes to become more rigid. This pattern of reduced reserves is repeated in most systems of the body. When one adds to these changes in physiology the increasing frequency of degenerative and other diseases, it is easy to appreciate what a strain the ego comes under to maintain the balance in the hypothetical life scales.

One can postulate, however, that constantly adapting and improving the environment might greatly reduce the effect of these aging and morbid changes. Indeed, if we could anticipate an ordered sequence of events, with muscle power reducing in the 50s and 60s, the cardiorespiratory reserve diminishing in the 60s and 70s, and the brain giving up thereafter, we might be able to plan the environment successfully. Of course, as is well known, things don't happen like that. While most people will move into old age with little morbidity and reasonably maintained function, others will be old before they realize it—and it will be too late to plan the environment satisfactorily. Because of the tendency of morbidity to interpose itself suddenly on the aging person, it is prudent to plan the environment before old age is reached.

The environment means more than the house in which the old person lives. While this is important, even more so are the personal contacts which the environment allows people to maintain. In a study of 1000 cases (3) referred consecutively to a geriatric department some years ago, the number of people available to help the ill old person was more important than the physical condition of the house. It was immaterial whether the helpers were relatives, neighbors, or home helps. This is a fact to bear in mind when planning a retirement home. An individual who does not want to live with relatives, although at times that may be inevitable, should continue in an area where he has plenty of friends and relatives. Just by being there they will give the individual confidence to continue to cope with life's stresses.

One cannot, however, be dogmatic, and the one essential in providing care for the old is flexibility. In Southern California, the enormous urban sprawl interlaced with five or six lane freeways which is Los Angeles and its satellite townships seems an impossible environment in which to be old. Human beings are adaptable, and in the massive parking lots of shopping centers one often sees a large automobile slide into a space and a fragile looking octogenarian emerge to do her shopping! For the well-to-do elderly Californian, there is always Palm Springs, where expensive suburbs have been created with every conceivable leisure activity and where for perhaps 8 months of the year the climate is ideally warm and dry. While the prospect of such a golden end to life may not appeal to everyone, for some it is perfect. The petty jealousies and continuing competitiveness of leisure activities may give an added spice to life.

Aging and morbidity may erode the old person's ability to cope with stress —by reducing mobility, impairing cardiorespiratory reserve, and clouding cerebral function. Adjustments to the environment can assist old people to maintain their independence by 1) easing physical problems through such measures as living on one level, easy on–off central heating, all types of electric power switches at waist height and so on, and 2) keeping the individual geographically placed among well-known neighbors, friends, or relatives who can provide emotional, moral, and, occasionally, physical support.

Because one cannot, in the majority of cases, anticipate when morbidity may strike, it is important to plan ahead to achieve the optimum environment for old age. For this to be possible, a wide ranging educational effort is required; society must consciously adopt a new and much more positive approach to old age as a time of life when increased leisure and an ability to do what you want where and when you want to can outweigh its too readily accepted and overemphasized physical disabilities.

If it is true that adapting and planning the environment can reduce the effects of morbidity, it is equally true that a sudden change in the environment can precipitate trouble. Removing an elderly person from home to hospital is often not the panacea it seems to be to the worn out relatives who have been providing care at home. Even if it does not prove to be the last straw which precipitates death, it will take time for the old person to accept and cooperate in the new scheme of things. Sudden loss of a spouse, near relative, or even a faithful neighbor or friend can similarly destroy the fragile structure of the old person's domestic support, and morbidity may quickly follow.

GERONTOLOGY AND GERIATRICS

Gerontology is the current game; the old, our current paranoia. There is a steadily increasing tendency to philosophize, dogmatize, verbalize, and semanticize over the unfortunate side issues inevitably thrown up by the dominance of sociologic aberrations in old age. These side issues have spawned a myriad of fascinating interwoven experimental facts sufficient to perpetuate this type of parasense indefinitely [with acknowledgments to Cameron of St. Michael's College in Toronto who fears today's students are slipping into a fate worse than illiteracy, a habit of talking an unintelligible polysyllabic jargon borrowed from the social "sciences" and the shallower forms of mysticism (7)].

Gerontology is derived from the Greek word *geron,* an old man, and the word means the study of aging. The true gerontologist is a research worker concentrating on particular aspects of the process of senescence. A physician who practices geriatric medicine is a geriatrician, from the Greek *geras,* old age, and *iatros,* physician (5).

We grow old for the good of the species. We each have a tiny piece of immortality in our germ cells encased in the soma, which is the rest of our bodies. The soma has its built-in obsolescence. Why? Because evolutionary processes need the chance of slowly, but surely, modifying and improving the race's ability to fend for itself. These are the harsh facts of biologic gerontology. Bullough (2) has suggested that it is like mass production. In order to stimulate sales and survive in business, manufacturers make minor modifications to titillate the fancy of the consumer. But to allow new generations of cars to be produced, all current models must have their built-in obsolescence—and after a very few years, the paint flakes and the doors fall off and we queue up for a Mark 2 or 3 or 4.

Aging means

to grow old, to develop the characteristics of old age . . . to retreat from a more developed complex or more fully grown state, to degenerate, to regress . . . to diminish, to become depleted, to become less available . . . to retreat, to become closed in, restricted, tied down . . . to become degraded or decayed.

Aging is not, according to Bromley (1) who wrote that definition, an extension of child development. That is a carefully programmed, genetically regulated, unidirectional process. Aging is a multidirectional, unprogrammed, disorderly process of deterioration.

EARLY EXPERIENCE

There have been old people in the world for a very long time. If we accept Biblical evidence of the ages of Abraham, Isaac, and their contemporaries, individuals lived for hundreds of years! No doubt the original authors of the more legendary portions of the Old Testament had a different idea of time from the one we have. It is interesting, however, to compare the attitudes of various civilizations to their elderly. The earliest historical note I have found is in Madame Christiane Desroches–Noblecourt's book on Tutankhamen (6). In describing the celebration of the jubilee of King Amenophis III in 1375 B.C. she refers to the barbaric ritual murders of the chieftains of prehistoric Egypt on the approach of senility.

The Greeks adopted a somewhat more humane attitude to their old people. In general they evolved the theory that in aging the heat of the body became exhausted. Hippocrates believed that a spare diet and exercise were the main factors leading to a long and healthy life. He lived some 2400 years ago, and yet he was able to describe a catalog of geriatric conditions—cataracts, dimness of vision, glaucoma, deafness, neuritis, pains of the joints, vertigo, cachexia, apoplexy, generalized pruritus, and what he called insomnolency. By modern standards this is still a good list and suggests that many diseases at this age affect the special senses, the central nervous and locomotor systems.

Six hundred years before Hippocrates, we read of geriatric treatment administered to King David.

Now King David was old and stricken in years; and they covered him with clothes, but he gat no heat. Wherefore his servants said unto him, let there be sought for my Lord the King a young virgin: and let her stand before the King and let her cherish him, and let her lie in thy bosom, that my Lord the King may get heat. So they sought for a fair damsel throughout all the coasts of Israel, and found Abishag a Shunammite, and brought her to the King. And the damsel was very fair, and cherished the King, and ministered to him: but the King knew her not.

Geriatric medicine is not new but has a long and interesting background.

EXPLAINING THE POPULATION EXPLOSION

If a number of lay people were invited to explain why there are more old people today, it is likely that most would attribute the change to advances in medicine.

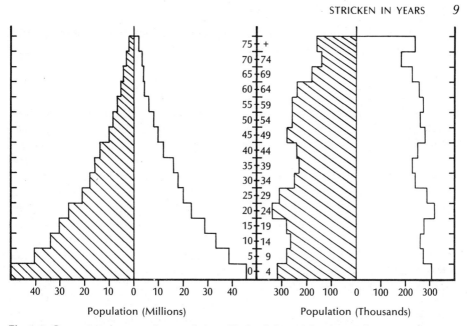

Fig. 1–2. Comparison between the population of India (**left**) and Sweden (**right**) in 1970. (Leaf A:
Getting old. Copyright © 1973 by Scientific American, Inc. All rights reserved)

They would be thinking that, because of new medical discoveries, physicians
are able to treat and cure many of the conditions which formerly kept individuals from reaching old age. This view is largely untrue; the major factor
responsible for the larger number of elderly has been the prevention of such
conditions. For example, improved hygiene and environment are due to public health services which, capitalizing on the discovery of the causes of infections and the methods by which they spread, instituted preventive programs. These have been of greater significance than improvements in the
treatment of such illnesses.

The direct result of the dramatic fall in infant mortality in the early decades
of this century was a rise in the life expectancy of the newborn infant. This
increased from 50 in 1900 to 67 in 1971 (males) and from 52 to 74 (females)
during the same period. The change in population structure which followed
became evident in the 1930s and 1940s with the apex of the population pyramid
broadening out in many countries. If one compares a country such as India,
which has extremely high birth and infant mortality rates, to a country such as
Sweden, which has extremely low birth and infant mortality rates, one can see
the completely different population structure that results (Fig. 1–2).

The Indian type pyramid was universal until the twentieth century. Today
every nation is developing the Swedish pattern, some much faster than others.
Countries to which a flow of young immigrants continues will not have such
a high proportion of elderly in the community. Considerable economic and
social strains build up with increasing numbers of old people because, although

many retain independence and vigor, a proportion, which slowly increases with age, will become unable to look after themselves.

BRITISH EXPERIENCE

In Britain, because of the Poor Law Amendment Act of 1834, many of the more helpless elderly found their way into Poor Law Institution Infirmaries. The principle of the Act was that the able-bodied poor were to be given accommodation in a workhouse under conditions inferior to those of the humblest laborer outside. The Commissioners responsible for supervising the implementation of the act did not intend that the elderly should suffer and condemned workhouses which mixed the elderly with others, preferring special institutions for the old. Most local Boards of Guardians, which were elected annually by the ratepayers of each parish, districts designated for the administration of the Poor Law, were too small, however, to allow separate homes for the aged to be erected, and thus a mixed pattern of residents developed throughout the country. The old, sick, mentally defective, able-bodied destitute, and even children were housed together.

The Act was successful in reducing obvious poverty from communities largely by sweeping it into corners out of sight, but it also created during the Victorian era an enormous dread and hatred of the workhouse. It was not until 1929 that a major change took place by the passing of the Local Government Act. Boards of Guardians were abolished and their duties taken over by County and County Borough Councils who were elected by the voters of a larger but still local community. Poor relief was renamed Public Assistance and was administered by Special Public Assistance Committees of the Councils. The most modern and best equipped buildings became municipal general hospitals, while many of the older and less suitable were used to house large numbers of the elderly and the chronically sick.

It was in the middle and late 1930s in this highly unsuitable environment that the pioneers of geriatric medicine began to create a new approach to illness in the elderly. Bred by necessity out of Poor Law Institution and foaled in Britain, geriatrics developed slowly. After years of being neglected and even derided by the medical profession, it finally established itself as a relevant specialty in the National Health Service. Other countries, without the numerous Poor Law Infirmaries of Britain, have been slower to develop the subject.

MEDICAL PROFESSION AND AGING

The general concensus of the world medical profession remains uncertain about the need for specialists in the clinical medicine of old age, and it is of interest to examine the reasons for this attitude. In the first place, it goes almost without saying that caring for old folk at the end of their lives offers a lower ratio of complete cures than the one which can be achieved with younger patients. Many of the purely medical problems of old age are aggravated by social difficulties with which the good practitioner must involve himself, and the major clinical features tend to be unattractive and difficult to elucidate. It is, therefore, understandable that members of the profession have not been eager to train in geriatrics. The impartial lay observer might be forgiven for raising an eyebrow at this. Are not these "unattractive" patients nonetheless entitled to good doctoring? If individuals are offered a long and expensive education by the community to become medical men or women, should they not provide a full service for all the people?

A second reason for the physicians' attitude stems from this long training itself. During the past two or three decades, great emphasis has been placed on an increasingly scientific approach to medicine. During lengthy studies of anatomy, physiology, biochemistry, pathology, and all the clinical subjects, the student associates the acme of medicine with difficult diagnostic problems and the skillful use of sophisticated laboratory tests. These are important and the frontiers of medicine must be pushed forward, but if too much time is spent on elaborate techniques of investigation, too little will be left for the consideration of the mundane human problems which are involved in providing clinical care for the elderly suffering, for example, from the aftereffects of a stroke. The balance of medical education between the scientific and the humane is dangerously tipped in favor of the former in many medical schools. Many students with their uncluttered minds and altruistic ideas recognize this. Later, however, as postregistration physicians with an eye on career prospects, the temptation to ignore a specialty which universities have largely excluded becomes too great.

A third reason for the lack of enthusiasm toward geriatrics is best described as emotional. Most of us can expect to live to be old, and many physicians share the popular belief that this is a time of life to be dreaded. They exclude old age, as far as possible, from their thinking. With such a conscious or subconscious attitude, the last thing such physicians wish to do is to devote their working lives to old age. One suspects there may also, in some cases, be guilt feelings which become rationalized into a rather supercilious rejection of both the specialty and those who practice it.

One might add as a footnote to these three reasons for lack of interest in geriatrics as a career specialty the rather less well acknowledged fact that it is not an easy one to practice. Not only may history taking be excessively time consuming and physical examination very difficult, but also the final interpretation of the clinical situation and decision on management demand mature, kindly judgment.

The final reason, which may well be the most significant, is that British geriatricians have placed great stress on the social and preventive aspects of geriatrics, and to some extent this has undervalued the clinical features. Links between gerontology and geriatrics have been scanty with the result that the scientific basis for the clinical specialty of geriatrics has gone unrecognized. Much has been written about the clinical medicine of old age but from a conventional systems point of view. The cardiologist is the expert on diseases of the heart from the cradle to the grave, for example. The definition of geriatric medicine by age is blurred for two reasons: people age biologically at varying chronologic times, and retirement at 65 has created an artificial division often accepted as the onset of old age and the end of middle age.

Geriatric medicine will become established, like pediatrics before it, only when good scientific reasons for its value as a specialty are demonstrated. The thesis set out in this book is that physical aging and the study of it constitute the scientific basis of geriatric medicine, that the clinical problems commonly encountered in elderly patients stem primarily from cerebral deterioration but span all systems, and that these problems are much more frequently associated with those over the age of 75. An attempt is made to define the data base of this branch of medicine by examining the physical changes associated with aging individuals and the rapidly increasing knowledge of biologic gerontology gained by study of animals in the laboratory. On this foundation, the major clinical problems unique to old age will be examined. It is hoped that this first cohesive attempt to define the content of geriatric medicine will stimulate discussion and research which will lead to advances in the future.

Our object is to preserve independence and make old age a time of life to be anticipated. As Lin Yutang has said

No one can really stop growing old. And since there is no use fighting against nature, one might just as well grow old gracefully. The symphony of life should end with a grand finale of peace and serenity and material comforts and spiritual contentment, and not with the crash of a broken drum or cracked cymbals.

REFERENCES

1. Bromley DB: Some current issues in the psychology of human ageing. In Cape RDT (ed): Symposia on Geriatric Medicine, Vol 3. Birmingham, England, West Midland Institute of Geriatric Medicine and Gerontology 1974, pp 16–23
2. Bullough WS: The Biology of Aging. Lecture at Conference on Essentials of Geriatric Medicine, University of Western Ontario, April 1977
3. Cape RDT: A geriatric service. Midland Med Rev 8:21–43, 1972
4. Cicero MT: De Senectute (c. 45–44 BC)
5. Concise Oxford Dictionary, Oxford, 1964, p 512
6. Desroches-Noblecourt C: Tutankhamen. London, George Rainbird Ltd, 1963
7. (Editorial): Globe and Mail, Toronto, April 6, 1977
8. Fry M: Public Oration in Old Age in the Modern World. Edinburgh, E & S Livingston, 1959, pp 4–12
9. Shakespeare W: As You Like It
10. Verwoerdt A: Clinical Geropsychiatry from Working with Older People, Vol IV, Clinical Aspects of Aging. US Department of Health Education and Welfare, Rockville, MD, 1971
11. Vital Statistics, Vol III, Deaths, Statistics Canada, 1973
12. Yutang L: The Importance of Living. Great Britain, Readers Union Ltd, 1939, pp 197–206

Chapter 2

PHYSICAL ASPECTS
OF AGING

A writhled forehead, hair gone grey.
Fallen eyebrows, eyes gone blind and red,
Their laughs and looks all fled away,
Yea, all that smote men's hearts are fled;
The bowed nose, fallen from goodlihead;
Foul flapping ears like water-flags;
Peaked chin, and cheeks all waste and dead,
And lips that are two skinny rags:

Thus endeth all the beauty of us.
The arms made short, the hands made lean,
The shoulders bowed and ruinous,
The breasts, alack! all fallen in;
The flanks too, like the breasts, grown thin.
                    Algernon Swinburne

Everyone is familiar with the general appearance of an old person. While there are some who remain remarkably ageless, most of us will slowly and irrevocably develop the characteristic skin and postural changes seen in individuals who have reached the later decades of life. It is important for the medical student, however, to be able to recognize the specific features of this process and to develop a facility for estimating the age of the patient.

SKIN

The skin becomes wrinkled on the face, with the appearance of "crow's feet" around the eyes. The reason for this change is the loss of subcutaneous supporting tissue and a resulting thinning and, on occasion, drying out of the skin. As with most age related changes, there is no regular chronologic sequence of events; some individuals will have a well-preserved, relatively young looking skin in their 80s while others will be considerably lined and shrivelled 20 years earlier. This variability is one of the most obvious features of biologic aging, and any theory which attempts to explain the process must take this into consideration.

Lax skin was recorded in 94% of a group of 163 community volunteers aged 64 or over who were studied in North Carolina (37). The two other most common findings were seborrheic keratoses in 88% and cherry angiomas (De Morgan's spots) in 75%. Dry scaly skin was observed in more than three-quarters of these individuals. Hobson and Pemberton (23) describe skin conditions as not disabling but a "major vexation" in the old. They found 32% of men and 28% of women in their Sheffield study with a significant degree of pruritus, a condition which begins as an insidious irritation but can culminate in loss of sleep and much misery. This condition is commonly associated with the dry skin found so frequently in the Duke study (37).

Other abnormal features are senile purpura and senile warts or papillomata, both associated with aging of the skin and found most commonly in the very old. The purpura appear to be related to the loss of subcutaneous tissue supporting the skin capillaries; the loss of this tissue makes it possible for a very minor trauma to cause small ecchymotic lesions. These are largely confined to the extensor surfaces of the forearms. There is no convincing evidence that deficiency of vitamin C plays any role in etiology. Describing this as "spontaneous bruising," Hobson and Pemberton found it in 40% of men and 77% of women. There was an increase in incidence with age noted in the men but not the women. The accumulation of small yellow, brown, or black warty papillomata seen frequently on the trunk and, at times, on the limbs and face, is also common to the very old. Tindall and Graham Smith noted such lesions in 63% of their North Carolina subjects. It is possible that the development of such benign multiple small growths is associated with the aging of skin in a number of mammals. They were noted in one notorious 13-year-old dog owned by the author!

The skin is composed of two layers, a superficial epidermal cellular layer and a deeper one composed largely of connective tissue. In the latter, called the corium or dermis, masses of fibrous strands form a mesh in which is contained a jellylike homogeneous matrix. Andrew (3) has described how the deeper layer loses its woven feltlike structure underneath the wrinkles and lines of the aging skin. Changes occur in both the cellular and the matrix part of the dermis. Young tissue will produce masses of refractile jelly with few fibrils, while in the old the situation is reversed.

The various cell types encountered in the skin include fibroblasts, endothelial cells, pericapillary cells, macrophages, and every kind of white blood cell. Andrew *et al.* (4) studied 419 specimens of human abdominal skin and counted the number of cells present in a measured area. They found that the number of cells declines with age examining an area under the microscope of 0.034810 sq mm for total cell population in each human subject. There was a decrease of almost 50% by the fifth decade with a later slight further loss (Fig. 2–1). A similar reduction in numbers of epidermal projections into the dermis occurs.

These changes confirm the clinical impression of a degree of atrophy of the skin with increasing years. Earlier work (14) suggested that there is a reduction

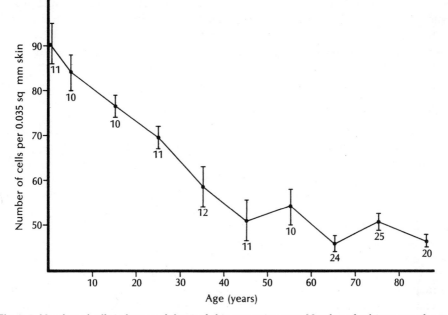

Fig. 2–1. Number of cells in human abdominal skin at varying ages. Number of subjects at each age noted with mean value $\pm$ standard error. (Composed from data of Andrew W et al.: Gerontologia 10:1–19, 1964)

in the thickness of the epidermis in spite of keratosis being a common associated factor. The combination of a thinning epidermis and changing collagen (see Ch. 3, Biologic Gerontology) probably combine to produce the characteristic "crow's feet" of old age.

EYES

A visual sign of aging is the yellowish white, opaque ring around the periphery of the iris, which is known as the arcus senilis. It originates from the deposition of fatty substances in Bowman's and Descemet's membranes and can become thick and very obvious. It never interferes with vision and is not related to the level of cholesterol in the blood. The condition occurs in about 40% of all old people, and it is believed there is a familial tendency to develop it. This appearance bears no relationship to the functional changes in the eyes which occur as individuals reach their fifth and later decades, when presbyopia causes many to require glasses for reading.

PRESBYOPIA

Presbyopia is a phenomenon which results from a diminishing ability of the lens to focus at different distances. This alteration in visual adaptability occurs both in those who undertake work which involves accurate and keen visual acuity and those whose occupation is less demanding from this standpoint. Both the schoolteacher and the garbage collector suffer in a similar manner. This is the most common change in vision which occurs with increasing age, but there are three other conditions of much more serious significance.

CATARACT

A cataract develops when age related changes in the lens cause opacification. The lens, which is the most protein rich of organs, doubles its weight and volume in the course of a lifetime. It is completely enclosed by a capsule, layers of which degenerate and form a hard nucleus inside the organ as it slowly grows with age. Simultaneously, the capsule becomes less elastic and accommodation of the nucleus progressively more difficult. The full explanation for these changes has not been established, but it is known that a critical part is played by anaerobic degradation of glucose in the metabolism of the lens protein. With age the sugar content of the organ and hence the availability of energy is reduced. A relative acidosis develops in the lens as a result of which proteolytic enzymes are activated and cloudiness develops. Senile cataract is almost always bilateral, and it has been noted that the manner of development in monozygotic twins is remarkable (29). The condition can be treated surgically, but only at a stage when the cataract is ripe for the procedure. The results of surgery depend on whether there is any underlying degenerative change in the retina.

SENILE MACULAR DEGENERATION

Senile macular degeneration results from ischemic changes in the retina which become increasingly common with advancing years. It is not, however, due solely to arteriosclerosis or hypertension but may arise as a natural accompaniment of aging. The retinal artery is an end artery, and its terminal branches supply blood to the periphery of the fundus. Poor vascular supply to this area results in hyaline infiltration, calcification, and fatty degeneration. At the periphery of the retina cystoid degeneration may in a very small proportion of cases result in retinal detachment. Similar changes can also occur at the foveal region of the retina where visual acuity is determined. Cystoid degeneration in this area may cause a hole to develop with a resulting hypertrophic overgrowth of pigmented epithelium, "ruptures of Bruch's membrane, penetration of the connective tissue, haemorrhage and transudation" (29). The central lesion may be surrounded by bright patches, a condition known as circinate retinopathy. The condition leads to almost total blindness, which may be very difficult for the patient to accept. The older the person, the more likely this is, and the loss of valuable sensory input may trigger other problems.

GLAUCOMA

With the increase in the size of the lens as its capsule develops new fibers, the anterior chamber of the eye becomes smaller. The angle between the root of the iris and the corneoscleral posterior surface becomes more acute, and the trabecular system through which aqueous passes to the episcleral veins may become clogged, resulting in an increase of pressure in the eye—glaucoma. That this disease occurs in only 3% of individuals over the age of 50 is due to the reduced amount of aqueous produced at this age, a mechanism which compensates to some extent for the age changes described previously.

Rintelen (29) comments on what he terms primary compensation: "a specific senile phenomenon which would of itself lead to a functional impairment can have its effects neutralized and offset by a second, roughly synchronous, process which occurs in other parts of the same organ independently of the first." He goes on to quote the example just given.

INCIDENCE OF POOR VISION

Eye changes thus illustrate the difficulty of differentiating biologic features due to an aging process from those that are signs of a morbid condition. Sheldon (30) reported that 410 out of a sample of 478 old people used glasses for reading. In the same account, he reported that 30 individuals (6.3%) did not need glasses, even for reading the newspaper or sewing. In these cases, the failure of accommodation, which manifests itself as presbyopia, did not occur. The incidence of significant deterioration in vision due to cataracts, macular degeneration, or chronic glaucoma is about 15%, which means that well over 80% of people retain reasonable sight throughout their lives. Hobson and Pemberton (23) found that 97.5% are likely to require glasses for near vision, however.

EARS

Ears are as vital for maintaining communication as the eyes are for observation. Any reduction or failure of ear function deprives the individual of one of the richest sources of sensory stimuli that man possesses. There is, with the ears as with the eyes, a slow progressive loss of acuity which is known as presbycusis.

This condition results from age changes in different parts of the hearing system, from the organ of Corti to the neurons of the dominant hemisphere. There is no clear chronologic sequence to these age changes, and as with all biologic changes associated with increasing age, the time at which presbycusis first becomes obvious varies. Although the onset is usually noticeable during the seventh decade, there is evidence to suggest that the noise and bustle of modern life which predispose an individual to arteriosclerotic heart disease also reduce the age at which hearing may begin to deteriorate. Pfaltz (28) quotes a study carried out in the Sudan which demonstrated that Mabaans, who lead an isolated existence in the South of the country, at age 60–65 showed an insignificant decline in their ability to hear sounds at higher frequencies compared with an American control group. An English comparison between urban and rural subjects showed a similar statistically valid difference favoring the country group.

The acoustic system consists of four main parts: 1) the middle ear responsible for sound conduction, 2) the inner ear for mechanical frequency analysis and stimulus transformation, 3) the peripheral neuron for conduction and acoustic selectivity, and finally 4) the central auditory pathway which is responsible for integration and interpretation. With increasing age the latter three become impaired. The sensory cells situated at the basal turn of the cochlea appear to be the first to be affected and, as a result, tones of high frequency are lost. Impairment of frequency analysis and reduced ability to recode acoustic signals may result in disturbed intelligibility of speech. There appears also to be a steady loss of intact ganglion cells of the auditory nerve, which interferes with the selectivity process. As a result the elderly person attending a cocktail party may be overpowered by the assorted sounds of people talking and be unable to discriminate or select individual conversation.

The most important disturbance to the old person's hearing is, however, in the central auditory pathway. This results in a marked deterioration in the central data processing which is of great significance in conversation and sentence comprehension. The old person experiences a statistically demonstrable difficulty in identifying a voice or understanding a message in an acoustically disturbed situation. This is an example of the significance of central nervous system function to the subject as a whole.

The incidence of impaired hearing is much greater than that of defective vision. In Sheldon's 1948 survey (30), 30% of those examined suffered from various degrees of deafness. In the later Sheffield study (23), 69.3% of the women had normal hearing, but only 47.7% of the men. Both studies found deafness more common in men. The Sheffield authors stated, "Early in the survey, it was found that deafness of the subject so often made it difficult to obtain a satisfactory history that a hearing aid was added to the equipment taken by the physician."

MUSCLES

Muscles are composed of nonmitotic cells, which means that they are irreplaceable. These vital structures, which clothe the bones and give the person shape, achieve their optimum size and strength when the individual reaches full maturity in the middle 20s. Thereafter, their state depends on the type of life which their host leads. The more robustly physical it is, the bulkier and stronger the muscles remain. One cannot repeat too often that the only way muscle power increases is by increased use, and vice versa failure to flex or extend muscles means their atrophy.

The manual worker and the athlete who keeps in training maintain their muscle bulk and strength well into the sixth decade, but then there is a slow steady atrophy, its pace depending on the mode of life of the person concerned.

This results in wasting of the former bulky muscles of trunk and limbs. These muscles are largely replaced by an increasing quantity of adipose tissue, which may not only compensate for the loss of bulk but also create new bulges in unwanted places.

Lean body mass is made up of muscles, liver, brain, and kidneys; this total weight diminishes 20%–30% by the age of 70–80. The tissue lost is replaced by fat (Figs. 2–2 and 2–3). Novak (12) studied 215 men and 305 women volunteers between the ages of 18 and 85, determining total body potassium by counting naturally radioactive ^{40}K in the whole body counter. Total body potassium was reduced with age in men from 56.1 mEq/Kg to 43.4 mEq/Kg and in women from 45.6–37.6 mEq/Kg (Fig. 2–2). Fat increased with age in men from 17.8%–36.2%, while fat-free mass and cellular mass diminished from 82.2%–63.8% and from 46.6%–36.2%, respectively (Fig. 2–3). Similar changes occurred in women. He found that it is noteworthy that the main changes occur beyond the age of 45 and that they are much more marked in men, although the same trends appear in both sexes.

The loss of lean body mass has clinical implications. In the first place the

Fig. 2–2. Total body potassium in mEq at varying ages. Mean values and numbers of subjects noted for each age group. (Composed from data of Novak LP: J Gerontol 27:438–443, 1972)

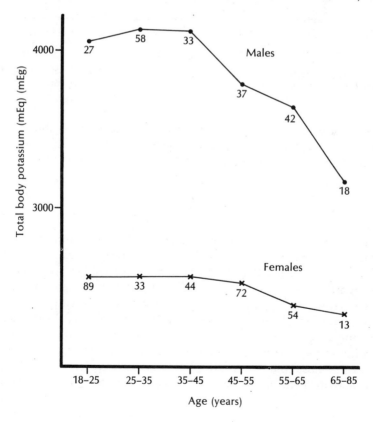

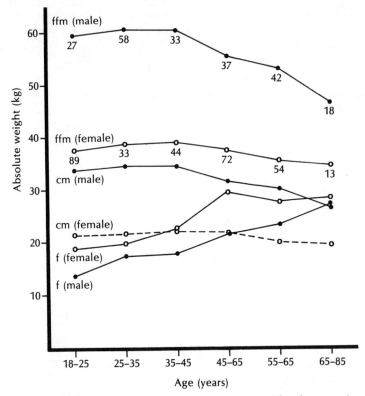

Fig. 2–3. Fat (**f**) fat-free mass (**ffm**), and cell mass (**cm**) of males and females at varying ages. Mean values and number of subjects in each age group noted. (Novak LP: J Gerontol 27:438–443, 1972)

individual's need for energy-providing food is reduced as is the target organ mass on which drugs may act. It follows that less food and smaller doses of drugs are required in old people (see Ch. 9, Iatrogenic Disorders).

BONES

Muscles cannot function without a rigid structure on which to contract. Bones are not inert structures, but are factories of unceasing chemical activity through-out life. It is established that after the menopause women lose calcium from these supports of the body, which results in the development of osteoporosis in old age. Gryfe et al. (22) have demonstrated that the quality of bone estab-lished in youth and adolescence governs the calcium state of the skeleton in old age. The incidence of osteoporosis in elderly men is lower than in women, and the condition is not so severe in men. Fractures of the wrist and the neck of the femur are the most common injuries in old age. These occur much more often in women than men, leading one to suspect that they result as much from metabolic bone disease as from the effects of falling (see Ch. 6, Falling). In about 10% of cases, the fracture occurs spontaneously or with very minor trauma.

Curiously enough, loss of calcium from bone is accompanied by calcification of costal cartilages and interspinal ligaments, causing the thorax to lose elasticity. The change impedes full ventilation of the lungs and reduces respiratory efficiency. Osteoporosis of vertebral bodies may lead to compression fractures with partial collapse. This, combined with disk degeneration, causes a reduction in the individual's height; an associated increased lordosis contributes the characteristic, slightly bowed appearance of the old person.

The observant student will note that these alterations in body conformation are not chronologically determined. There are as many octogenarians with straight backs and erect postures as there are people 20 years younger already bowed down by the years. The round-shouldered, bent-backed, pot-bellied old man peering through spectacles with his presbyopic eyes, one hand clutching a stick and the other raised to try and catch the words being addressed to him makes a useful picture to act as a mnemonic device for the student—but one which, like so many "classic" conditions in medicine, is not seen very often.

INTERNAL SYSTEMS

While these externally obvious changes are occurring, a similar slow progressive deterioration of function takes place in all internal systems. An outline of some of these physiologic decrements between the ages of 30 and 80 was shown by Bourlière (7) at the Canadian Conference on Aging, 1966 (Fig. 2–4). Deteriora-

Fig. 2–4. Involution of various functions with age. **GFR.** Glomerular filtration rate. (Attributed to Shock. Bourlière F: Report of Canadian Conference of Aging, 1966, pp 23–36)

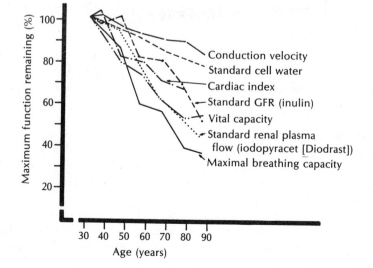

tion is the rule, but to different degrees in the various systems. While maximal breathing capacity falls by 60%, basal metabolic rate is reduced by only 20% between 20 and 90.

There are five essential functions involved in the process of living. These are nutrition, metabolism, circulation, elimination, and homeostatic control. Aging has an effect on each of these functions.

NUTRITION

Food, air, and water are the three essentials for biologic existence. The demand for these varies with the activity, environment, and age of the individual concerned. Dunlop used to emphasize this point to his students in Edinburgh by contrasting the need for energy food of an active, hunting Eskimo living on blubber in the Arctic Circle with that of a thin, elderly seamstress contemplating her navel while sitting under a tree on the Equator. The former required 6000 or more calories daily; the latter, a modest 1200. The older the individual, the less the demand for such energy food. There are two main reasons: the first is the reduction in lean body mass already described, and the second is the less active life which the majority lead.

It is usual for the average intake of food to diminish by about one-quarter by the time the seventh, eighth, and ninth decades are reached. It is important to recognize this and avoid the temptation to encourage excessive eating which would only result in further accumulation of neutral fat stores. Not only are such fat stores unnecessary but they are also actively harmful because they embarrass the heart's action and impair respiratory efficiency. In general, an optimum diet for an old person 75 or over contains 1600–2400 calories, depending on the sex and height of the individual. The only other essential is an adequate supply of first class protein, minerals, and vitamins.

This has been elegantly shown by the studies of Exton–Smith and Stanton (15, 34). Sixty women from two London, England boroughs were included in their survey of nutrition which was originally carried out in 1962 and repeated 7 years later. Great pains were taken to obtain accurate assessments of the diets consumed. An initial visit and explanation was followed by a second visit to take a detailed dietary history. On this occasion scales, pencil and paper, and plastic bags for keeping plate and preparation waste were left. Investigators then visited each woman daily for 7 days, checking larder stocks from day to day, encouraging her to weigh items of food, and totaling each 24-hour consumption. Club meals and meals on wheels were noted and calculated separately. The study details each individual's consumption of calories, protein, calcium, and iron. In addition a table showing intake of calories and nutrients is included (Fig. 2–5). With age there is a remarkably consistent reduction in food intake on the order of 20% between age 70 and 80 and above.

When the authors repeated their program in 1969, they found that the same change had occurred on a longitudinal basis over 7 years as had been shown by the earlier cross-section study. The mean caloric intake diminished by 17% in 13 subjects, although their protein intake fell by 20%. On the other hand, there

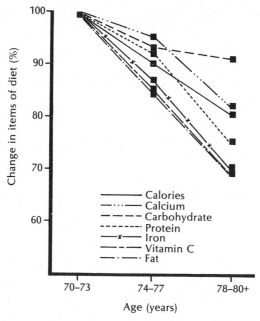

Fig. 2–5. Alteration in mean dietary intake after age 70. (Composed from data of Exton–Smith AN, Stanton BR: Report of an Investigation into the Dietary of Elderly Women Living Alone. London, King Edward's Hospital Fund for London, 1965)

were nine survivors who continued to eat as much as or more than they had before. The latter group maintained their health and weight more effectively than the former.

A more extensive longitudinal survey of nutrition and aging was carried out in San Mateo, California in 1948 with follow-up in 1952, 1954, and 1964 (9, 20, 35). The same general progressive fall in intake with age was noted, but the importance of personal habit was exemplified by the fact that higher protein consumers continued to eat more of this food as they aged. There is an association between good eating and good health, but it would seem likely that those in good health maintain interest in food and cooking, rather than the reverse. There is no good evidence, for example, that vitamin supplements contribute anything extra to what is accomplished by the normal daily requirement.

Absorption of Food

Food enters the body via the gastrointestinal system. The initial reception of food in the mouth is sometimes a problem for the old person because ptyalin secretion may be reduced by 20%, but a much more significant factor is the state of the teeth. Some persons are proud that they have retained their own teeth, even though the teeth may be a number of yellowish decayed stumps only good for supporting a rich source of commensal and pathogenic organisms; others exhibit dentures which fitted 20 years earlier, but which now act as loose impediments to mastication and are often removed for comfortable gnawing by gums on the food. This is probably the major stumbling block to good digestion in the elderly, and adequate dental care can achieve a great deal to reduce this problem.

Frolkis (18) has demonstrated that with aging there is a progressive reduction in the quantity of digestive enzymes produced in the stomach and intestine, the largest decrement being for trypsin and pepsin. By the 80th birthday, the production of these two enzymes falls to 30% and 20%, respectively, of production at age 20. In spite of this there is little evidence of failure to digest a normal diet, although Bender (6) suggests there may be slower and less complete absorption of certain substances.

Bender reviewed the literature on carbohydrate, fat, calcium, iron, and vitamin absorption (6). There is evidence to suggest a slowing of absorption of some sugars such as 3-methyl-glucose or galactose, and xylose absorption is reduced by nearly 50%. When two groups, one young and one old, were given 25 g xylose, the former reached a higher peak of average blood xylose level than the latter, and the 5-hour urinary content was reduced in the old subjects by about 50% (16). Production of pancreatic lipase and amylase is reduced by age 70 to 60%–70% of what it was at age 20 (18). This fact has been blamed for a poorer absorption of fat in old age.

Calcium absorption depends partly on an active transport system. A group of rats given Ca^{45} were sacrificed at the end of 96 hours. The older the rat, the more radioactivity was found in the stool, indicating a low level of absorption (6). A similar situation occurs with iron. In spite of slowing down of absorption there is no good evidence that aging *per se* prevents the absorption of any natural food that is available. Obesity is a greater danger to longevity than starvation. Capricious appetite occurs in old people but is likely to be due to physical or psychiatric illness and not to aging alone.

Metabolism

Basal metabolic rate is slowly reduced from maturity onwards, falling by about 20% between the ages of 20 and 90 (Fig. 2–6). The quantity of oxygen used by every tissue is reduced by an amount which varies from organ to organ. According to Frolkis (17), this change is accompanied by an increase in anaerobic glycolytic activity and alterations in permeability of cell membranes, the general effect being to reduce efficiency of energy provision and restrict the older person's working capacity.

The supply of oxygen reaches the body through the respiratory system. Skeletal changes cause a steadily increasing rigidity of the thorax; as a result ventilation and maximal breathing capacity are reduced (Fig. 2–4). At age 80 the latter has fallen to only 40% of its capacity at age 20. It is reasonable to postulate that the increase in glycolytic activity is the result of this progressive deterioration in respiratory capacity. In the healthy old person this is not enough to restrict normal activities but does make it necessary to limit energetic exercise. As is the case for all bodily functions, training can improve performance. The old person

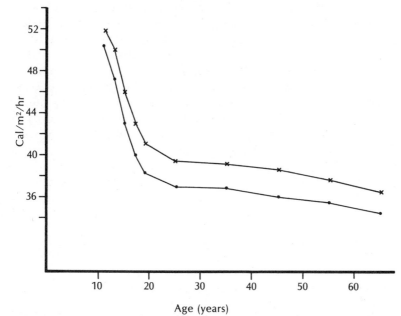

Fig. 2–6. Change of basal metabolism with age. (Adapted from Trémolières Geissler–Brun: Nutrition and Metabolism. From von Hahn HP [ed]: Practical Geriatrics. Basel, S. Karger 1975 p 55–75, 1975)

who has followed a regular exercise regime throughout life finds fewer restrictions in old age than a person who spent more time driving than walking.

Changes associated with aging take place in the lung parenchyma with coalescence of alveoli, due to atrophy and loss of elasticity in the septa, and result in varying degrees of senile emphysema. Thus both intra- and extrapulmonary factors affect the body's intake of oxygen. These are further reinforced by major changes in the neurohumoral control of respiration. Chemoreceptors at the carotid sinus become hypersensitive to oxygen lack. The respiratory center becomes more sensitive to carbon dioxide, catecholamines, and acetylcholine. These changes are accompanied by a reduction in the efficiency of oxygen diffusion, which makes the old person more sensitive to hypoxia. For example, most young people tolerate heights of 10,000 feet without oxygen supplements, but the octogenarian becomes seriously embarrassed at 6000 feet.

Glucose Tolerance

It is accepted that the incidence of diabetes mellitus increases with age. According to the United States National Center for Health Statistics (39) approximately 5% of each sex are diabetic at the age of 75. There is agreement that the response to an oral glucose tolerance test (GTT) alters with age, and Andres (1) cites nine large studies to demonstrate that the blood glucose level 1 hour after a 50 g oral bolus ranged from 100 mg/100 ml at age 20 to 170 mg/100 ml at age 75. There were variations in the findings of different workers in the United States, Australia, Sweden, and England, but the trend was unequivocal. For each decade of life the blood glucose level at 1 hour rose by 10 mg/100 ml $+$ 4 mg/100 ml. On the basis of these figures, Andres proposed a nomogram for the oral glucose tolerance test whereby one can place an individual on a percentile rank according to age and blood glucose level 2 hours after 50 g glucose (Fig. 2–7).

Lauvaux and Staquet (24) had earlier demonstrated increasing numbers of glucose levels between 150 and 250 mg/100 ml as people aged, which they attributed to a lower glucose tolerance. Grobin (21) confirmed this general trend when he reported a 25% incidence of abnormal glucose levels 2 hours after a 50 g glucose challenge at a Jewish Home for the Aged in Toronto, Canada. About half of these individuals were regarded as diabetic after further investigation. The question posed by such studies is does diabetes mellitus increase in incidence with age or does the aging process reduce the effectiveness of carbohydrate metabolic controls?

To try and answer this question Smith and Hall (32) studied 53 very old

Fig. 2–7. Oral glucose tolerance test nomogram. (Andres R: Med Clin North Am 55:835–846, 1971)

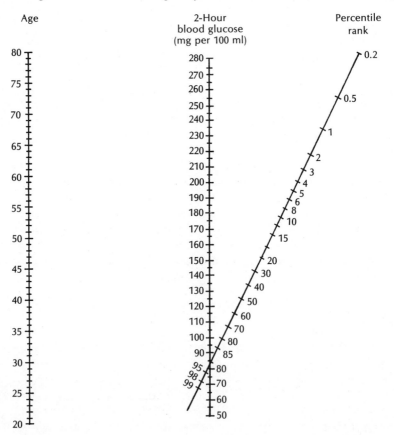

individuals between the ages of 86 and 95. Their object was to determine whether carbohydrate tolerance does diminish and is this a state common to the aged, or does the higher blood glucose level represent an age linked condition such as arterial disease which is associated with hyperglycemia? A randomly selected group of patients awaiting discharge from a geriatric ward were given a standard glucose tolerance test after 3 days of a fixed carbohydrate diet (300 g daily). The results obtained were compared with those from two other groups, one composed of 19 women (mean age 30) who had been delivered of a baby of normal birth weight within the previous 2 years and the other of 21 healthy women (mean age 52) being investigated for postmenopausal bleeding. Of the 53 very old subjects 34 had a normal glucose tolerance apart from a delayed peak value at 1 hour (*cf.* 30 min with both younger groups). One small group of 6 had a probable diabetic curve with a delayed high peak of almost 200 mg/100 ml, while the remaining 13 fell into an intermediate range (Fig. 2–8). When the insulin levels are examined (see Fig. 2–9), it can be seen that in the old subjects

Fig. 2–8. Glucose tolerance curves in young women, postmenopausal women, and very elderly subjects of both sexes who were given 50 g glucose. **ma.** Mean age. **n.** Number of subjects. (Smith MJ, Hall MRP: Diabetologia 9:387–390, 1973)

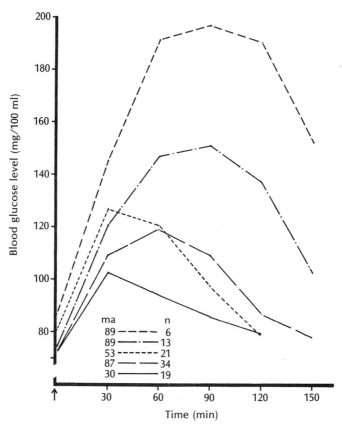

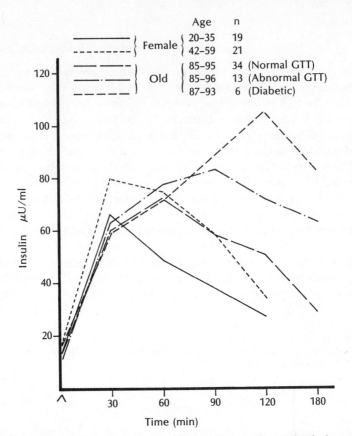

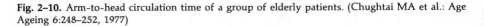

Fig. 2–9. Production of insulin in response to 50 g glucose given orally to individuals at varying ages. **n.** Number of subjects. (Smith MJ, Hall MRP: Diabetologia 9:387–390, 1973)

Fig. 2–10. Arm-to-head circulation time of a group of elderly patients. (Chughtai MA et al.: Age Ageing 6:248–252, 1977)

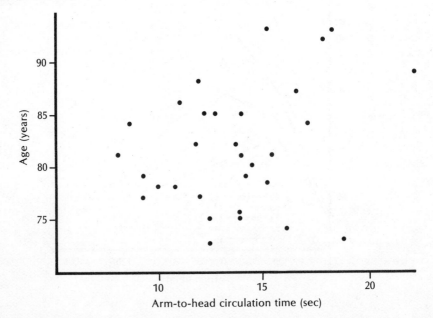

insulin production is a little slower and appears to be less effective. In the two groups with higher glucose levels the production of insulin continues to increase until 90 and 120 min., respectively, without reducing glucose levels to a significant extent. Smith and Hall suggest that either the insulin is less biologically active or is ineffective because of an as yet unknown antagonist preventing it from fulfilling its normal action.

It is wise, therefore, to proceed with caution in the elderly patient whose blood sugar levels are higher than normal. The probability is that these are harmless to the individual. Careful evaluation with glucose tolerance curves, a trial on a carbohydrate reduced diet, and inquiry about symptoms such as polyuria and polydipsia may be all that is required in the first instance. Diabetic ketosis is not common in this age group, but degrees of hypoglycemia can be a real danger in that they may cause permanent cerebral damage.

CIRCULATION

An impoverished circulation due to hardening of the arteries is regarded as the cause of most of the ills of the old. There is no doubt that heart disease is the most common cause of death in most of Europe and North America and that it is directly responsible for almost one-third of deaths in the old. To balance the picture, however, one must state that over a quarter of octogenarians have normal hearts when they die. From a purely physical standpoint the old heart shows few differences from the young one. There is a definite reduction in muscle, with an increase in fatty tissue. In a varying number of cells there is an accumulation of brown or yellow lipid pigment, the significance of which is not clear, but it represents an alteration in the internal milieu of the cell and probably results in less satisfactory function.

Accompanying these anatomic changes are a number of parallel physiologic alterations. There is a slower myocardial contractility, a reduction in cardiac output, and an increased rigidity of the arterial wall. As a result of this latter change, the pulse wave travels more quickly but the circulation time tends to increase. These general statements are subject to a wide variation (Fig. 2–10). While studying a group of elderly patients with and without senile dementia for evidence of associated circulatory disturbance, Chughtai *et al.* (10) found a significant relationship between age and circulation time, but also found increasing variations between individuals. Changes in the arterial walls are also responsible for the steady increase in peripheral resistance of about 1% per year from the age of 50 upwards.

Homeostatic mechanisms which control the complex management of so many bodily functions ensure that vital organs are protected from the effects of these adverse changes in circulation. Cerebral blood flow shows a relatively slight fall in old age, while the heart itself occupies a middle place in terms of reduction of blood flow and availability of oxygen. In the old person with an aged but not a diseased heart, therefore, exercise tolerance is perfectly adequate for all normal purposes, including quite vigorous activity. The degree of vigor is related to the speed of the action. In general the slower and more deliberate the action, the greater the amount which can be carried out by the elderly person. There is, therefore, no reason to tell the patient to stop all the usual activities, but rather a caution to carry them out more slowly, for shorter periods, is wise. One of the more difficult accomodations to age is the acceptance of a slower pace. Some feel this is the last straw, one which cannot be borne, and depressive illness may follow.

A considerable controversy has arisen over the need to treat high blood pressure in individuals beyond the age of 70. The increased thickening and rigidity of arterial walls which may come with age means that the pulse pressure tends to rise from 35–45 to 55–70 or even more. Because of the increased rigidity of the brachial arterial wall, conventional methods of measuring blood pressure with a sphygmomanometer may not be accurate. A recent study (33) has demonstrated that measuring the level by intraarterial transducer, in some cases, reveals diastolic pressures which are 20 or 25 mm Hg lower than when a sphygmomanometer is used (Table 2–1).

There is no doubt that the use of antihypertensive drugs may cause serious side-effects from the patient's standpoint of postural hypertension on the one hand or depression, lethargy, and apathy on the other. Medicine is an art, not solely a science, and this particular topic is one in which the competing claims of life expectancy and its quality may be to some extent opposed. In the final years the latter should perhaps win the day, but there are no easy or quick solutions to this problem.

The literature demonstrates very clearly that adequate treatment of sufferers from essential hypertension who have not yet reached the age of 65 results in lower mortality and fewer strokes (5, 8, 25, 36). Curiously enough the incidence of myocardial infarction is not affected. Beyond the age of 70, however, there is good reason to believe that the potential gain in terms of reduced mortality and strokes is much less and the side-effects of treatment are much greater (8, 19, 26). The truth may only be known when there are more accurate methods of measuring blood pressure in old people.

ELIMINATION

Renal Function

It must now be clear that the total effect of aging on bodily functions is to alter them, almost always in a deteriorating direction. One of the first functions to be carefully studied by Shock and his colleagues in Baltimore was that of the kidney. This was a classic piece of research and probably the first to demonstrate unequivocally that aging *per se* can cause significant and consistent changes in function of a particular organ system. For this reason it is worth recalling in some detail the main paper of the series by Davies and Shock (12).

Seven groups of 9–12 males between the ages of 24 and 89 were studied, each group representing a decade from the third (20–29) to the ninth (80–89). No subject in any group had evidence of previous renal disease, cerebrovascular

TABLE 2-1. Direct vs Indirect Arterial Blood Pressure (mmHg)

Sex	Age	Indirect (Adult cuff)	Indirect (Thigh cuff)	Direct	Mean
		Patients over age 60			
M	62	260/118	220/100	244/106	157*
M	62	190/95	165/100	145/74	102
M	62	170/110	150/105	166/85	114
F	63	>300/168	>300/188	292/131	195
F	64	190/120	180/110	180/80	123
F	64	220/90	235/90	260/82	154
F	65	198/100	190/90	193/82	128*
F	65	238/140	230/120...100	175/98	138
F	65	150/88	150/88	156/76	105
F	67	245/120	230/110	184/86	122
M	71	210/158	200/160	227/115	158
M	72	178/130...112	180/110	162/112	140
F	72	224/118	252/112	235/87	144
F	73	220/108	200/90	197/77	112*
F	73	250/135	250/130	219/88	142
M	74	170/94		203/60	100
F	74	160/120		184/109	139
F	75	188/118...110	140/90	165/77	110
M	77	158/96	140/84...70	155/64	106
F	79	190/100	190/90	209/81	124
M	79	226/130	220/120	230/106	153
F	80	240/110	250/100	220/66	115
M	83	180/100	170/110	160/90	128
F	84	186/88	198/94	236/83	130†
		Patients under age 60			
M	29	122/90	118/80	118/73	88*
M	35	156/106...88	130/86...78	142/95	115*
M	38	158/100...96	146/96	141/84	100*
M	43	162/110	162/110	145/67	97
F	49	210/110	200/100	233/108	152*
M	50	242/140...134	190/108...100	207/91	132
F	51	144/80	100/64	154/84	108
M	52	228/116	190/104	135/68	89
M	53	138/98	126/85	136/84	102†
F	54	168/110...100	154/100...96	153/107	120*
F	55	220/110	224/120...90	272/98	149*
F	55	210/118...110	200/102	186/92	130
F	56	150/90		134/94	113
F	56	162/108	140/88...80	135/68	97*
M	57	188/102	176/98	186/81	78
M	59	228/116	180/108...98	208/98	140

*thin arms
†fat arms
(Spence, Sibbald, Cape RDT: [in press])

accident, coronary artery disease, syphilis, rheumatic heart disease, hypertension, or any recent alteration in body weight. Hypertension was defined as a blood pressure in which the diastolic level was greater than 90 mm Hg. Only two tests were performed on patients with systolic pressures greater than 160 mm Hg. Under carefully controlled basal conditions, four clearance and four Tm periods (each of 10–14 min) were carried out using the constant infusion technique of Smith, Goldring, and Chasis (31).

The average insulin and iodopyracet (Diodrast) clearances and iodopyracet (Diodrast) Tm decreased linearly with age (Figs. 2–11 and 2–12). At that time, Davies and Shock were unable to comment on the likely mechanisms involved, but later Andrew (2) demonstrated that the changes which occur in the kidney histologically in old age include a reduction in the number of glomeruli. The current view is that the reduction in renal function which has important clinical repercussions is thus due to loss of nephrons.

The effect of these changes is not only to make the kidney a less effective waste disposal system but to reduce its efficiency in homeostatic control. Under the direction of the hypothalamus the kidney is largely responsible for maintaining normal water and electrolyte balance, but if kidney function is halved, this becomes more difficult. Variations in the state of hydration occur frequently in the old, who have a tendency to become dehydrated. Embarrassed by the symptom, the sufferer from precipitancy of micturition (see Ch. 7, Incontinence) who reduces intake to conceal it and the individual on diuretics whose heart failure has cleared but who continues to dry out are two examples of subjects at risk.

A more recent suggestion is that the chronic renal failure of later years may have a significant role to play in osteoporosis (see Ch. 6, Falling). This is certainly the reason why drugs such as digoxin which are excreted solely by the kidney must be given in more cautious dosage in the elderly (see Ch. 9, Iatrogenic Disorders).

Bowel Function

There is little evidence of specific age changes in the colon, other than thinning of the muscle layers. The lifelong dietary and excretory habits of the individual are more important than any aging effects *per se*. A diet which has contained an ample supply of fiber and bulk, added to a regular routine of bowel clearance, is the most effective way of maintaining good colonic function. Unfortunately the diet of the mass of North Americans is lacking in fiber, and the speed and urgency of modern life in their countries are not conducive to good bowel habits. Misuse of laxatives complicates the picture. All these factors, poor diet and eating habits with overdosage of irritant purgatives, tend to result in diverticulosis (in about 50% of people over the age of 80).

It has been shown that aging brings about a change in the secretion of digestive enzymes by the intestine, and it is likely that there are also alterations in motility of different portions of the alimentary tract. Whether these play a significant role in the disturbances of colon function seen quite commonly in the elderly is difficult to judge. From a practical point of view there seems little doubt that the key to maintaining satisfactory colonic excretion is a good mixed diet with plenty of fiber, plenty of fluid, and regular habits.

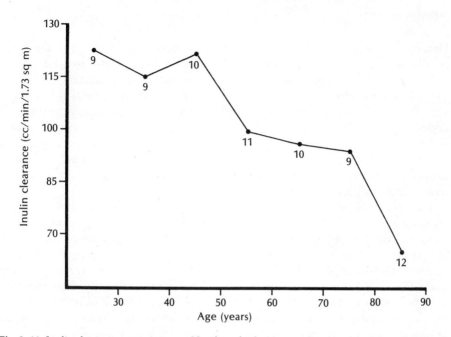

Fig. 2–11. Inulin clearance at varying ages. Number of subjects at each age noted. (Davies DF, Shock NW: J Clin Invest 29:496–507, 1950)

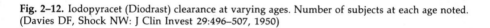

Fig. 2–12. Iodopyracet (Diodrast) clearance at varying ages. Number of subjects at each age noted. (Davies DF, Shock NW: J Clin Invest 29:496–507, 1950)

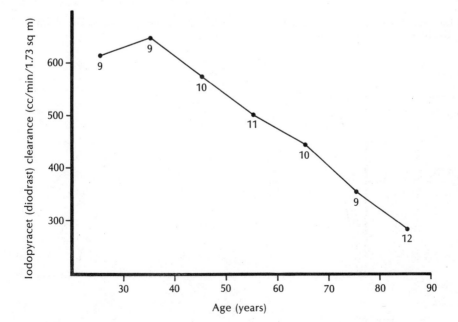

HOMEOSTASIS

Homeostasis is the word used to describe arrangements to preserve the *milieu intérieur* of the body at a constant level of temperature, acid–base and water–electrolyte balance. These are based on neurohormonal regulation under the overall direction of the hypothalamus and pituitary with peripheral aid from the autonomic nervous system and the kidneys. The young person is generously endowed with kidney, liver, and glandular tissue which acts as "over insurance," in Comfort's terms, to maintain homeostasis. Complex mechanisms depend on the individual components of the system. The progressive deterioration of function of the kidneys, lungs, bone, and muscle may all be involved to a greater or lesser extent in homeostasis.

The efficiency of the process is, therefore, progressively impaired with increasing age. Comfort (11) has drawn attention to the teaching of physiology using the mature young adult as the norm. Unfortunately none of us remains at that point for more than a moment of time; we spend most of our lives either on the road to the pinnacle of fitness or on the slope towards senescence and death (Fig. 2–13). The gerontologist is interested in the constantly changing state of homeostasis as it evolves in later years. One of the difficulties is that chronologic age is an unsatisfactory clue to what might be expected in any given system at any given time, as each person ages at an individual pace.

If one accepts Smith and Hall's data on glucose metabolism as an example of a working homeostatic system, it appears that 34 (64%) of the 53 very old people (mean age 88) were still capable of maintaining satisfactory control. There is an increase in the scatter or range of physiologic measurements of older people, as

Fig. 2–13. Hypothetical representation of human homeostatic function. (Davies DF, Shock NW: J Clin Invest 29:496–507, 1950)

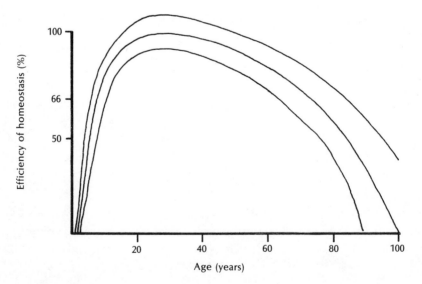

was illustrated by cerebral transit times (Fig. 2–10). As homeostatic efficiency diminishes so does the difference between individuals with the result that while a few of the biological elite retain considerable efficiency, some have it reduced by 80% or more (Fig. 2–13).

There is an increase in the scatter or range of physiologic measurements of older people which has been included in Figure 2–13 by fanning out the band of homeostatic function in later years. Figure 2–10 is one example of this. This sometimes makes it difficult for the clinician to distinguish normal from abnormal conditions within this widened range. If one studies a particular system in detail, however, one suspects that any deviation in the old person from the norms recognized and accepted in young and middle-aged people is usually due to pathology. An example of this is the high frequency of lower hemoglobin levels in groups of old people, which suggests that there might be a lower norm for such individuals. More detailed study of such cases, however, suggests that the lower levels are due to disease, *i.e.,* anemia with a specific cause, and not the aging process (13).

Homeostatic mechanisms in the elderly usually succeed in maintaining norms for temperature, blood pressure, acid–base balance, and state of hydration under basal conditions. The control, however, becomes increasingly brittle and subject to a degree of impairment or even collapse on exposure to only mild stresses (see Ch. 8, Homeostatic Impairment).

LOSS OF ADAPTABILITY

The aging organism becomes progressively less able to adapt to challenge or stress, until finally the stresses are too much and death occurs. From skin to bone and in every part of the body changes are constantly taking place. No one stands still at the optimum peak of physical perfection. Having achieved that state each individual is inexorably moved on.

The clinician looks at such changes as they affect the symptomatology of disease and has a system oriented approach. The gerontologist examines the changes at a more fundamental level—in the cell—in a bid to resolve the reasons for aging changes. For years there was little common ground between them. As knowledge has accumulated, however, clinicians have been probing more deeply into the alterations of function which take place, such as the secondary effects of failing renal function on bone, and the biologist has been contributing new information on the structure and functioning of aging cells such as evidence on the nature of lipofuchsin.

Frolkis (17) reviewed regulation and adaptation processes in aging. In his view, "longevity is a species sign." It is likely, he asserts, that the aging process is represented in the genes. Structural genes which control biosynthesis of protein act in response to regulatory genes. The latter are affected by and may be responsible for age related changes. Frolkis analyzes inductive synthesis of enzymes by hydrocortisone. Young rats (8–10 months) were given hydrocortisone, and liver tyrosine–aminotransferase activity was stimulated; the larger the dose, the greater the increase in activity. When old rats were given the same amounts of hydrocortisone the results were different; the smallest dose produced the greatest effect (Fig. 2–14).

At the Institute of Gerontology in Kiev cellular homeostasis has been studied in considerable detail (17). Concurrent with the altered response to hydrocortisone, Frolkis claims that there is a reduction in potential possibilities of biosynthetic systems, which would mean a loss of adaptability at the cellular level. A critical feature of cells is the membrane potential, which depends on the proportion of ions of sodium, potassium, and chlorine and on the permeability of the membrane. Changes in the quantities of these elements in and out of the cell do occur with aging. There is a loss of potassium from muscle cells of the rat, with an increase extracellularly, and the reverse is true of sodium. This is presumably an adaptive mechanism to maintain the critical cell membrane potential.

Energy is required for this process, and there appear to be changes in the method by which the old obtain energy, such as a greater use of glycolysis. These studies suggest that aging is not simply the result of loss of cells but of altered function at every level, including the cellular one. Frolkis (17) concludes that "the reduced reliability of self-regulation at different levels of the activity of the organism plays the most important role in the mechanism of aging." These

Fig. 2–14. Effect of rats' age on the stimulation of liver tyrosine–aminotransferase activity by hydrocortisone. (Adapted from Frolkis VV: Main Problems of Soviet Gerontology. Kiev, USSR, 1972, pp 54–84)

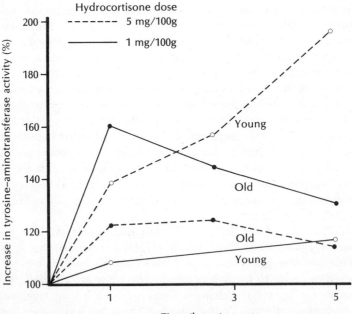

changes, he claims, form the basis for the reduced adaptive possibilities, the greater incidence of disease, and the growing chance of death with increased age.

If clinicians are to make a significant impact on the aging process in their patients, much greater knowledge of how the adaptive mechanisms operate at the cellular level and what is likely to maintain their adaptive potential will be needed. In spite of much new knowledge we still seem some distance away from this ability. Nonetheless, more difficult problems have been solved; inevitably the day will dawn when the pieces of the jigsaw puzzle will fall into place, and we shall understand the nature of the aging process.

The characteristic changes which occur with age are thus seen on close inspection to add up to a steady, remorseless loss of the ability to adapt to any stress or unusual series of events that may require quick reactions on the part of the individual. As long as life produces no such happenings, all is well with the elderly person. The picture may seem gloomy, but provided one uderstands the nature of the changes which are occurring and makes allowances for them, old age does not mean a continual series of abandoning one's favorite pursuits. What may be needed is a reorganization which will allow these activities to be conducted in a more leisurely and temperate manner.

REFERENCES

1. Andres R: Aging and diabetes. Med Clin North Am 55:835–846, 1971
2. Andrew W: The urinary system. In Anatomy of Aging in Man and Animals. New York, Grune & Stratton, 1971, pp 172–182
3. Andrew W: The skin and fascia. In Anatomy of Aging in Man and Animals. New York, Grune & Stratton, 1971, pp 71–93
4. Andrew W, Behuke RH, Sato T: Changes with advancing age in the cell population of human dermis. Gerontologia 10:1–19, 1964
5. Beevers DG, Hamilton M, Fairman MJ, Harpur JE: Antihypertensive treatment and the course of established cerebral vascular disease. Lancet I:1407–1409, 1963
6. Bender AD: Effect of age on intestinal absorption: implications for drug absorption in the elderly. J Am Geriatr Soc 16:1331–1339, 1968
7. Bourlière F: Aging in the Individual. Report of Canadian Conference of Aging. Toronto 1966, pp 23–36
8. Carter AB: Hypotensive therapy in stroke survivors. Lancet I:485–489, 1970
9. Chope HD, Breslow L: Nutritional status of the aging. Am J Public Health 46:61–67, 1956
10. Chughtai MA, Cape RDT, Harding LK, Mayer PP: Mean cerebral transit time in demented and normal elderly persons. Age Ageing 6:248–252, 1977
11. Comfort A: Physiology homoeostasis and ageing. Gerontologia 14:224–234, 1968
12. Davies DF, Shock NW: Age changes in glomerular filtration rate, effective renal plasma flow and tubular excretory capacity in adult males. J Clin Invest 29:496–507, 1950
13. Ehtisham M, Cape RDT: Protocols for diagnosing and treating anemia. Geriatrics 32:91–99, 1977
14. Evans R, Cowdry EV, Nilson PE: Aging of human skin. Anat Rec 86:545–566, 1943
15. Exton-Smith AN, Stanton BR: Report of an investigation into the dietary of elderly women living alone. London, King Edward's Hospital Fund for London, 1965
16. Fikry ME, Aboul-Wafa MH: Intestinal absorption in the old. Gerontol Clin 7:171, 1965
17. Frolkis VV: Regulation and adaptation processes in aging. In: The Main Problems of Soviet Gerontology. Kiev, 1972, pp 54–84

18. Frolkis VV: Physiological aspects of aging. In von Hahn HP (ed): Practical Geriatrics. Basel, S Karger, 1975, pp 1–20
19. Fry J: Natural history of hypertension. A case for selective non-treatment. Lancet II:431–433, 1974
20. Gillum HL, Morgan AF: Nutritional status of the aging. J Nutr 55:265–303, 1955
21. Grobin W: Diabetes in the aged: underdiagnosis and overtreatment. Can Med Assoc J 103:915–923, 1970
22. Gryfe CI, Exton-Smith AN, Payne PR, Wheeler EF: Pattern of development of bone in childhood and adolescence. Lancet I:523–526, 1971
23. Hobson W, Pemberton J: The Health of the Elderly at Home. London, Butterworth & Co, 1955, pp 53–68
24. Lauvaux JP, Staquet M: The oral glucose tolerance test: a study of the influence of age on the response to the standard oral 50 g glucose load. Diabetologia 6:414–419, 1970
25. Marshal J, Kaeser AC: Survival after non-haemorrhagic cerebrovascular accidents. Br Med J II:73–77, 1961
26. Merrett JD, Adams GF: Comparison of mortality rates in elderly hypertensive and normotensive hemiplegic patients. Br Med J II:802–805, 1966
27. Novak LP: Aging total body potassium, fat-free mass, and cell mass in males and females between ages 18 and 85 years. J Gerontol 27:438–443, 1972
28. Pfaltz CR: Diseases of the ear and vestibular system. In von Hahn HP (ed): Practical Geriatrics. Basel, S Karger, 1975, pp 397–421
29. Rintelen F: Diseases of the eye. In von Hahn HP (ed): Practical Geriatrics. Basel, S Karger, 1975, pp 422–436
30. Sheldon J: The Social Medicine of Old Age. Oxford, Nuffield Foundation, 1948, pp 46–106
31. Smith HW, Goldring W, Chasis H: The measurement of the tubular excretory mass, effective blood flow and filtration rate in the normal human kidney. J Clin Invest 17:263, 1938
32. Smith MJ, Hall MRP: Carbohydrate tolerance in the very aged. Diabetologia 9:387–390, 1973
33. Spence JD: Personal communication, 1977
34. Stanton BR, Exton-Smith AN: A longitudinal study of the dietary of elderly women. London, King Edward's Hospital Fund, 1970
35. Steinkamp RC, Cohen NL, Walsh HE: Resurvey of an aging population: fourteen-year followup. J Am Diet Assoc 46:103–110, 1965
36. Taguchi J, Freis ED: Partial reduction of blood pressure and prevention of complications in hypertension. N Engl J Med 291:329–331, 1974
37. Tindall JP, Graham Smith J Jr: Skin lesions of the aged. In Palmore E (ed): Normal Aging. Durham, Duke University Press, 1970, pp 50–57
38. Trémolières J, Geissler-Blun C: Nutrition and metabolism. In von Hahn HP (ed): Practical Geriatrics. Basel, S Karger, 1975, pp 55–75
39. United States National Center for Health Statistics: Glucose tolerance of adults, United States, 1960–1962. Diabetes prevalence and results of a glucose tolerance test by age and sex. Washington DC, Department of Health, Education and Welfare, US Public Health Service Publication, 1964

Chapter 3

BIOLOGIC GERONTOLOGY

Spring it is cheery,
Winter is dreary,
Green Leaves hang, but the brown must fly;
When he's forsaken,
Wither'd and shaken,
What can an old man do but die?

Thomas Hood

PERSPECTIVES IN LONGEVITY

In 1971 The National Institute of Statistics in Ecuador recorded that Vilcabamba, a small village in the Andes, had a total population of 819. Nine of this number were over 100 years old, and 16.4% of the population were over the age of 60, a figure which contrasted sharply with the 6.4% for rural Ecuador as a whole. The valley that shelters Vilcabamba is 4500 feet above sea level, and its vegetation is lush. The people live by farming, but their methods are extremely primitive and only a bare subsistence is extracted from the land.

Leaf (26) describes how a team of physicians and scientists from Quito, under the direction of Salvador, studied this unique community. The average daily caloric intake of an elderly adult was found to be 1200 calories, of which the protein content was 35–38 g, fat 12–19 g, and carbohydrate 200–250 g. There is no modern sanitation, cleanliness, or medical care, and a small river which skirts the village is used for drinking, washing, and bathing. The inhabitants live in mud huts with dirt floors, sharing their quarters with chickens and pigs. Infant mortality is high. The people appear to be of European rather than Indian descent, and there has been a Roman Catholic church in the village for generations. Its baptismal records validated the ages of the elderly population. Gabriel Erazo, reported to be 121 years old, had a desire to live for one more day. All the centenarians were born locally and had worked hard to scratch a livelihood from the soil. The mountainous terrain demands continuous, vigorous activity even for the very old. Tobacco and sugar cane are grown in the valley, and the local rum drink, zuhmir, is popular but is not consumed to excess.

Leaf found a similar group in another remote and circumscribed community hidden in the Karakorum range in Kashmir near Pakistan's border with China

39

and Afghanistan. The valley is surrounded on all sides by peaks towering more than 20,000 feet high. Although the valley itself is dry, a system of irrigation canals built over the past 800 years carries water from the high surrounding glaciers, converting the valley into a terraced garden reminiscent of Shangri-La. According to Leaf, a Pakistani nutritionist surveyed the diet of the inhabitants of this village, called Hunza, and examined in detail the diet of 55 males. Their average energy intake was 1923 calories with 50 g protein, 36 g fat, and 354 g carbohydrate. As in Vilcabamba, everyone worked hard to wrest a living from the rocky hills.

In Hunza, there is no written language, and no records of birthdates such as the Vilcabamban baptismal ones are available. The inhabitants are Ismaili Moslems of limited education; their ruler, or Mir, is a well-educated man who confirms the suggested longevity of many Hunzacots. Leaf's party was unable to establish any memories of the British invasion of 1891, but was impressed by the appearance of a number of "aged but lean and fit-looking Hunzacots who can climb the steep slopes of their valley with far greater ease than we could." Both in Vilcabamba and Hunza, there was evidence of almost unique genetic isolation.

A considerable number of very old people was observed by Leaf in a third place: the Caucasus in South Russia. This is a much wider area covering three Soviet republics; Georgia, Azerbaijan, and Armenia. The climate varies from a humid, subtropical Black Sea coast with an annual rainfall of about 60 in. to drier continental conditions marked by extremes of summer heat and winter cold. More old people are found in the mountainous regions than at sea level, and the incidence of atherosclerosis among those who live in the mountains is only half that in the sea level villages. The 1970 census placed the total number of centenarians in the Caucasus at 4500–5000. The incidence for this group in Georgia was 39/100,000 and in Azerbaijan 63/100,000. The figure for the United States is 3/100,000. The Gerontological Center in the Republic of Georgia has records of 15,000 persons over the age of 80, more than 70% of whom continue to lead active lives.

DEVELOPMENT OF GERONTOLOGY

In the past 30 years gerontology, the study of the aging process, has advanced from a minor rather esoteric, biologic science into one of the more active and innovative. The question to which everyone would like the answer is whether there is a predetermined limit to the life of an animal and, if so, what factor or factors are responsible for it? Are "age changes, like developmental changes, programmed into the original pool of genetic information and played out in an orderly sequence just as developmental changes are?" to quote Hayflick (23). Before examining the various theories which have been put forward, one should review the facts which have been established by scientists studying different aspects of the aging process in a variety of zoologic species.

SURVIVAL CURVES

If one examines graphs of the numbers of survivors of any particular population, it is possible to note both similarities and differences. Graphs based on data concerning Canadian males in the years 1926, 1950–1952, and 1970–1972 illustrate the striking effect of reducing infant mortality rates between 1926 and 1970–72 (Fig. 3–1) and demonstrate that this is the major factor in increasing life expectancy. Each male born in Canada today can expect to complete his 70 years and each female her 76 or 77 summers. Contrasting with the Canadian male curves is one of Indian women in whom the infant and child mortality was very high. From the gerontologic point of view, the most interesting fact is that all four lines end at the same point on the base line, between the ages of 90 and 100. All the advances in public health and improvement of the environment, plus the small contribution of therapeutic medicine, have succeeded in saving many infants and younger people but not in increasing the longevity of the species.

Similar survival curves for other animals reveal the same situation (11). There is an allotted span on this earth for the rat and horse, and if one multiplies the rat's age of peak mortality, 22 months, by 35 and the horse's 22 years by 3.5, one can establish similar mortality curves for the rat, horse, and man (Fig. 3–2). Without going into more detail of the specific evidence, it can be confidently stated that each animal species has its own characteristic life span. The shape of survival curves may be varied by environmental or therapeutic measures, but these influences have not affected the mean length of life of the species. It follows that, for every species, even under optimal conditions the span of life is fixed. There are variations around a mean, but there is a predetermined maximum age beyond which no one survives. Until more objective evidence has been produced, the individuals in Vilcabamba who reached 120 can be taken to represent this maximum for human beings. Survival curves also suggest the possibility of a built-in mechanism which governs the timing of senescence and death.

DIET

One of the most thoroughly researched areas of gerontology is the effect of variations in diet. It has been shown that controlled undernutrition in childhood slows down growth and increases life span. Evidence in support of this statement has come from studies on a variety of animals ranging from rats to fish, including protozoa. McCay, Dilley, and Crowell (28) made the first observations on brook trout in 1929, but McCay's classic studies on the effect of a restricted diet on rats were not reported until 1939 (29, 30). He and his coworkers showed that on a diet which was severely restricted in calories but adequate in protein, vitamins, and minerals the time taken to reach maturity was extended, but the length of the animal's life was increased substantially. It was possible to double the life span and move the survival curve well over to the right (Fig. 3–3). Similar prolongation of life has been achieved by Berg and Simms (4) without slowing

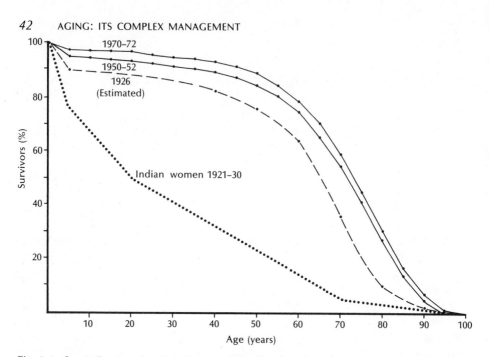

Fig. 3–1. Survival curves for Canadian males based on provincial and regional life tables for 1950–1952 and statistics Canada, 1970–1972. Estimated curve is included for 1926 based on comparison of mortality statistics. (Curve for India from Leaf A: Getting old. Copyright © 1973 by Scientific American, Inc. All rights reserved)

Fig. 3–2. Programmed aging; distribution of deaths by ages for rat, horse, and man, showing peaks of mortality at 22 months, 22 years, and 76 years, respectively. In the upper series of curves time scales have been adjusted 30 times for the rat, 3.5 times for the horse, and unaltered for man to illustrate the general resemblance of curves of natural death as a function of life span. (Burnet FM: Genes, Dreams and Realities. New York, Basic Books, 1971, pp 151–154)

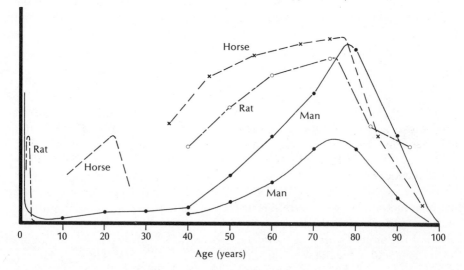

the maturing poccess. Of underfed male rats on their regime 81%–87% were alive at 800 days, while only 48% of controls, which were fed freely, survived for that time.

According to Walford (40b), in addition to extending life span, the restricted diet appears to protect the animal from a number of diseases of aging such as tumors, cataracts, hair discoloration, dry skin, chronic nephrosis, periarteritis, and myocardial degeneration. Berg (3) studied the effect of a restricted diet on the size and health of rats and noted that, while restricted diets (by 33% or 46%) resulted in smaller, lighter animals their "health and female fertility were better" than those of the freely fed controls. If the dietary restriction is carried out before the animal is weaned, however, it can be harmful. In a similar manner, if restricted diets are introduced after maturity, they are much less effective and may not add to the life span at all. The critical period is between weaning and maturity, and the ideal diet from this standpoint is one in which a normal rate of growth to maturity occurs on a diet with strictly controlled reduced calorie intake. It is interesting to recall that the men and women of Vilcabamba and Hunza exist throughout their lives on a diet which is sparse compared with the typical North American one.

TEMPERATURE

Animals whose temperature varies with the atmosphere live longer if they are maintained in a cooler environment. Examples cited by Walford are *Daphnia, Drosophila,* and rotifers. Walford, with Lui (27), demonstrated the same phenomenon in *Cynolebias adloffi.* The effect is variable, and the influence of temperature, unlike diet, was most noticeable if the organism was exposed to a change later rather than earlier in life. This was true for *Drosophila* and rotifers. When the former were subjected to changes of temperature early in life, a temperature of 16°C delayed their emergence as flies, but did not affect life span as a flying insect. In one inbred strain, the effect of the low temperature in the pupal stage was adverse on the life span of males, without affecting the females in this way.

Rotifers react quite differently to changes of diet and temperature (Table 3–1). Early life is not affected by temperature changes, but later life is; the reverse is true for underfeeding. The suggestion of Bourlière (7) that the effect of temperature is related to reduction in basal metabolic rate was not accepted by Walford. He and Lui (27) showed that annual fish reared at a reduced temperature display a faster growth rate and become larger than others developed in warmer water. For present purposes, it is perhaps enough to point out the association of low temperature with increased life span and vice versa in poikilothermic creatures.

IRRADIATION

Exposure to radiation, in the majority of cases, shortens life span. Curtis (14) has shown that there is a linear relationship between the percentage reduction in life span and the amount of radiation (Fig. 3–4). This applies to all but very small

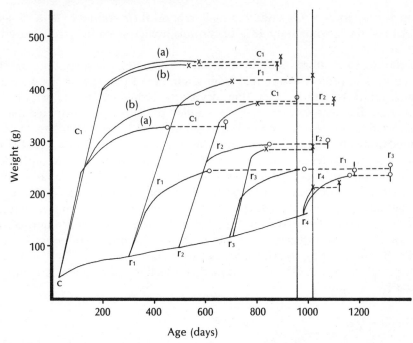

Fig. 3–3. Effect of growth retardation by low calorie diet on the survival and longevity of rats. **C.** Point of weaning C_1. Control groups (a) fed carotene and (b) fed cod liver oil. R_1, R_2, R_3, R_4 represent growth rates of rats retarded for 300, 500, 700 and 1000 days, respectively. The solid line continues to point of reaching mean maximum weight for the same sex and group; hatched line continues to death of last survivor of that sex and group. **O.** Female, **X.** Male. I death of final survivor. (McCay CM et al: J Nutr 18:1–13, 1939. Copyright © 1939 by American Institute of Nutrition)

TABLE 3–1. Effects of Temperature and Nutrition on Age Changes in the Rotifer

	Interval	Temperature			Nutrition		
		25°C	31°C	35°C	Diet I	II	III
Early Life	AB	4	4	4	4	4	4
	BC	7	6	8	8	21	29
	AC	11	10	12	12	25	33
Late Life	CD	4	4	4	4	4	4
	DE	19	8	2	18	16	18
	CE	23	12	6	22	20	22
	AE	34	22	18	34	45	55

Diet I Fresh filtered boiled pond water + algae suspension
Diet II Fresh filtered boiled pond water
Diet III Fresh filtered boiled pond water 3 days/week
A = day hatched   B = start of egg production
C = end of egg production
D = decrease in malic dehydrogenase to lactic dehydrogenase
E = death
Duration of intervals in days
(Fanestil DD, Barrows CH Jr: J. Gerontol 20:462–469, 1965)

doses. Much of the effect of such exposure may be reparable, but Curtis points out that there is no recovery from damage caused by densely ionizing radiation such as that of neutrons. Repeated small doses of x-rays are more potent than their sum given at one time.

There are, however, enough inconsistencies between them to indicate that radiologic effects cannot be equated with a true model of aging. Some animals, such as insects, are quite resistant to radiation. Insects are composed almost entirely of nonmitotic cells, which may be the reason for the resistance. Doses of 400R or 500R in mice produce marked mutation of germ cells, but 10,000R increases the life span of *Drosophila.* The increase is due in this instance to ovarian damage and interference with egg laying (25).

A similar situation accompanies the use of radiomimetic drugs such as nitrogen mustards. Curtis (13) did not find any life-shortening effects in mice with these drugs, while Upton *et al.* (38) did. These apparent contradictions were explained by the different dosage used. Curtis used a nontoxic dose repeated frequently over a period of months, while Upton and his coworkers used a single very large dose, discarding the animals which died within 30 days.

In a mammoth study which involved 3904 RF/J female mice, Storer (36) explored the idea that, if the effects of irradiation were analogous to an "accelerated aging" process, they should be illustrated by a shift to the left of survival curves. This was the case in his study (Fig. 3–5). Not satisfied with that, Storer excluded cases suffering from certain diseases which occurred frequently in irradiated animals. Having done so, he was still able to demonstrate a definite shortening of life span after irradiation.

The time when a disease of aging occurs should also be responsible for a shift to the left on a survival curve. Walford (40c) gives evidence that graying of hair is speeded by irradiation, but age pigment does not develop in nondividing cells (14). Perhaps the most significant feature of the effect of radiation, however, is that comparing it to the known changes in connective tissue normally associated with aging, reveals relatively young collagen in the radiation aged animal. Walford (40c) confirmed this when he studied four age-dependent chemical parameters in two groups of normal and irradiated hamsters (Table 3–2).

Storer's data convincingly demonstrates the life-shortening effect of radiation. On the basis of his results he suggests a probable loss of 24 days from the life span of the RF/J female mice which he studied for every 100R radiation exposure. He concluded, however, that the effect was achieved by selective damage to certain organ systems and could not be accepted as due to a true premature aging. Curtis (14) attributes the effect of radiation to its capacity to cause cell mutations. In the cells of normal elderly livers there are a number of such changes. The numbers are significantly increased following irradiation. All degenerative diseases, he suggests, result from a complex series of events. Radiation accelerates at least one of these events for virtually all diseases, but, while Curtis admits that it is tempting to give it a key role in the aging process, he concludes that there are too many inconsistencies for this to be accepted.

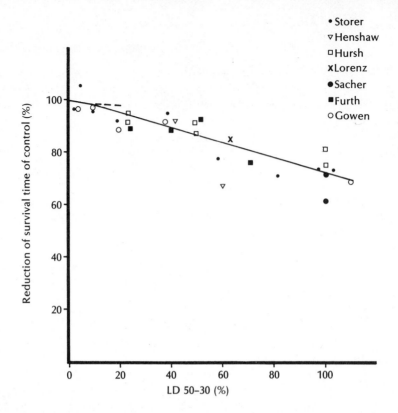

Fig. 3–4. Percentage shortening of life span for mice by irradiation, comparing survival time with dose expressed as a fraction of the LD 50 dose. Data from various investigators plotted by Curtis, who deemed it reasonable to draw a straight line through the points until very low doses are reached. At this point the line curves to approach the origin at about 25% of its slope at high doses (**broken line**). (Curtis, HJ: Biological mechanisms of delayed radiation in mammals. In Ebert M, Howard A [eds]: Current Topics in Radiation Research. Amsterdam, North Holland 1967, pp 141–174)

Fig. 3–5. Percent survival of control and irradiated rats as a function of age. (Storer R: Radiat Res 17:884, 1974)

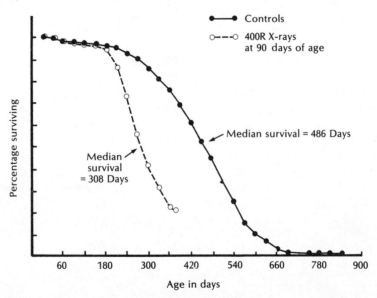

TISSUE CULTURES

Goldstein (17) has described the three major types of cells which are found in mammals: continuous mitotics, intermittent mitotics, and nonmitotics, which are sometimes referred to as postmitotics. The first group includes cells of the blood, intestine and skin which are constantly replaced at intervals of a few days to a few months throughout life; in the second category are cells of the liver and kidneys, organs which have a potential for repair replacement after damage, injury, or loss of tissue; muscle and nerve cells belong to the third group (Fig. 3–6).

Hayflick (22) has studied continuous mitotic cells in culture. He demonstrated that there was a definite limit to the number of generations which such cells could sustain. When he grew embryonic human fibroblasts in an optimum culture medium, the cells continued to divide and reproduce themselves in euploid form for 50 ± 10 generations. Beyond that, they either ceased to divide or became aneuploid with chromosomal abnormalities and, therefore, were analagous to tumors. This finding was taken as an indication of the finiteness of the force of mortality. Confirmation for this view came from the fact that adult human fibroblasts multiplied for only 20 generations when they were cultured.

Further support for the idea of a limit to a cell's potential doubling capacity came from a study of fibroblasts cultured from sufferers of the rare condition

Fig. 3–6. Mitotic capacity of cells during life. Cells are classified according to their mitotic capacity after cessation of somatic growth. Ascending arrows indicate discrete events on a time scale that is otherwise a gradual and continuous sequence. Descending arrows indicate stimuli for cell division at various stages of the life span. (Goldstein S: The biology of aging. N Engl J Med 285:1120–1129, 1971. Reprinted by permission)

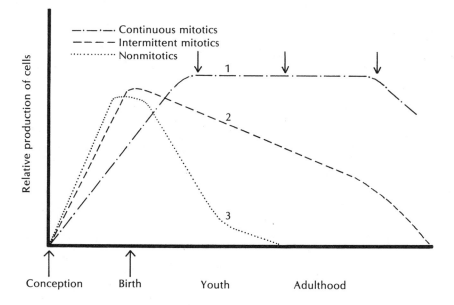

TABLE 3-2. Chemical Parameters of Aging in Normal Hamsters and in Hamsters Irradiated with 420 R at 3 Months of Age

Age Months	1*		2†		3‡		4§	
	Normal	Irradiated	Normal	Irradiated	Normal	Irradiated	Normal	Irradiated
3	1.00 (5)		13 (8)		12 (8)		0.9 (8)	
8	0.75 (5)	0.75 (5)	48 (5)	52 (5)	14 (5)	13 (5)	1.4 (5)	1.4 (5)
22	0.38 (5)	0.34 (5)	200 (7)	175 (5)	16 (7)	15 (5)	1.6 (7)	1.8 (5)
29.5	0.23 (4)		303 (4)		16 (4)		2.6 (4)	

*Soluble/insoluble collagen in skin, numbers referring to ratio of total hydroxyproline in acetic acid extract, pH 2, to that in residue.

†Ethanol-non-extractable liver pigment expressed in arbitrary units of color standard.

‡Liver—activity in units in reference to mg protein in supernatant of liver homogenate.

§Renal lysozyme expressed as mg lysozyme equivalents per g protein in supernatant of liver homogenate.

Figures in brackets are numbers of subjects. Average values given in table.

(Walford RD: The Immunologic Theory of Aging. Copenhagen, Munksgaard, 1969) of premature aging known as progeria. Unlike normal cells such cells undergo only 2–10 doublings (23). This suggests that the survival of cells may be linked to some kind of biologic timing mechanism which determines the age at death in terms of numbers of divisions. Attempts to modify this *in vitro* situation by serially transplanting tissue from breast, skin, and marrow into isogenic hosts have failed (23). It was claimed that the trauma of the procedure was not a factor in this failure, but rather that survival time depended on the age of the transplanted material.

The hypothesis is appealing, and there can be no doubt that the concept is an important one. Hayflick tentatively draws parallels between the range of population doublings for cultured normal embryo fibroblasts from five species and mean maximum life span of each in years (Table 3–3).

CELLULAR CHANGES

The development of more sophisticated techniques for studying histologic specimens has resulted in the discovery of much new anatomic data on cellular structure and characteristics in old animals. Protozoa, unicelled organisms multiplying by simple division, have long been thought to be immortal. Andrew (1a) demonstrates, however, that even these simple basic creatures are subject to senescence.

A suctorian, tokophrya infusionum, has been studied for its aging characteristics by Ruczinska, and some of his results are described by Andrew. This ciliated unicellular organism averages a body diameter of 30μ when young, but this doubles during its 2–3 weeks of existence. There are two nuclei, a micronucleus and macronucleus; the latter undergoes continual alteration in appearance throughout life. Originally spheroid, it becomes oblong or irregular and contains a number of chromatin bodies. The number of these increases from 40 to 300 as the organism ages. While young, embryos are produced every 2–4 hours, but the old animal produced none. There is a decrease in the number of tentacles from 60 to 15 or less in very old animals.

Three general observations can be made about the history of cell aging:

TABLE 3–3. Finite Lifetime of Cultured Normal Embryonic Human and Animal Fibroblasts

Species	Range of population doublings for cultured normal embryo fibroblasts	Mean maximum life span (years)
Galapagos Turtle	90–125	175 (?)
Man	40–60	110
Mink*	30–34	10
Chicken	15–35	30 (?)
Mouse	14–28	3.5

*Data from 20 embryos.
(Hayflick L: N Engl J Med 295:1305, 1976)

1. It is often accompanied by the accumulation within the cell of a pigment, lipofuscin, seen commonly in aging nerve cells.
2. There is a tendency for numbers of large aberrant cells which have hyperchromatic prominent nucleoli and a tendency to amitotic division to appear in, for example, the kidney and intestinal mucosa.
3. There is an accumulation of colloid material in sites such as renal tubules.

These three features were studied and illustrated by Andrew and Pruett in 1957 (1b).

The kidneys of 50 Wistar Institute rats were examined; there were four groups of animals: young (75–100 days), middle-aged (300 days), senile (868–983 days and 1000–1170 days). Among the findings was a reduction in size of the glomeruli in the two latter groups compared with the younger groups. There was little in the way of glomerular fibrosis, which occurred in only 10% of the senile groups, but there was some thickening of the basement membrane. There were also accumulations of lymphocytes and plasma cells in the adventitial layers of arteries, arterioles, and veins, quantities of colloid in the lumina of tubules apart from the collecting ones, and the presence of some aberrant cells as previously described.

Walford (40a) has drawn attention to evidence of reduced mitotic activity in a variety of organs in rats (Table 3–4). Other examples of age related cellular changes which can be cited are the Alzheimer senile plaque and neurofibrillary tangle found in the brain. It may be that one should regard these changes as pathologic rather than senescent, but the differentiation is difficult. At present, there is a gray area between abnormal appearances due to pathology and those due to aging.

CHEMICAL CHANGES

Hayflick (23) has recently described a whole series of metabolic and cell characteristics of normal human fibroblasts. He points out that some substances in the cells increase with age, such as glycogen, lipid, protein, ribonucleic acid (RNA), lysosomes and their enzymes; some decrease, such as transaminases, deox-

TABLE 3–4. Average Number of Mitoses in Standard Area in Organs of Rats

Organs	Young rats	Senescent rats
Adrenals	2.4	0.1
Thyroid	5.6	0.0
Parathyroids	31.7	3.4
Liver	77.7	2.5
Kidneys	11.0	1.0
Spleen	262	49

(Adapted from Korenchevsky by Walford RD: The Immunologic Theory of Aging. Copenhagen, Munksgaard, 1969).

yribonucleic acid (DNA), ribosomal RNA, alkaline phosphates; some remain unaltered, such as respiratory enzymes, glutamic acid dehydrogenase, nucleohistones. Whether these changes occur *in vivo* is not known, but it is likely that the aging cell alters significantly in its detailed chemical composition as its function begins to deteriorate.

A great deal of work has been done on connective tissue composed of cellular and extracellular material. The latter consists of collagen and elastin. Collagen is a protein containing hydroxyproline, proline, and glycine; its molecule is a triple helix with 14 hydrogen bonds in a long, relatively straight and strong rod. This can be seen with an electron microscope and special techniques. Hall (21) has described changes in the physicochemical composition of collagen which occurs as it ages. When it is heated to 60°C at pH 7, it becomes degraded to form gelatin. The amount of gelatin which can be obtained from a given quantity of collagen diminishes with increasing age. Its solubility in acetic acid or appropriate buffer solutions also diminishes in proportion to its age. If submitted to electrophoresis, three different component chains, alpha, beta, and gamma, are revealed. The molecular weight of the alpha chain is about 100,000; of the beta, approximately 200,000; and of the gamma, 300,000. With increasing age, the quantity of low molecular weight alpha chains tends to fall, the heavy gamma chains increase, and the beta chains remain constant.

Physical changes in the behavior of collagen occur concurrently with these chemical alterations. Brocas and Verzar (7) have demonstrated that contraction of collagen fibers in response to heat can be counterbalanced by weights, resulting in isometric tension in the fiber. This tension can be measured, and results indicate that the tensile strength of single collagen fibers increases with the age of the animals.

Walford (40a) provides evidence that serum globulins, particularly of the gamma type, are increased with advancing years. It must be added that others have countered this. In a detailed study by Woodford–Williams *et al.* (42), which carefully excluded old people with disease, there was no significant rise in globulins with age. Walford, however, cites other species in which a rise in globulin occurs with age, including gerbils, rats, chickens, dogs, bulls, and goats.

Von Hahn and Fritz (20) studied DNA prepared from livers of rats and demonstrated that the effect of thermal denaturation of DNA in young and old animals was different. DNA has an increasing thermal stability with age. The authors suggest that their findings are in keeping with their concept of cellular aging as due to progressive, irreversible blocking of genes by protein repressors.

GENETIC FACTORS

The final evidence concerning the nature of aging comes from the geneticists. Kallman (24) describes the results of a study of twins in New York over a period of years. A significant difference between monozygotic and dizygotic twins was demonstrated. Involving hundreds of same sex pairs over 60, the study showed that the intrapair life span differences were twice as great for those who were dizygotic as for those who were monozygotic. Later, Kallman pointed out that longitudinal twin data show that, compared to the limited degrees of similarity between two-egg twins or ordinary sibs, all measurable similarities between aging one-egg twins are consistently more pronounced, frequently in spite of very different environments.

He cited physical and mental signs of aging, social adjustment, intellectual performance and its rate of decline as examples.

It has long been known that members of long-lived families are more likely to reach old age than those whose ancestors died young. Using life insurance statistics, Rockstein (33) reaffirmed that individuals with long-lived parents are more likely to live into old age than are those whose parents died young. One formula that has been suggested is that if the total ages at death of a person's grandparents and parents add up to more than 400, the odds are that the person will reach 70. Rockstein also suggests that the "almost universally observed phenomenon" of a sex difference in longevity which favors the female is evidence of a genetic factor at work. The species-specific life spans of a variety of animals as well point to the same conclusion. Thus, longevity for any animal depends, to a considerable degree, on the genetic material from which it sprang.

SOMATIC MUTATION, CROSS LINKAGE, AND FREE RADICALS

Before considering further general theories, it is important to describe briefly three chemical happenings which are advanced as causes of the aging process. Somatic mutation occurs throughout life spontaneously or as a result of ionizing radiation. Sinex (35) believes that "aging hits are relatively common, modifying and unbalancing cellular control and function." As such, they are clearly a possible cause of senescence and death. Their random nature may also be consistent with Burch's approach. Aging hits are not subject to repair, while other, simpler types of injury are quickly repaired. An example of such a change which is cited by Sinex is the hydrolysis of the phosphate diester bonds of DNA. Because the latter is a stable double-stranded molecule, this chemical reaction occurs only very occasionally and is quickly corrected by the system of repair polymerase and ligase.

Sinex claims that there are three types of mutation: spontaneous hydrolysis, radiation induced mutation, and aging. Their degree of repairability is in the order listed, with least repair possible with aging hits. Sinex also believes that somatic mutation has a particularly significant role to play in the aging process of animals that are relatively long-lived (longer than 2 years) and sensitive to radiation in small doses. Man is such a species.

Cross linkage is the chemical reaction which produces the greatest amount of damage by the least amount of interference. The process is accomplished by an agent such as a small molecule with a chemically active site at each end. Apparently, such molecules exist in cells, and they may latch on to a strand of the DNA double helix. Once this has occurred, one of two things happen. Either the cell's reparative process cuts out the piece of the helix to which the linking agent has attached itself (Fig. 3–7), or the other end of the molecule, which is spinning around in perilous proximity to the other strand of the DNA double helix, may secure a grip on it. When this happens, the DNA molecule becomes permanently defective and unable to replicate itself; spontaneous cell death results (Fig. 3–8). Formaldehyde which, according to Bjorksten (5), is formed in at least eight normal metabolic reactions, acts as a cross-linking agent of DNA very readily. Unsaturated fatty acids and triglycerides are other such agents.

Cross linkage of DNA is of great importance, but even more important may be a similar event which occurs in a large number of large molecules. It seems likely that hyalinization and amyloid formation may be produced by a conglomeration of cross-linked macromolecules. It is also worth noting that ionizing radiation may cause cross linkage as well as fission of molecules. As somatic mutation results from ionizing radiation, there is a connection between the two processes. Free radicals may also act as cross-linking agents.

Pryor (31) defines **free radicals** as highly reactive cellular components derived from atoms or molecules in which an electron pair has been transiently separated into two electrons that exhibit independence of motion. This gives the radicals a large amount of free energy, and they attack and oxidize any available neighboring molecules. It is not difficult to understand how they may become involved in cross linkages. The effect of free radicals is to create peroxidation of unsaturated fatty acids in organic substances rich in such acids. One important area for such activity has been shown to be mitochondrial and microsomal membranes, according to Gordon (18). In this area, the application of results of *in vitro* experiments to the *in vivo* situation is controversial. While numerous workers have demonstrated *in vitro* peroxidation, Green (19) failed to identify lipid peroxides in a study of vitamin E deficient rats. On the basis of his work, he does not accept that peroxidation of unsaturated fats by free radicals occurs in the living animal.

On the other hand, Gordon (18) brought together evidence in support of the idea that free radical peroxidation of fatty acids can cause far-reaching changes *in vivo* during aging. He reports alteration of permeability of cell membranes to electrolytes, microsomes deficient in cholesterol, and accumulation of products of lipid peroxidation within cells and in body fluids which, along with a variety of other changes, have all been suppressed by the addition of antioxidants to the subject's diet.

There seems little doubt that somatic mutation, cross linkages, and peroxidation by free radicals all occur and perhaps form the cracks in the body's physiology which begin the aging process. It is unlikely, however, that one of them alone could be totally responsible or that any generally applicable theory of aging could be constructed on them.

SIGNIFICANCE OF EVIDENCE

It would be ludicrous to suggest that the preceding few paragraphs represent more than a skeleton outline of the very considerable volume of work that has been undertaken in this field over the past 30 and more years. For clinicians, it

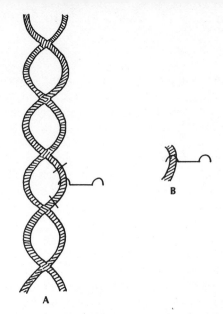

Fig. 3–7. A. Cross-linking agent attached at one point of a DNA molecule, involving one strand only. B. Agent excised by defense mechanisms together with a piece of the DNA affected. The damage is then repaired, the unaffected strand being the template. (Bjorksten J: In Rockstein M [ed]: Theoretical Aspects of Aging. New York, Academic Press, 1974, pp 23–31)

Fig. 3–8. A. Cross-linking agent attached to the second strand of DNA before the defense mechanism could excise it. When this happens, the cell is doomed. If the cross-linking agent is excised, there is no template for repair, as both strands are involved at the same point. B. Cross-linking agent blocking the normal parting of strands in mitosis at a stage where the resultant DNA can neither return to normal nor complete the division. (Bjorksten J: In Rockstein M [ed]: Theoretical Aspects of Aging. New York, Academic Press, 1974, pp 23–31)

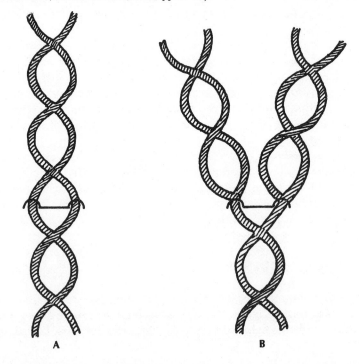

is important to realize that scientific colleagues have made considerable strides in their pursuit of knowledge of the aging process. Many of the answers to questions about why we age may be known within the next few decades. This does not necessarily mean, in my view, that we shall be able to extend the natural life span of the human race. Knowing more of the mechanisms of aging, however, will help physicians to assist patients to avoid many of the ills that currently beset old people. My object in describing very briefly the main areas in which evidence on the nature of aging is accumulating is to alert my clinical colleagues of current progress. We must all be ready to avail ourselves of this new knowledge as soon as it produces possibilities for clinical application.

Curiously, perhaps, clinicians have shown little enthusiasm for research into aging, although they have been anxious to learn biochemical and other parameters of normal old people to assist them clinically. Their lack of curiosity about biologic gerontology has contrasted with the considerable enthusiasm for studies in sociologic and psychologic aging shown by their colleagues in those fields. It may be that biologic gerontology has appeared to be an interesting, but esoteric, cul-de-sac from the clinical standpoint. It now assumes potential importance as the breakthrough in knowledge approaches. When definitive answers to some parts of the question, "How do we age?", come through, they will undoubtedly have very great clinical relevance.

THEORIES OF AGING

It has been said that there are as many theories about aging as there are gerontologists. It is true that there are differing views about what is most important in dictating time factors and about the significance of emotion, intellect, and natural catastrophes in the aging process. The first major argument concerns whether aging is a predestined, programmed affair or not. Wilson (41) has strongly supported the view that death, and hence aging, is a fact of human life that offers the species direct or indirect advantages by limiting life span. Without committing himself on the particular steps in the program, he uses an eloquent, common sense approach to plead a good case for there being a thread of design throughout the whole process.

Burch (9), on the other hand, in a review of the various theories of aging (Fig. 3–9) discards the concept of an ordered programmed process proceeding from conception and embryogenesis through childhood to maturity, senescence, and death. The small spread in age at which each specific stage is reached, he believes, contrasts with the very wide range of ages at which features of senescence appear. Teeth and hair may be lost, for example, before full maturity is reached. The idea that aging is a toxic process which results from an accumulation of poisons in the body fails to explain the anatomic specificity of many age related conditions such as polyarthritis. Wear and tear may appear to explain changes in teeth and weight-bearing joints but can scarcely be a convincing reason for the development of arcus senilis or graying of hair. Burch himself strongly favors the theory that aging is based on errors.

Discussing the possible theories of senescence due to a proliferation of errors, Burch comments on the three possible sites where these may occur (Fig. 3–10). These are the cell, the extracellular tissue, or a combination of the two. By cellular errors, he means alterations in the cell by mutations in complex proteins and suggests that the aging process may be governed by such changes in nonmitotic cells. As these persist, a disturbance of function of the host tissue, brain or muscle, would occur. Should similar cytologic errors occur in mitotic tissue, the result would be the development of clones of cells arising from one originally damaged parent cell; again, such a clone may have a destructive effect on the organ concerned. Extracellular errors do occur and have been studied in collagen (see Chemical Changes).

Burch believes, however, that if there is an aging process encompassing the whole organism, it must be more generalized. His experimental evidence suggests "relational" error theories. He postulates that cells which have undergone somatic mutation may stimulate an alteration in the immunologic system. The individual becomes progressively less able to cope with assaults on his defense mechanisms, suffers self-impairment and finally death.

Fig. 3–9. Outline of the main approaches to aging and senescence. (Burch PJR: The biological nature of ageing. In Cape RDT [ed]: Symposia of Geriatric Medicine, Vol 3. Birmingham, England, West Midland Institute of Geriatric Medicine and Gerontology, 1974, pp 3–14))

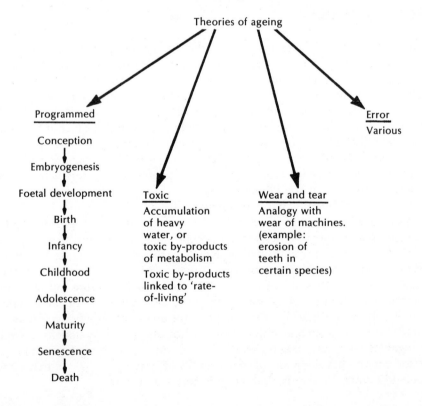

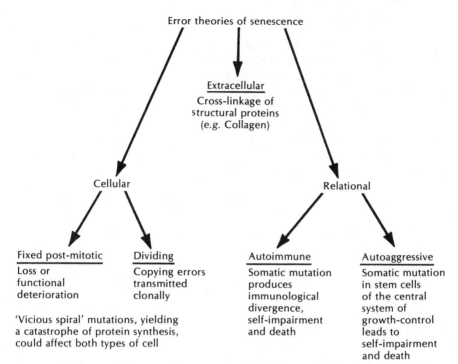

Fig. 3–10. Outline of error theories of senescence. (Burch PJR: The biological nature of ageing. In Cape RDT [ed]: Symposia of Geriatric Medicine, Vol 3. Birmingham, England, West Midland Institute of Geriatric Medicine and Gerontology, 1974, pp 3–14)

Burch and his co-workers believe that there are two cytologically distinct systems involved in the central control and coordination of growth of a target tissue. When tissues are situated on the blood side of a blood–tissue barrier, such as endothelium, the cells that regulate growth are probably thymus-dependent lymphocytes. On the other side of this barrier, they believe that there must be a humoral factor that can pass from one side to the other. To control growth, there must be a feedback homeostatic mechanism which, in turn, requires a measuring element or "comparator" to determine whether the target tissue has achieved its appropriate size. These comparators, according to Burch, are a "fixed number of growth-control stem cells" for each tissue. When mutations occur in these cells, they give rise to abnormal clones of cells in the target tissue and these forbidden clones become responsible for initiating morbid processes with a wide range of effects, from degeneration to uninhibited growth, as in cancer. Burch and his co-workers maintain, therefore, that aging or senescence is not deterministic in the way that growth and development are, but is initiated by random errors which cause autoaggressive disorders. The process is stochastic in nature.

PROGRAM OF AGING

Development is a well-ordered sequential process with well-established land-marks along the way. Is senescence similar? Is there a genetically determined step-by-step process of deterioration ultimately ending in death? One major biologic fact which appears to deny that senescence is in any sense programmed is the remarkable variability of individuals who are the same chronologic age. In their ninth decades, at which time lesser surviving mortals are struggling to maintain their wits, Bertrand Russell was demonstrating volubly in Trafalgar Square, Gladstone and Churchill were Prime Ministers of Britain, and Agatha Christie was still captivating her readers. Hayflick (23) has suggested that there is a "mean time to failure" which allows for substantial variation. After all, we are not dealing with genetically controlled biologic robots, but with human beings of extraordinarily varied random composition who treat their biologic selves with a wide range of care or abuse. It is not illogical to find wide differences in mortality and life span.

Burnet has developed a very plausible theory linking the "clock" to the survival of the thymus gland. He first described this idea in 1970 (10) and claimed in 1973 (12) that support for his views had developed in the meantime. His suggestion was that, if the Hayflick limit functioned as a life span controller, it was likely to do so through one particular tissue essential to life which uses up its generations more quickly than any other similar line. The early atrophy of the thymus in mammals and its importance in the production of T lymphocytes led to the suggestion that these essential elements of the immune system constitute such a line relevant to aging. Three characteristics of this process emerge from Burnet's general consideration of its biologic nature:

1. There are genetic limits to the number of generations of somatic cell proliferation *in vivo,* as Hayflick has demonstrated *in vitro.*
2. Somatic mutations occur and increase with age, resulting in altered and less effective cell function.
3. The older the organism, the less effective its immune responses.

This is one of the most clearly stated immunologic theories of aging. Burch (9) and Walford (40 b, c) both support the view that the body's immune defense system is critical to the aging process, although Walford's view is closer to Burnet's than Burch's.

TISSUE CONTROL

Bullough (8) believes that the key to an animal's life span lies in its tissues which, no matter how they vary in detailed structure and function, are controlled throughout life by a common plan. He postulates that every tissue has to be maintained at a mass which is constant relative to the total mass of the animal and must preserve a rate of function which is appropriate to the body's needs at any given moment. These two properties Bullough calls cellular and molecular homeostasis, respectively.

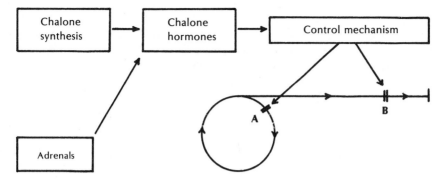

Fig. 3–11. Diagram of the chalone control mechanism in a typical mitotic tissue such as epidermis. Chalone action is strengthened in the presence of the two stress hormones from the adrenals. An inhibition of mitosis at point A is accompanied by an inhibition of cell aging at point B. (Bullough WS: Ageing of mammals. Nature 229: 608–610, 1971)

Fig. 3–12. Diagram of the situation in a typical non-mitotic tissue. With mitosis permanently blocked all the cells pass very slowly along the aging pathway to their death. It is suggested that point B of the chalone mechanism (see Figure 3–11) remains operative. (Bullough WS: Ageing of mammals. Nature 229:608–610, 1971)

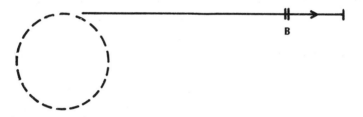

Cellular homeostasis is achieved through varying the rate of mitosis in tissues consisting of cells retaining this potential. A number of tissues have been studied by Bullough and his coworkers: epidermis, sebaceous glands, melanocytes, lung alveoli, kidney, liver, granulocytes, erythrocytes, and lymphocytes. In all cases, these cells synthesize a tissue-specific antimitotic messenger molecule called a chalone which controls new cell production. Every tissue which consists of cells capable of mitosis is constantly changing, because as new cells are created, old cells are dying. After a certain period, which varies from tissue to tissue (14–21 days for epidermal cells, but only 2 days for those of duodenal mucosa), the cells lose the capacity for mitosis and become aging and postmitotic. The faster the rate of mitosis, the shorter the life span of the cell, which allows the balanced size and function of the tissue to be maintained. This means, in effect, that the time of death of the cell is dictated by the antimitotic messenger molecule which is controlling affairs at its birth. Therefore tissues composed of mitotic cells are, theoretically at least, potentially immortal (Fig. 3–11).

Nonmitotic tissues, the neurons, skeletal and cardiac muscle, which during embryonic development, are mitotic, lose this capability at birth. In reaction to the increasing size and maturity of the host, each individual cell of these tissues enlarges to the necessary degree. Because the process of mitosis can no longer occur, the length of life of the nonmitotic cell is greatly prolonged. Instead of a matter of days or weeks, life span for a neuron is many years. Throughout life, however, there is a slow but steady loss of both neurons and muscle cells. The chalone antimitotic messenger substance continues to control these nonmitotic cells, but its role becomes to determine when a cell's death is dictated (Fig. 3–12). A reduction in mitotic potential leads to a slowing of the aging process for the cell.

INFLUENCE OF STRESS

Bullough cites evidence that aging may be inhibited considerably by stimulation of the adrenal glands. Tannenbaum and Silverstone (37) studied the incidence of tumor formation in mice maintained on reduced calorie diets. They found that it was possible to lower tumor incidence in this way and discovered, as McCay had done earlier, that the mice lived for a prolonged life span. It was also noted that the mice had unusually large adrenal glands. Bullough postulates that the mice's fruitless search for extra food acted as a stress which caused the adrenal enlargement and that it was this factor and not the diet *per se* which lengthened life because it inhibited both cell gain and cell loss.

For different reasons Friedman *et al.* (16) and Bellamy (2) treated rats and mice, respectively, with glucocorticoid hormones. In both cases there was prolongation of the life span, and the animals remained in excellent physical shape, suggesting loss of fewer nonmitotic cells from muscle or brain.

CRITICAL ROLE OF THE BRAIN

Why should there be mitotic and nonmitotic tissues? The former are potentially immortal, the latter not. Bullough suggests that the reason may be to set a limit on the life span of the animal, because this has an ultimately beneficial effect on the species. If an evolutionary process is to continue, there must be a continuous discarding to encourage recreating. If this is the purpose of nonmitotic tissues, then according to Bullough, it is probable that they have a critical role in determining life span. He postulates that with its many controlling and regulating functions the brain is the most probable site of the determination of life span.

Shock (34) has also looked at the question from the viewpoint of the whole organism rather than from a cellular level, and he agrees with the general concept of zoologist Bullough. He believes that control mechanisms are the key to the timing of the aging process. He cites the increasing tendency of homeostatic mechanisms related to blood pressure and temperature to break down in older individuals. The examples of breakdown of endocrine control mechanisms to which he draws attention include the kidney's response to antidiuretic hormones and the reduction in glucose tolerance. Shock concludes with the advice the "further investigations should be focussed on the general hypothesis that aging, at least in the total animal, may be a reflection of the breakdown of control mechanisms." Appealing to the clinician, who no longer expects one all-embracing theory to explain all diseases, he adds that the same principle applies to aging: aging is a highly complex phenomenon requiring different explanations for different parts of the process. In his view, the endocrine and nervous systems are the prime controlling agencies.

If one accepts the general direction of Bullough's and Shock's ideas, the brain emerges as the probable seat of decision in the aging process. Not only does it exert the controlling influence over the entire nervous system, but located in it are the hypothalamus and anterior pituitary, which largely direct the function of the second main monitoring agency, the endocrine system.

REFERENCES

1a, b. Andrew W: The Anatomy of Aging in Man and Animals: Protozoa. New York, Grune & Stratton, 1971, pp 3–10, a; 171–182, b

2. Bellamy D: Long-term action of prednisolone phosphate on a strain of short-lived mice. Exp Gerontol 3:327–333, 1968

3. Berg BN: Nutrition and longevity in the rat. I. Food intake in relation to size, health and fertility. J Nutr 71:242–254, 1960

4. Berg BN, Simms HS: Nutrition and longevity in the rat. II. Longevity and onset of disease with different levels of food intake. J Nutr 71:255–263, 1960

5. Bjorksten J: Cross linkage and the aging process. In Rockstein M (ed): Theoretical Aspects of Aging. New York, Academic Press, 1974, pp 23–31

6. Bourlière F: The comparative biology of aging. J Gerontol [Suppl 1] 13:16, 1958

7. Brocas J, Verzar F: Measurement of isometric tension during thermic contraction as criterion of the biological age of collagen fibres. Gerontology 5:223–227, 1961

8. Bullough WS: Ageing of mammals. Nature 229:608–610, 1971

9. Burch PJR: The biological nature of ageing. In Cape RDT (ed): Symposia on Geriatric Medicine, Vol 3. Birmingham, England, West Midland Institute of Geriatric Medicine and Gerontology, 1974, pp 3–14

10. Burnet FM: An immunological approach to ageing. Lancet II: 358–360, 1970

11. Burnet FM: Genes, Dreams and Realities. Aylesbury, England, MTP, 1971, pp 151–154

12. Burnet FM: A genetic interpretation of ageing. Lancet II: 480–483, 1973

13. Curtis HJ: Biological mechanisms underlying the aging process. Science 141:686, 1963

14. Curtis HJ: Biological mechanisms of delayed radiation in mammals. In Ebert M, Howard A (eds): Current Topics in Radiation Research. Amsterdam, North Holland, 1967, pp 141–174

15. Fanestil DD, Barrows CH Jr: Aging in the rotifer. J Gerontol 20:462–469, 1965

16. Friedman SM, Nakashima M, Friedman CL: Prolongation of the life span in the old rat by adrenal and neurohypophyseal hormones. Gerontologia 11: 129–140, 1965

17. Goldstein S: The biology of aging. N Engl J Med 285:1120–1129, 1971

18. Gordon P: Free radicals and the aging process. In Rockstein M (ed): Theoretical Aspects of Aging. New York, Academic Press, 1974, pp 43–59

19. Green J: Vitamin E and the biological antioxidant theory. Ann NY Acad Sci 203:29–44, 1972

20. Hahn JP Von, Fritz E: Age related alterations in the structure of DNA. Gerontologia 12:237, 1966

21. Hall DA: What has gerontology to offer geriatrics? In Cape RDT (ed): Symposia on Geriatric Medicine, Vol 3. Birmingham, England, West Midland Institute of Geriatric Medicine and Gerontology, 1974, pp 32–38

22. Hayflick L: The limited in vitro lifetime of human diploid cell strains. Exp Cell Res 37:614–636, 1965

23. Hayflick L: The cell biology of human aging. N Engl J Med 295:1302–1308, 1976
24. Kallman FJ: Twin data on the genetics of ageing. In Ciba Foundation Colloquia on Ageing, Vol III. London, Churchill, 1975, pp 131–142
25. Lamb MJ: The relationship between age at irradiation and life shortening in adult drosphila. In Lindop PJ, Sacher GA (eds): Radiation and Aging. London, Taylor and Francis, 1966, p 163
26. Leaf A: Getting old. Sci Am 229:44–54, 1973
27. Lui RK, Walford RD: Increased growth and life-span with lowered ambient temperature in the annual fish—cynolebias adloffi. Nature 212:1277–1278, 1966
28. McCay CM, Dilley WE, Crowell MF: Growth rates of brook trout reared upon purified rations, upon dry skim milk diets, and upon feed combinations of cereal grains. J Nutr I:233–246, 1929
29. McCay CM, Maynard LA, Sperling G, Barnes LL: Retarded growth, life span, ultimate body size and age changes in the Albino rat after feeding diets restricted in calories. J Nutr 18:1–13, 1939
30. McCay CM, Maynard LA, Sperling G, Barnes LL: Chemical and pathological changes in aging and after retarded growth. J Nutr 18:15–25, 1939
31. Pryor WA: Free radical reactions and their importance in biochemical systems. Fed Proc 32: 1862–1869, 1973
33. Rockstein M: The genetic basis for longevity. In Rockstein M (ed): Theoretical Aspects of Aging. New York, Academic Press, 1974, pp 1–10
34. Shock NW: Physiological theories of aging. In Rockstein M (ed): Theoretical Aspects of Aging. New York, Academic Press, 1974, pp 1–10
35. Sinex NW: The mutation theory of aging. In Rockstein M (ed): Theoretical Aspects of Aging. New York, Academic Press, 1974, pp 23–31
36. Storer JB: Evaluation of radiation response as an index of aging in mice. Radiat Res 17:878–902, 1974
37. Tannenbaum A, Silverstone H:. Quoted by Bullough DS: Ageing of mammals. Nature 229: 608–610, 1971
38. Upton AC, Conkling JW, McDonald TP, Christenberry KW: Preliminary studies on late somatic effects of radiomimetic chemicals. In Harris RJC (ed): Cellular Basis and Aetiology of Late Somatic Effects of Radiation. London, Academic Press, 1963, pp 171–175
39. Vital Statistics: Vol III, Ottawa, Statistics Canada, 1973
40. Walford RD: The Immunologic Theory of Aging. Copenhagen, Munksgaard, 1969, pp 37–43, a, 149–160, b; 180–197, c
41. Wilson ED: The programmed theory of aging. In Rockstein M (ed): Theoretical Aspects of Aging. New York, Academic Press, 1974, pp 11–21
42. Woodford-Williams E, Alvarez AS, Webster D, Landless B, Dixon MP: Serum protein patterns in 'normal' and pathological aging. Gerontologia 10:86–93, 1964

Chapter 4

BRAIN FAILURE

"You are old, Father William," the young man said,
"And your hair has become very white;
And yet you incessantly stand on your head—
Do you think, at your age, it is right?"

"In my youth," Father William replied to his son,
"I feared it might injure the brain;
But now that I'm perfectly sure I have none,
Why, I do it again and again."

Lewis Carroll

EVOLUTION OF THE BRAIN

There are larger, stronger, and faster animals on the earth than man, but *Homo sapiens* totally dominates the world and even beyond. This has been possible because of the development of the human brain, which is probably the most complicated and versatile computerized system in biology. As an illustration of the brain's effectiveness and the reasons for man's supremacy over all other creatures, it is relevant to relate what is known of prehistoric and more recent man to the size and function of the human brain.

Detailed knowledge of the Pleistocene in terms of human history is negligible and is based on archeologic and anthropologic studies of a few isolated discoveries. About 1–2 million years ago the prehuman beings inhabiting the world were the Australopithecines. Between their heyday and the arrival on the scene of Cro-Magnon man about 35,000 years ago, the size of the brain trebled. In evolutionary terms this was a much greater change than any other which occurred in our species over this million year plus period. It is strong evidence for the view that the brain is the single most important factor in man's evolutionary development.

During the period between the Australopithecines and Cro-Magnons, man's lifestyle is unlikely to have varied a great deal. By examining the current living pattern of baboons and chimpanzees, it is possible to make intelligent assessments of the social organization of groups of primitive man. These were probably small in size—perhaps 50–100—living in relatively circumscribed areas. Each group would have had its own hierarchical structure and means of communication between its members. Apart from the inevitable male competition for the most desirable females, resolved by triumph of the strongest and most determined, there was probably relative peace within the group. The relationship between inhabitants of neighboring areas might have been another matter. Primitive languages would have been varied, the index of suspicion high, and the likelihood of intergroup fights strong.

Bigelow (4) has suggested a new concept of evolution based on the premise that those groups which always triumphed in the local wars were, on the average, those that had better communication within the group and therefore acted as a more cohesive team. Accepting that physically, man-for-man, there may not have been much difference between them, the deciding factors were likely to be leadership, strategy, and good teamwork; these qualities were better developed in those with higher levels of intelligence. In advancing this hypothesis which emphasizes the importance of cerebral function to man, Bigelow was seeking an explanation for the remarkable increase in the brain's size. He emphasizes three major clues to account for the increased size of the brain:

1. The brain is a "social instrument," therefore the force that caused its expansion will be "related to social life."
2. This force has "acted on man alone."
3. It "was acting against men with the smallest brains."

If one keeps these factors in mind, one can build up a credible idea of how this remarkable evolutionary process occurred.

The original areas of the world, which were inhabited by Australopithecines, would have varied then as now in their desirability and suitability to support life. Favored zones would have contained many groups; less popular regions, fewer. The most important factor would have been the availability of food and water. Competition between neighbors would have been more intense and ferocious, with frequent wars between those nearest to the most desirable areas. Those who proved weaker would have been either slain or pushed out of the attractive geographic spot. A type of concentric arrangement of groupings would have developed (Fig. 4–1), with fewer settlements further from the center and those consisting of the groups less able to war successfully. Survival of the fittest in this type of constantly fluctuating situation would have resulted in the destruction of those with the least intelligence and smallest brains. If one envisages this evolving process occurring in many areas, for thousands of generations, it becomes possible to understand the reason for the brain's development.

Two further accompaniments of this process are the ferocity, including wholesale slaughter, with which man has always treated his human enemies and the polygamy which was a feature of human life until the relatively recent religious eras. Because the strongest and most intelligent were dominant, both resulted in an increase of genes associated with superior brains. The known history of the past 10,000 years adds credence to what must be a matter of conjecture in relation to earlier times. The Bible recounts stories of endless small but ferocious wars between the Israelites and a variety of neighboring tribes. Classical history continues the same story, with larger and larger groups coming

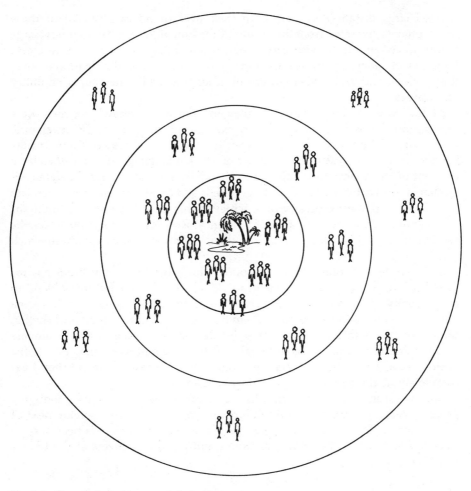

Fig. 4–1. Groups clustering around desirable terrain.

together and eventually forming the great empires of the Greeks, Persians, and Romans.

At a more social level there have also been major advances. For thousands of years our ancestors found food where they could, scavenging and hunting, or eating berries and fruit in the wild. About 8,000–10,000 years ago they discovered the nature of seed, which allowed them to grow their own crops and cultivate the land in an organized manner. About the same time they realized it was possible to domesticate certain animals, and the creation of flocks and herds kept hunger at bay.

Until relatively recent times in the story of man, our forbears traveled on foot, but about 5000 years ago the potential of the horse to pull chariots and later to carry men was developed. Modern civilization took a rapid leap forward. Large armies of Mongols and Caucasoids dominated the Central Asian plains and covered large distances quickly with their new found cavalry. All of these developments stemmed from the ability of the human race, with their now large brains, to communicate with each other, to rationalize, to improvise to create tools and weapons, and most importantly, to continue their domination of even the strongest and most united groups of other animals by their superior ability for strategy.

At this time in the Dordogne Valley in France and elsewhere, men were creating art forms in their caves—an example of the constantly developing complexity of the brain. This can be seen as an innovative way of communicating and, in a sense, was the forerunner of written language. If one thinks for a moment of the enormous complexity of modern life and studies the details of human brains with their billions of nerve cells and dendrites, one can appreciate that the evolutionary process which achieved this must have required millions of years to reach its current state of efficiency. Recorded history illustrates the sudden burgeoning of this process into the prolific and productive phase which continues today.

If the endless adaptability and resourcefulness of the human brain has resulted in extremely capable human individuals, the brain's failure is likely to have equally important consequences. Where the mature human with a keen mind can to a certain extent control environment and obtain food and shelter, the old person with brain failure is as helpless as the young infant, as aimless as the rudderless ship, and as vulnerable as the weaponless soldier. This is the position of a large number of elderly people who, as a result, live out their lives completely at the mercy of their fellow human beings.

We have seen that the brain may play a dominant role in regulating the aging process. Varying degrees of brain failure are implicated in the development of four major medical problems of old age. To understand this it is necessary to state briefly some of the known anatomic and physiologic facts of the brain's function.

STRUCTURE OF THE CENTRAL NERVOUS SYSTEM

There are 15,000–20,000 million nerve cells in the human body, each with 10,000 processes linking it to other nerve cells (Fig. 4–2). The enormous complexities of the brain and nerves are responsible for the wide range of activities which are initiated and controlled by the central nervous system. The brain substance consists of cell bodies encased in a great mass of interlacing dendrites known as a dendritic field. Every axon is encased in myelin, and the speed of conduction of impulses varies with the thickness of the axon. Each axon finally splits up into a number of terminal filaments, which means that each nerve cell may be concerned, for example, with a number of different muscle fibers. The stimuli which the boutons terminaux exert on other nerve cells may be added to by those from other boutons (Fig. 4–2). The speed of transmission of impulses is measured in milliseconds. The process is largely similar to passage of an electric current but is much slower. All boutons connect with other nerves at synapses,

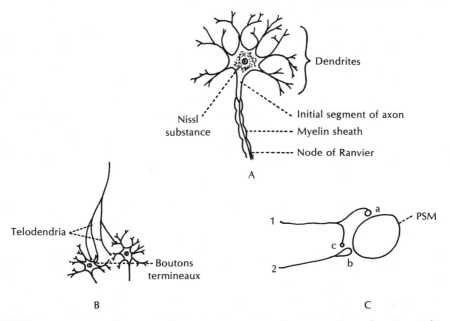

Fig. 4–2. Basic neuron unit. A. Cell body and its processes. B. Terminal portion of an axon within CNS. C. Detail of terminal knobs **a** and **b** of two axons which can excite the postsynaptic membrane (**PSM**) of another neuron. Axon 1 also has another terminal knob **c** which establishes axoaxonal contact with **b** of axon 2 and is able to exert presynaptic inhibition on it. (Bowsher D: Introduction to the Anatomy and Physiology of the Nervous System. Blackwell, 1970, pp 39–46)

and the link across these is by release of chemical substances such as acetylcholine or noradrenaline.

The direction of flow of impulse is from dendrites to axon, with the position of the cell body varying with the type of cell.

RECEPTORS AND EFFECTORS

Receptors turn a variety of stimuli into nervous energy which results in transmission of an impulse from the periphery to the center. These impulses may be consciously experienced by the individual, such as touch, heat, or pain. Others, such as proprioceptive stimuli from muscles and joints, are not although they allow us to control limb and trunk function. A third group is linked to the special senses of vision, hearing, taste, and smell.

There are three important general properties of such afferent arrangements (7):

1. Each stimulus requires a certain threshold strength to trigger the nerve impulse. A Pacini corpuscle will respond, for example, to a minute deformation or vibration on the skin maintained for only 0.1 sec. Such stimuli from several sensory end organs may converge on one afferent axon. While some responses are extremely sensitive, others may require a much stronger stim-

ulus. Bowsher (7) suggests that under optimal atmospheric conditions the human eye can detect the light of one candle at 28 miles.

2. The frequency of impulses passing up the nerve is proportional to the intensity of the applied stimulus—this is the meaning of frequency coding. There is, thus, a quantitative as well as a qualitative signal dispatched by the sensory nerve.

3. Adaptation refers to the response of the receptors to a continued stimulus. Some receptors, but not all, will relay impulses as long as the stimulus is applied. These are slowly adapting receptors which signal a *steady state*. A different type of signal emanates from Pacini corpuscles; impulses quickly cease if the stimulus is maintained. This type of receptor signals a *change of state*.

These qualities of receptors give an indication of the sensitivity of the information-gathering function of the nervous system.

The *effectors* are typified by the motor unit. Each striated muscle has a large number of such units, the size of the units varying with the type of muscle. The small muscles of the hand which are concerned with fine, skillful movements have small motor units (10–20 fibers) innervated by a single axon, while the muscles of strength (such as those of the proximal parts of limbs) may have as many as 1500. The motor unit is a separate entity. There is a limit to the length of time for which any such unit can maintain a contraction, and in no muscle do all units fire at once. At any given point the muscle's contraction is maintained by a proportion of the component units while the others relax and pass through their refractory phase.

Both receptors and effectors come under the influence of other parts of the central nervous system. Sensory messages are relayed through reticular formations in the medulla, pons, and midbrain before being directed through the thalamus to the sensory cortex. Impulses from the motor cortex are modified by information transmitted from cerebellum, red nucleus, substantia nigra, basal ganglia, midbrain, and pontine and medullary reticular formations. The dendritic fields simplify the need and capability of the brain to establish a most complex series of links between sensory and motor parts of the system as well as between the component parts of each. This simple account of sensory and motor systems emphasizes the complexity of neutral pathways and interrelations. One further component must be included.

AUTONOMIC NERVOUS SYSTEM

The autonomic nervous system controls most visceral functions of the body, and its influence is distributed widely through the sympathetic and parasympathetic nerves. Most of the control which it exerts is involuntary, in contrast to the motor and sensory systems which relate more to voluntary activity. The transmission of sympathetic stimuli plays a major role in control of blood pressure levels, temperature control, and intestinal motility. Eyzaguirre and Fidone (15) describe how control of the autonomic system is vested in the hypothalamus and other higher centers in the brain (see Ch. 8, Homeostatic Impairment).

AGING OF THE BRAIN

What effect does age have on the brain, both anatomically and physiologically? There is a widely held belief that the changes which occur in cerebral function in older people are due to vascular disease. It is important therefore to examine this view and allot cerebral vascular disease its proper place in the etiology of syndromes of cerebral failure.

SENILE PLAQUES, NEUROFIBRILLARY TANGLES, AND SOFTENING

Tomlinson, Blessed, and Roth (22, 23) carried out a thorough and meticulous pathologic study of 78 brains, 50 from demented and 28 from nondemented elderly people who died in Newcastle. The pathologic details recorded included the number of senile plaques, presence of neurofibrillary tangles and granulovacuolar degeneration, and a measurement by volume of areas of softening, which were attributed to vascular disease. This resulted in quantitative data in the case of plaques and softening, with less definite estimates of tangle formation and granulovacuolar degeneration, using the terms "none," "occasional," "numerous," or "considerable."

In addition to the pathologic studies, clinical diagnoses were considered. Particular care was taken to differentiate cases of senile dementia from functional psychoses and delirious states. The nondemented group, which acted as a control, were physically ill from a variety of causes. Each subject was assessed on a dementia scale (0=full competence, 28=complete dependence) and a test score (37=full marks, 0=complete failure). The object of the study was to correlate pathologic, clinical, and psychologic data. The results (Table 4–1) indicate a strong link between the number of senile plaques and a clinical diagnosis of senile dementia, poor scoring on the dementia scale, which involved activities of daily living, and poor scoring on the test, which was of memory and cognitive function (5).

The pathologic examination of the 28 brains from nondemented subjects showed softening visible with the naked eye in 13, the volume of which varied 0–91 ml with a mean of 13.2 ml. There were also senile plaques in 22 with a count per high-power field of 3.3, neurofibrillary tangles in the hippocampus only in 14 subjects and in the cortex in 3, and granulovacuolar degeneration in 14 (Fig. 4–3). Thus in this group of brains from nondemented subjects, one could identify four major pathologic features usually associated with dementing disease (22).

In the brains of the 50 subjects with dementia, 25 showed a combination of the three histologic changes associated with senile or Alzheimer's dementia: plaques, tangles, and granulovacuolar degeneration. The difference between the

TABLE 4-1. Mean Plaque Counts and Mean Dementia and Test Scores in Diagnostic Groups

Diagnostic groups	No. of cases	Mean plaque counts	Standard deviation	Mean dementia scores	Standard deviation	Mean test scores	Standard deviation
Senile dementia (78.15)*	26	20.85	12.17	13.92	5.03	10.5	9.15
Depression (71.86)	7	1.14	1.22	2.14	1.35	28.6	8.42
Paraphrenia (75.00)	5	5.00	4.18	2.80	1.64	25.0	6.08
Functional cases continued (73.17)	12	2.75	3.33	2.42	1.44	27.1	7.45
Delirious states (76.36)	14	2.64	4.16	2.00	1.71	20.8	8.28
Physically ill controls (76.88)	8	5.13	4.32	2.25	1.75	31.8	4.40
Total	60						

*Mean age of groups in parentheses; standard deviation 4.14–8.26
(Blessed G, Tomlinson BE, Roth M: Br J Psychiatry 114: 797–811, 1968)

Fig. 4–3. Pathologic changes in the brains of 28 nondemented subjects. **m.** Mean. (Composed from data of Tomlinson BE, Blessed G, Roth M: J Neurol Sci 7:331–356, 1968)

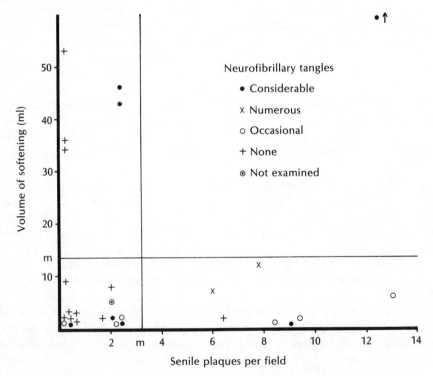

brains of the demented and the nondemented was essentially one of degree. The authors emphasized the consistency of a finding of widespread neurofibrillary degeneration throughout the cortex. In only 6 of these 25 cases was there no evidence of ischemic softening, and it was very small (less than 3 ml) in 11; the volume in the remaining 8 varied 10–53 ml. Of the remaining 25 cases, 6 had gross vascular lesions, and they were regarded as cases of pure arteriosclerotic dementia since they had a mean volume of softening of 186 ml. None of the 6 had neurofibrillary degeneration. Four cases presented a combined picture with much softening added to the other features. Eleven cases exhibited less severe changes, although all four pathologic features were present. Tomlinson and his coworkers judged three of these as having features favoring arteriosclerotic etiology, three were judged as senile dementia, and the remaining five as mixed. Of the final four cases, two presented no significant lesions of senile or ischemic disease, there was one probably due to trauma, and one case of Wernicke's encephalopathy. Thus of the 46 with recognizable pathologic features of dementia, 28 were of the senile or Alzheimer type of the disease, 9 were arteriosclerotic, and 9 had evidence of both conditions.

The study described the mean age of the subjects in the different diagnostic groups (Table 4–1) but found no significant correlation between mean plaque count and age, because in their view the effects of age were "presumably overshadowed in this material by the influence of other factors." Tomlinson, however, found that there is a tendency for plaque counts to increase with age when he examined the brains of subjects who died from injury or physical disease. Ball (1) demonstrated the same association in neurofibrillary tangle occurrence in his quantitative study on this condition (Fig. 4–4).

The evidence from these studies strongly suggests that ischemic softening, senile plaques, neurofibrillary tangles, and granulovacuolar degeneration will be found in virtually all brains of elderly subjects. These changes represent the pathologic features of brain failure. The older the patient, the more frequently senile plaques and neurofibrillary tangles occur, which is not necessarily the case with vascular damage. This knowledge needs emphasis because the prevalent view is that the main cause of failing cerebral function is arteriosclerotic disease. While there has been an enormous continuing research effort into this condition so prevalent among affluent societies, an equal program into the etiology of plaques and tangles is long overdue.

LIPOFUSCIN ACCUMULATION

Another well-recognized feature of the aging brain is the slowly increasing quantity of pigment granules which accumulates in neurons and glial cells. The precise nature of this material has not yet been established, but it is fatty in nature, may be derived from lysosomes, and consists of enzymatic material (21). Siakatos and Armstrong (21) discuss the question of whether the pigment represents inert material of no further value to the cell or whether it is a form of end product from an effete enzyme system. The role of peroxides and free radicals in the genesis of the lipopigment is described,

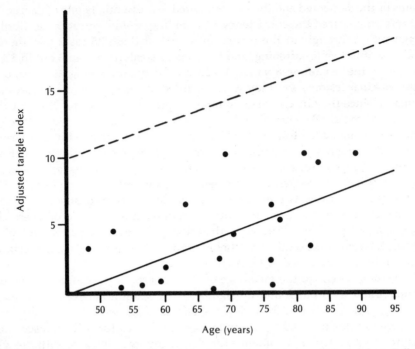

Fig. 4–4. Adjusted tangle index in 19 control subjects of varying ages. (Adapted from Ball MJ: Neuropathol Appl Neurobiol 2:395–410, 1976)

and the hypothesis is advanced that peroxidase deficiency may be responsible for the formation of ceroid pigment in cases of Batten–Spielmeyer–Vogt syndrome.

Brizzee, Ordy, and Kaack (8) studied a group of rhesus monkeys ranging in age from a few days to 20 years to establish changes in brain weight during development, maturity, and aging; the earliest appearance of lipofuscin in neurons; the comparative incidence of this in different parts of the brain; and the precise site of pigment in glia and neuropil. They demonstrated that there were gradations in the amount and character of pigment which first appeared in animals about 3 months old. These workers assessed the quantity on the basis of three criteria: fine granules, larger discrete scattered particles, and congregated masses. Their results showed a steady increase in quantity from nil at the newly born stage to 77% involvement of cells of the medulla at age 19.5±0.95. The quantity of pigment varied from zone to zone of the brain. The least was in the cerebellum and neocortex (21% and 22% respectively); the most, in midbrain —hippocampus (62%) and medulla (65%).

The variations in quantity of pigment in different anatomic sites remains unexplained. Brizzee *et al.* speculate that there may be an association between lipofuscin and respiratory enzyme activity or the variations may have a relation to differences in the regional use of energy. This remains an unsolved mystery.

BRAIN CHEMISTRY

Quite apart from the question of cell loss, aging is accompanied by significant alterations in brain cells. Confirmatory evidence can be found by comparing the gross chemistry of the brain in old people with that of young people. The amount of water in the brain decreases from 92% at birth to approximately 76% at age 90; total lipids rise from 3.5% at birth to 10.5% at age 30 and decline to 7.5% at 90; DNA, RNA, and protein similarly increase by three times from birth to maturity. The 140 g protein in the brain's dry weight at maturity decreases to 100 g by 90 years of age (19). These are crude measures of a highly complex process of constantly altering states, but they confirm once more the concept of a series of changes going on in neuronal and glial cells as the individual passes through development and maturity to senescence.

More recently, attention has been drawn by Davies and Maloney (13) to the reduction in choline acetylase activity in cases of Alzheimer's dementia. They found this most marked in the hippocampus, where neurofibrillary tangles are

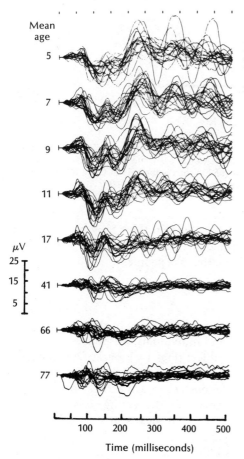

Fig. 4–5. Changes in the visually evoked responses of the brain during maturation and aging. Each age group was composed of 20 subjects (10 males, 10 females). (Beck EG, Dustman RE, Schenkenberg T: In Ordy JM, Brizzee KR [eds]: Neurobiology of Aging. New York, Plenum Press, 1975, pp 175–192)

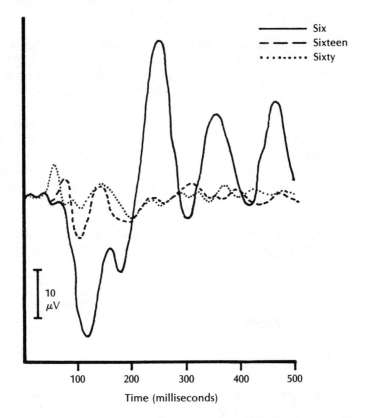

Fig. 4–6. Visually evoked responses of the brain in 3 subjects of different ages. The high amplitude of the response during formative years and the potentiation of early and attenuation of late components in later years are shown. (Beck EG, Dustman RE, Schenkenberg T: In Ordy JM, Brizzee KR [eds]: Neurobiology of Aging. New York, Plenum Press, 1975, pp 175–192)

found to the greatest extent (2). It seems possible that there may be an association between these biochemical and pathologic findings which are present, to a much smaller degree, in the brains of healthy old people.

ELECTROENCEPHALOGRAPHY

Another indication of the same phenomenon can be seen in the electrical patterns of the brain in young, mature, and old individuals. Responses to visually evoked stimuli vary with the age of the subject (Fig. 4–5). Beck, Dustman, and Schenkenberg (3) point out the advantages of using an evoked response technique as opposed to examining the spontaneous electrical activity of the brain. The response is brisker and more immediate in the young, less marked in amplitude in the mature and the senescent, and slower to complete in the senescent (Fig. 4–6). The implication is again of alteration in electrical functioning of the older brain, confirming and adding to the evidence.

SENSORY EFFICIENCY

The importance of sensory input cannot be overemphasized, and it is likely that progressive blunting and reduction in the capability to recognize and process a wide variety of external stimuli is of the greatest importance (see Eyes and Ears, Ch. 2). If one remembers that the key function of the brain is communication in the broadest sense, it becomes obvious that the first step in this complex process must lie in the recognition of messages. Advancing years make it increasingly difficult because of deterioration or loss of receptors, diminution in numbers of afferent neurons, and loss of the relevant areas in nuclei and cortex of the brain. The fact that there is a slowing in reaction times and increased difficulty in inhibiting irrelevant signals suggests that central processing of information may perhaps be the most crucial aspect.

In 1975 Corso (12) discussed the effect of age on vision, hearing, taste, pain, touch and vibration and concluded that the pattern of age related sensory deficits was such as to suggest a mixed etiology. He added that, in the older person,

there is a marked impairment of information processing in tasks involving irrelevant stimuli, coding and decoding of stimuli and the abstraction of information from a complex stimulus configuration, which suggest that the behavioural measures in these situations encompass cognitive processes beyond the level of simple perceptual functions.

Of great importance to this information processing are the inhibitory capabilities of much of the brain. Recent work in relation to the cerebellum has suggested that its role may be predominantly an inhibitory one. Llinas (18) described how he and Wolfe demonstrated that the activation of Purkinje's cells by mossy fibers increases about 25 milliseconds before an eye movement begins, the implication being that cerebellar regulation of movement is capable of correcting mistakes (in this case to ensure visual coordination) before impulses have reached the relevant muscles.

CEREBRAL BLOOD FLOW, OXYGEN UPTAKE, AND CEREBRAL METABOLISM

The brain comprises 2% of the body in terms of weight but consumes 15% of the total cardiac output and uses 20%–25% of oxygen which is inhaled. Of the total consumption of glucose 25% goes to provide the necessary energy for the brain. As the individual ages, however, these demands are reduced in absolute terms. Cerebral blood flow has been estimated at 106 ml/100 g brain tissue/min at age 6, and this declines to 62 ml at age 21 and 58 ml at 71 (19). Oxygen uptake presumably diminishes in proportion. These changes are concomitants of increasing age, not the result of ischemic disease. In individuals with a severe degree of generalized arteriosclerosis or cerebral vascular disease, these changes become very much more striking.

LOSS OF NEURONS

Some doubt has been expressed by Hanley (16) that the evidence favoring fall-out of neurons throughout life was valid. In a careful review of the literature he found reason to state that the case was by no means proven. Since then, using a sophisticated counting arrangement, Ball (2) has provided clear-cut evidence of neuronal loss in the hippocampal cortex. He was able to express the number of neurons "per cubic millimetre of (paraffin-impregnated) cortex." His results show a drop from 7890/mm³ at age 45 to 5800 at 90, a loss of 26% (Fig. 4–7). Although this study provides information about only one area of the cortex, it seems likely that a similar loss occurs elsewhere in the brain.

MEASUREMENT OF CEREBRAL FUNCTION

The efficiency of most of the visceral organs and systems can be measured with relative ease. With the brain securely enclosed in its bone case and inaccessible to our prying attempts to learn its secrets, however, the situation is different.

Fig. 4–7. Neuronal loss from the hippocampal cortex with age in 19 control subjects. (Ball MJ: Acta Neuropathol [Berl] 37:111–118, 1977)

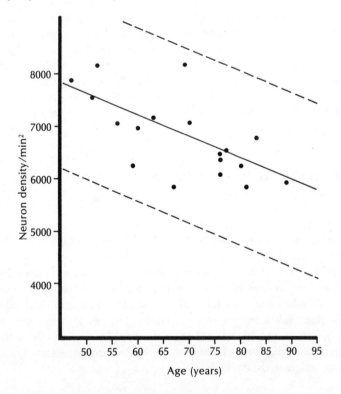

We do know that the individual who retains strength and suppleness in his or her muscles must have a brain in which the motor units are functioning well. We can judge that the skilled but elderly musician who continues to play or conduct with unabated vigor into the 80s has a brain which is performing well. How can we assess brain function in those humbler mortals who have no obsessional devotion to fitness or unique musical talent? There are two measures that can be used: 1) a test of intelligence and cognitive functions and 2) an assessment of the ability to perform activities of daily living in a competent manner.

It is fair to suggest that the scientist has to some degree regarded attempts at defining and marking intelligence as an activity of dubious validity. Psychologists have, however, developed their tests with skill and care, and they can offer much valuable information to help the clinician. As a vindication of psychologic testing as a measure of brain function, one can cite the fact that young people with above average intellectual ability are physically healthier and live longer (9).

PSYCHOLOGIC TESTS

Bromley (9) points out that psychologic tests aim to assess intellectual endowment. They are not an indication of an individual's capacity to do a particular job well, nor are individuals whose IQ is high guaranteed success in life. They have the potential in terms of above average intelligence, but success depends on a number of additional factors such as motivation, environment, family background, and occasionally even less predictable chance occurrences. Knowledge of the effect of age on intelligence stems largely from the work of Wechsler (24, 25). He based his studies on 10 tests of intellectual ability (Fig. 4–8).

The first three tests are a measure of stored knowledge and are affected by the educational attainments of the individual. These are little affected by age and, indeed, may improve as vocabulary and commonly used verbal skills increase. There is no speed factor in these tests, and the individual has time to think and ponder over the replies.

Simple *arithmetic* problems (Fig. 4–8) measure the subject's ability to calculate and handle figures. "How many apples for a dollar at 12¢ each, and how much change?" As can be seen there is a modest decline with age in results of such tests. *Similarities* refers to a Wechsler subtest in which the individual is asked to explain an association between two objects, such as a diary and logbook or birds and bees. Old people, according to Bromley, are less able to think in abstract terms and therefore do less well in this activity.

Picture completion involves the presentation of an incomplete representation of a common object, and the subject is asked to supply the missing part or parts. *Picture arrangement* involves placing in appropriate order a group of pictures which compose a nature sequence. *Object assembly* uses jigsaw puzzles, while *block design* is constructing a model with colored cubes according to a small given design. Finally, *digit symbol substitution* measures the ability to transfer a statement from one set of symbols to another, using a master code provided.

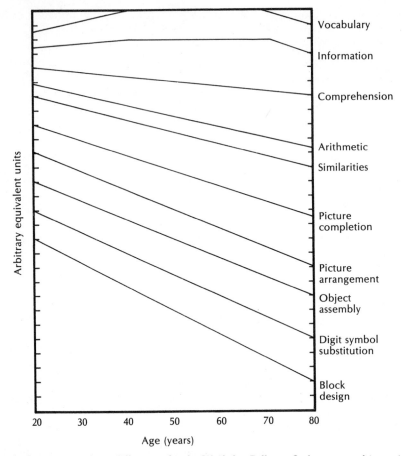

Fig. 4–8. Cross-sectional age differences for the Wechsler–Bellevue Scale, expressed in equivalent units (rank differences). (Bromley DB: The Psychology of Ageing, 2nd ed. The Effects of Ageing on Adult Intelligence. Penguin Books, 1974, pp 178–210)

When the results obtained in these tests are plotted against age (Fig. 4–8), the pattern is similar to that for a variety of physical parameters (see Ch. 2, Physical Aspects of Aging), namely a falling away in performance of varying degree. It is reasonable to hypothesize that this reduction in intellectual competence is comparable to the loss of physical abilities. It should be pointed out that these results were obtained by cross-sectional studies in the early days of this type of psychometric testing. Since then, there have been several longitudinal surveys, but

despite differences in the composition of samples with regard to age, intelligence, education, socio-economic background, and other relevant variables, there appears to be at least one common thread leading toward a cohesive pattern of intellectual functioning in the later years of life. That thread seems to be a remarkable stability of verbal scores

—whenever health has been preserved—accompanied by a relentlessly progressive decline in performance on speeded tasks. Thus our longitudinal studies have led us to rediscover the classical pattern of aging! [20]

ENVIRONMENTAL COMPETENCE

Observing an individual's skill at activities of daily living is commonly considered a means of assessing progress in a rehabilitation program. If one widens the concept to include all daily physical and mental activities, one can document obvious declines in performance with increasing age. Between ages 30 and 40 few can continue to play violent competitive sports such as hockey or football. This may be blamed on cardiorespiratory problems, but equally if not more important is eye-hand-feet coordination and reaction speed of the individual's brain. (What is sadder than to see a former world class baseball player dropping catches in the outfield which would have been easy for him in his prime?)

Both psychometric tests and activities of daily living assessments point to a reduction in cerebral competence in the elderly. The question should now be asked: "Does this fact have any implications for clinical medicine?"

CLINICAL RELEVANCE OF BRAIN FAILURE

Cerebral function involves sensory input and its translation into intellectual, motor, and neuro-regulating activity. The brain achieves its optimum potential between the ages of 16 and 20 (9), after which there is a slow decline in its capabilities (Fig. 4–9). This decline is more rapid beyond the age of 75. A concept of global cerebral function is used to imply the widespread nature of the brain's many activities. The theory is that, paralleling the rapid development of the brain during the pediatric era, there is a considerable reversal during the geriatric years. If this is true, one might postulate that

1. The loss of agility and increasing clumsiness of the failing motor system would lead to an increasing number of accidents and falls—and so it does.
2. It is likely that failing receptors—visual, auditory, and cognitive—will lead to misunderstandings and confusion—and so it does.
3. The more complex of the nervous system's regulating mechanisms will be most susceptible to the deteriorating efficiency of the aging brain, and control of micturition or defecation can be expected to break down—and so it does.
4. Finally, reaction to sudden stress—physical, mental, or emotional—activated by the brain's hypothalamic control of homeostasis may collapse—and so it does.

What are the common medical problems encountered in old age? The findings in a series of 1000 consecutive referrals to the Department of Geriatric Medicine at Selly Oak Hospital (10) in Birmingham, England, showed loss of mobility, mental confusion, and incontinence as the three most common problems (Table

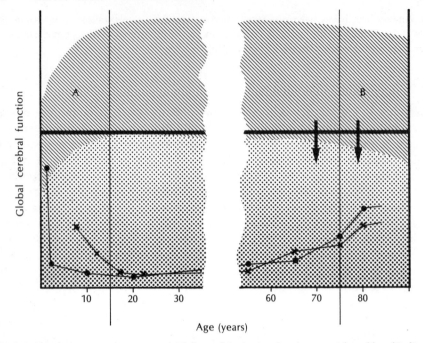

Fig. 4–9. Development, maintenance, and failure of the brain related to age. A broad band indicates the wide variation in functional activity from person to person. The straight black line represents the hypothetical level of function necessary for an individual to be fully capable of an independent existence. A. Pediatric era. B. Geriatric era.

4–2). The same features occurred with similar frequency in 731 elderly people in institutions in London, Ontario (Table 4–3) (10). This experience is by no means unique, as Droller (14) and Isaacs (16) had earlier reported similar findings. Homeostatic breakdown is the fourth most common medical problem of old age.

These are not diagnoses, but clinical problems which stem from aspects of brain failure aggravated by a wide variety of conditions. It may not be possible to offer effective treatment to patients developing cerebral deterioration at the present time. The danger is that, in our anxiety to make some effort to help the situation, we enthusiastically employ a number of agents to treat the heart failure, infections, metabolic upsets, cancer or other associated pathology, forgetting that increasing numbers of drugs means greater risk of adverse reactions (see Table 9–6). These tend to occur most frequently in elderly patients and constitute a fifth major problem, iatrogenic disorders. This is not a mere theoretical hypothesis. In a study of 731 institutionalised individuals of London, Ontario, it was found that 19.3% were taking 6 or more medications daily on a regular basis (Fig. 9–2). During their first 10 days in a chronic hospital 78 patients had a total of 644 drug orders written for them, 8 per patient (6).

The clinical relevance of brain failure lies in its being the predisposing factor

TABLE 4-2. Incidence of Most Common Aging Problems in Birmingham, England Survey*

Problem (no. of patients surveyed)	Findings (no. of patients)	Findings (% of patients)
Mobility (955)		
Fully Mobile	156	16
Ambulant with Difficulty	312	31
Immobile	487	49
Mental Confusion (970)		
None	569	59
Mild	249	26
Severe	152	15
Urinary Incontinence (928)		
None	647	70
Intermittent	82	9
Persistent	199	21

*Age<70, 165: age 71–74, 141; age 75–79, 211; age 80–83, 275; age 84, 206

TABLE 4-3. Incidence of Most Common Aging Problems in London, Ontario Survey*

Problem (no. of patients surveyed)	Findings (no. of patients)	Findings (% of patients)
Mobility (728)		
Fully mobile	407	56
Ambulant with difficulty	171	23
Immobile	150	21
Mental Confusion (731)		
None	469	64
Confused	197	27
Unable to communicate	65	9
Urinary Incontinence (730)		
None	451	62
Intermittent	126	17
Persistent	153	21

*Age<70, 151; age 70–74, 78; age 75–79, 119; age 80–84, 128; age 85–89, 149; age 90+, 106

in four of the five main problems which constitute, in all their ramifications, the essentials of geriatric medicine.

THE O COMPLEX

Falling, confusion, incontinence, homeostatic disturbance, and iatrogenic illness form the geriatric quintet and will be found separately or together in almost every acute or long-term problem posed by the elderly (Fig. 4–10). They constitute an interrelated complex of old age syndromes that are the essence of clinical

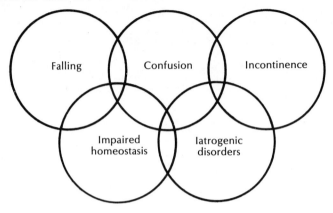

Fig. 4–10. O complex of geriatric medicine.

geriatric medicine. The older the patients, the more common the problems. Little attention is given to them in medical curricula, and what emphasis there is may be offered in unrelated courses such as neurology, orthopedics, and urology. The interlinking rings of this O complex underline the close relationship between the problems and their common association in the individual patient. The symbol represents the core of knowledge unique to the medicine of the very old. Because of this it offers an effective core for the teaching of geriatric medicine.

Since there is strong evidence of the brain's dominant role in timing and masterminding the aging process (see Ch. 3, Biologic Gerontology), it is not surprising to find that failure of this organ has equally important clinical implications. The key to solving the problems of the O complex lies in the brain. Cerebral cellular metabolism is of greater importance to the very old than to anyone else. This being the case, the need for redoubling research effort in this area is obvious. A small gain in this field that would permit more elderly people to maintain their independence would pay enormous human and economic dividends.

Recognition of the O complex means that useful explanations can be offered to patients. Understanding some of the background facts of a clinical problem may not cure it, but it can suggest to each individual possible methods of managing it and adopting rational countermeasures.

REFERENCES

1. Ball MJ: Neurofibrillary tangles and the pathogenesis of dementia: a quantitative study. Neuropathol Appl Neurobiol 2:395–410, 1976
2. Ball MJ: Neuronal loss, neurofibrillary tangles and granulovacuolar degeneration in the hippocampus with ageing and dementia. Acta Neuropathol (Berl) 37:111–118, 1977
3. Beck EG, Dustman RE, Schenkenberg T: Life span changes in the electrical activity of the human brain as reflected in the cerebral evoked response. In Ordy JM, Brizzee KR (eds): Neurobiology of Aging. New York, Plenum Press, 1975, pp 175–192

4. Bigelow R: The Dawn Warriors: Man's Evolution Toward Peace. London, Hutchinson of London, 1969

5. Blessed G, Tomlinson BE, Roth M: The association between quantitative measures of dementia and of senile change in the cerebral grey matter of elderly subjects. Br J Psychiatry 114:797–811, 1968

6. Borda I, Jick H, Slone D, Divan B, Gilman B, Chalmers TC: Studies of drug usage in five Boston hospitals. JAMA 202:506–510, 1967

7. Bowsher D: Introduction to the Anatomy and Physiology of the Nervous System. England, Blackwell, 1970, pp 39–46

8. Brizzee KR, Ordy JM, Kaack B: Early appearance and regional differences in intraneuronal and extraneuronal lipofuscin accumulation with age in the brain of a non-human primate (macaca mulatta). J Gerontol 29:336–381, 1974

9. Bromley DB: The Psychology of Ageing, 2nd ed. The Effects of Ageing on Adult Intelligence. Great Britain, Penguin Books, 1974, pp 178–210

10. Cape RDT: A geriatric service. Midland Med Rev 8:21–43, 1972

11. Cape RDT, Shorrock C, Tree R, Pablo R, Campbell AJ, Seymour DG: Square pegs in round holes. Can Med Assoc J 117:1284–1287, 1977

12. Corso JF: Sensory processes in man during maturity and senescence. In Ordy JM, Brizzee KR (eds): Neurobiology of Aging. New York, Plenum Press, 1975, pp 119–144

13. Davies P, Maloney AJF: Selective loss of central cholineogic neurons in Alzheimer's disease. Lancet II:1403, 1976

14. Droller H: Age with a Future: Evaluation of Medical Needs of Older People. Copenhagen, Munksgaard, 1964

15. Eyzaguirre C, Fidone SJ: Physiology of the Nervous System: The Autonomic Nervous System. Chicago, Year Book Medical, 1975, pp 315–342

16. Hanley T: "Neuronal fall-out" in the ageing brain: a critical review of the quantitative data. Age and Ageing 3:133–151, 1974

17. Isaacs B: Current Achievements in Geriatrics: Morbidity in Elderly Hospital Patients. London, Cassell, 1964, pp 29–40

18. Llinas RR: The cortex of the cerebellum. Sci Am 232:56–71, 1975

19. Ordy JM: Nervous system, behavior, aging. In Ordy JM, Brizzee KR (eds): Neurobiology of Aging. New York, Plenum Press, 1975, pp 107–108

20. Rudinger G: Correlates of changes in cognitive function. In Thomae H (ed): Patterns of Aging. New York, S Karger, 1976, pp 20–35

21. Siakatos AN, Armstrong D: Age pigment, a biochemical indicator of intracellular aging. In Ordy JM, Brizzee KR (eds): Neurobiology of Aging. New York, Plenum Press, 1975, pp 369–399

22. Tomlinson BE, Blessed G, Roth M: Observations on the brains of nondemented old people. J Neurol Sci 7:331–356, 1968

23. Tomlinson BE, Blessed G, Roth M: Observations on the brains of demented old people. J Neurol Sci II:205–242, 1970

24. Wechsler D: Wechsler Adult Intelligence Scale. New York, Psychological Corporation, 1955

25. Wechsler D: The Measurement and Appraisal of Adult Intelligence, 4th ed. Baillière, Tuidall and Cox, 1958

Chapter 5

CONFUSION

I am a very foolish fond old man
Fourscore and upward, not an hour more or less;
And, to deal plainly,
I fear I am not in my perfect mind:
> *Shakespeare, King Lear*

WHAT IS CONFUSION?

Confusion is a state of transient or long-term memory loss which leads to disorientation in time and space, a failure to recognize relatives or friends, and a marked tendency to repeat sentences, phrases, or actions—a phenomenon known as perseveration. The confused person may also suffer from an associated behavioral abnormality such as depression, mania, paranoia, or belligerence. The word confusion, defined by the *Concise Oxford Dictionary* as "thrown into disorder, mixed up in the mind," is used more frequently than any other in connection with old people suffering from the condition described. It is for this reason that the word is used here. For the purists, dementia (from the Latin *de*—out of and *mens*—the mind) might be more acceptable, but this suggests a more permanent change. Because this is not always the case, confusion is preferred to describe the problem.

CASE REPORT 5–1

Mr. and Mrs. Brown were both aged 74. Each was the other's fourth spouse, and they had been married for only 4 years. They lived contentedly together in a senior citizen's apartment. Having few close relatives, they depended on their own resources.

Mr. Brown had trained as an accountant and worked part time until 2 years before his accident. Apart from mild chronic bronchitis, he enjoyed good health and was fully active prior to his hospital admission. A jovial, rather hearty, big man, he admitted freely to having had a drinking problem in the past, but claimed those days were now over. He was extroverted, loud-voiced, and likeable.

Mrs. Brown retired about 8 years earlier than her husband. She had sustained a myocardial infarction 2 years before and required maintenance treatment with digoxin and a diuretic, which kept her in reasonably good physical health. In contrast to this, she had suffered from a moderate degree of dementing illness for the preceding 2–3 years.

Mr. Brown was the organizing force in the household, carrying out the shopping and cooking and prompting his wife to appropriate action from time to time. There was an obvious deep bond of affection between them, and they managed admirably together.

Catastrophe struck on the evening of day 1 after Mr. Brown, perhaps mildly intoxicated, had shown a visitor to the door. When he returned to the living room, he caught his foot on the doorstop, tripped, and fell awkwardly, fracturing his left hip. The friend heard the crash and returned, and an ambulance was summoned. In the hospital, early surgery and mobilization were carried out. Mentally clear on admission, Mr. Brown made good progress for the first 2–3 days, after which he developed episodes of delirium, particularly at night. A restraint jacket was brought into use, which served only to increase his belligerent confusion. Over the next 10 days the confusional outbursts became more frequent, and his rehabilitation progress was halted. He was given increasing doses of sedatives and tranquilizers in efforts to control his outbursts. Mr. Brown talked incoherently about his wife and seemed to be concerned about her welfare; at times he tried to telephone her. By the end of 2 weeks, several members of the hospital staff recorded in his chart that he was "irreversibly demented."

During this time Mrs. Brown had been having considerable difficulty coping at home on her own. A neighbor who tried to help her did not realize it was necessary to supervise her medication. Without her husband to guide her, Mrs. Brown became more confused and, since she had not been taking her medication, drifted into mild congestive cardiac failure. Finally, about 3 weeks after her husband's admission, she arrived at the emergency department of the hospital at 2:30 A.M., asking to see her husband. At this point, both had reached their nadir. Mrs. Brown was admitted to the psychiatric ward. On their respective charts on day 20 was written: (Mr. Brown's) "Confused and disorientated, apparently due to atherosclerosis—psychopathic personality . . . possibly organic. Confabulating, disorientated in time and space. He will require some sort of custodial care and could not possibly look after himself." and (Mrs. Brown's) "Moderate dementia— general deterioration with memory loss—loss of judgment, moderate disorientation, bland, unconcerned affect. No agitation, delusions, hallucinations or paranoid behavior."

The geriatrician was asked to see both patients. Mr. Brown was assessed as having a toxic confusional state due to dehydration, oversedation, and fecal impaction. It was thought that the physical constraints were making things worse. Fluids were encouraged, laxatives and enemas given, and sedation reduced. Attempts at mobilization were intensified. Mr. and Mrs. Brown were able to visit with each other on the orthopedic ward. On this regimen, Mr. Brown's confusion improved, and 6 weeks after his accident he was transferred to a geriatric hospital to complete his rehabilitation. During this time his wife's physical state improved with regular drugs and diet, and she followed her husband to the geriatric hospital.

At this venue they were, at last, really together again on the same ward. There was a striking improvement in the morale of both. Within 2 weeks, Mr. Brown was not taking any sedatives. Three months after day 1, they were able to return together to their senior citizen's apartment (Fig. 5–1)

This episode occurred 2 years ago and, to date, all has gone well.

The problem of a confusional state is one of the most common encountered in old people. So closely do we associate age with failing mental powers that we rather derisively use the word *senile* to describe those individuals unfortunate enough to have lost their abilities to remember and to think. The word suggests an article fit only for the scrapheap, hardly a person. Mr. Brown was so de-

Instability ⟵—— Stability ——⟶ Instability

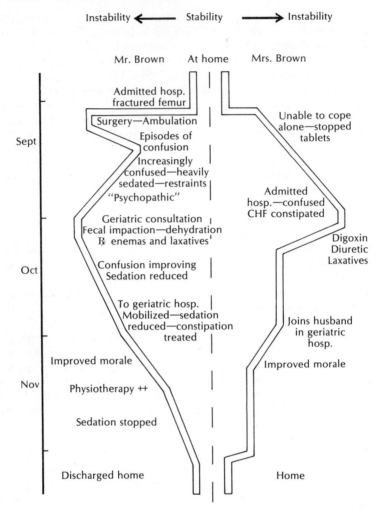

Fig. 5–1. Progress of the Browns.

scribed, although events later proved this to be far from the truth. To approach this difficult problem in a constructive way requires wide-ranging knowledge and understanding. Proper management of such situations demands a systematic approach which reviews all relevant factors.

ENVIRONMENTAL PROBLEMS

The great increase in the number of old people in the community has paradoxically been accompanied by steady changes in the environment which make life more difficult for them. Think of the main features of modern life—cars, airplanes, supermarkets, television, speed, noise; all of these can create tension and insecurity. Remember that the present octogenarians were born into a different world, a world in which those who went fastest were those who had the best horses! The social and scientific revolutions that followed two world wars have completely transformed the late Victorian way of life. Without hankering after a lost age, one may point out that our go-getting twentieth century, with its subservience to the gross national product, appears to have little room for the old who need to travel at a rather slower pace. For example, the old person who can safely walk to a local shop or variety store to buy food is lucky. Buying of such essentials may involve driving a car or a perilous bus journey, coupled with a nerve-racking visit to a somewhat bewildering supermarket, where deteriorating vision and hearing can add greatly to the individual's difficulties. The business of existing becomes a struggle which consumes all the old person's energy. It is no wonder that old people are mentally disturbed! Or is it?

CASE REPORT 5–2

Some years ago, an expostman of 86 came to the outpatient clinic. He complained of an aching back and aching right leg, general tiredness, and mild depression. He lived alone, was a keen gardener, enjoyed cooking, and kept his house very clean. Two or three days a week he traveled by bus some 2 or 3 miles to do his shopping. He presented no serious physical abnormalities on examination. In order to cheer him up and give him the opportunity of meeting other people, it was suggested that he go to the sheltered workshops for the elderly in his local area, provided he could manage the journey. He said, "Oh yes, that would be fine, but you know, Doctor, I really do not have the time!" In spite of his malaise, he was responding to the challenge which life posed for him.

The element of challenge is as important to the old as to those in their prime. Maintaining standards which give a reassuring boost to one's self-respect is something that may not make life more comfortable, but is potentially more valuable. Many well-meaning people fail to understand this need of the elderly. It is pleasant to offer an annual outing to the seaside or lake, and it is very kind to provide television sets. It may be ungracious to criticize the attitude behind such projects, but the fundamental flaw in them is that they provide packaged entertainment and reduce the recipients to a passive role as spectators, existing in a limbo between life and death. There are, one should remember, thousands of 70- and 80-year-old people flying off to escape the winter or to visit relatives in other continents taking the complexities and frustrations of modern air travel in their stride. Others resolutely refuse to be defeated by the North American winter and continue to shop, visit the hairdresser, go to exercise classes, and play bridge in spite of the inclement weather. The infinite variety of abilities encountered in the old cannot be overstressed.

Not only is the environment itself important, but so is what we do in it. Occupation in the widest sense can make or mar one's life. It is not surprising that many men become disheartened and physically ill on retirement and that some women develop psychiatric problems when the children have all left home. Much satisfaction in life stems from the belief that we are making our contribution to the community, however small that contribution may be. Much of life's enjoyment stems from contacts with other people, particularly contemporaries. If both these emotional props are removed, there are psychologic strains which affect both sexes. The social consequences of retirement and isolation are therefore important to the clinician in assessing morbidity in elderly patients.

The actions of grown children toward their elderly parents are almost always, kindly and well-intentioned. At times, however, their attitude may be overprotective and smothering. The children may even introduce a form of regimentation. These approaches reduce the self-respect of the elderly parents and diminish their zest for living. Meeting one challenge after another and taking risks produce some of the deepest pleasures and satisfactions in life. When old, one still needs these episodes. If it is a struggle to reach the supermarket or visit friends, the elderly person may respond to the stimulus and feel a warm glow of achievement. Young people should be urged to help the old to help themselves, by all means, but don't mollycoddle them! Recognizing these facts of life can assist the physician offering advice to patients and their families.

ASSESSMENT

The first step in assessing the problem of confusion in an elderly patient is to establish whether the patient's mental function is in fact abnormal. This may be straightforward when the individual is seen in the familiar surroundings of his or her own home and there is no significant loss of hearing or vision to complicate communication. It is much more difficult when one is faced with a belligerent, active octogenarian in a busy hospital emergency department. In both cases, a suitable validated technique of testing mental capacity should be used to reach a firm conclusion as quickly as possible. Much of the day-to-day management of geriatric patients is based on what are apparently reasonable common sense assumptions. Welford (37) has pointed out that ". . . research findings confirm popular beliefs about old age, but with important qualifications, so that common knowledge alone is an unreliable guide to practical action." Therefore a simple clinical method is required to provide a clear qualitative and an approximate quantitative answer to the question, "Is this patient confused?"

TESTS

Wechsler (39) was the first to produce a carefully compiled series of psychologic tests designed to quantify memory (see Ch. 4, Brain Failure). Since then, a considerable number of variations and elaborations on his general themes have been suggested, including a revival of color-naming tests originally described in 1915 and 1935 by Brown (8) and Stroop (35), respectively. Dixon (11) included these in his comprehensive but time-consuming battery of tests described in 1965.

Of more practical clinical value was the Roth and Hopkins (31) study of psychologic test performance in patients over 60 suffering from senile psychosis and the affective disorders of old age. They used four tests: 1) the vocabulary subtest from the Wechsler–Bellevue Scale, 2) the digit span subtest from the same scale, 3) progressive matrices (1938 version), and 4) an information test consisting of ten questions concerning orientation for time, place, and person and ten concerning well-known public events, persons, and dates. The authors demonstrated that, while both their groups of patients (20 with senile psychosis, 46 with affective disorders) had a similar ability to define words and repeat digits, there was a clear distinction between them in the other two tests. The demented patients with an organic brain syndrome (senile psychotics) were quite unable to manage the matrices and could not answer 15 or more of the questions of the information test. Individuals with affective disorders, on the other hand, found both these tests well within their capabilities.

The question and answer test has become increasingly popular as a simple clinical method for establishing significant mental confusion. Kahn, Goldfarb, Pollack, and Peck (20) showed in 1960 that it correlated well with the evaluation of a psychiatrist using a standard structured interview technique. More recently, Hodkinson (14) has demonstrated that such a test made a good, practical distinction between patients who were normal and those confused, either acutely or on a more long-term basis. He went further and offered evidence that the test could be conveniently reduced to a total of ten questions and would still cover details related to the subject, time, and simple general knowledge. His abbreviated mental test included

1. Age
2. Time (to nearest hour)
3. Address for recall at end of test—this should be repeated by the patient to ensure it has been heard correctly.
4. Year
5. Name of hospital
6. Recognition of two persons (doctor, nurse, etc.)
7. Date of birth
8. Year of World War I
9. Name of present monarch
10. Counting backwards 20–1

This was composed and published in Britain, but with a suitable change in question 9 (President or Prime Minister) it would be equally applicable in other parts of the world. If the patient is not in a hospital, the address or name of the house or institution in which the interview takes place could be substituted for question 5, and the identity of appropriate relatives, neighbors, or home staff for question 6.

This type of questioning is the most reliable method of establishing quickly whether or not a patient is disoriented. It is wise to include the questions as part of the normal history-taking process, interspersing them with others aimed at trying to obtain clinical information.

The importance and validity of this approach has been more recently confirmed by Pfeiffer (28), whose only variation on earlier work was to count errors rather than correct answers. Without this systematic approach, mistakes can be easily made. Apathy or dejection from a depressive state, mild obtundity, or failure to hear or understand the physician may lead to an erroneous label of dementia or worse still senility being put on a patient's chart. It is important to use a validated method of establishing a state of confusion and to record the detail briefly. Too often the comment "confused and disorientated" appears without any corroborative evidence. The old person, particularly in the middle or later years of the senium, may well be bewildered and anxious on arrival at a hospital. Such individuals require reassurance and encouragement before the clerk or physician starts the questioning to assess mental status. For the blind and deaf, even more care is required. Slow, deliberate questioning of the blind patient (after the speaker has clearly introduced himself) and large print cards of the questions for the deaf patient are necessary. Fears engendered by the hospital are not a factor when the patient is at home, but the family physician must remember that overanxiety about some physical problem may produce apparent confusion. There may also be a fear that he or she has been summoned to be "put away."

DEVELOPMENT PATTERN

Having established that the patient is in a confused state, the physician should collect all available knowledge about its development from whatever reliable source may be available. The one person who cannot help is the patient, and if there is no easily traceable relative who knows about it, it will be necessary to seek out neighbors and friends for information. The two crucial questions are: How long has it been since the patient was last fully sensible? In what manner did the disorientation develop?

ACUTE VS. CHRONIC CONFUSION

Confusion is a symptom, not a disease, and presents a characteristic clinical problem in the Weed (38) sense. The questions posed in the previous paragraph differentiate broadly acute from chronic confusional states. It should be stressed that the two are more closely linked than may be obvious at first sight. It has been suggested that deterioration of cerebral function is the predisposing factor which results in confusional states becoming increasingly common in older patients (see Ch. 4, Brain Failure). The older the individual, the greater the chance of confusion occurring. It may well be, although no one has to date produced firm evidence to this effect, that acute confusional states occur only in those who are on the brink of a true senile dementia. There is good evidence that an appreciable number, about 25% according to Kral (25), of patients in acute states will not recover, but will have continuing dementing illness. While it is therefore not only convenient but also important to differentiate between the two types, one should be aware that there are close links between them.

The overall objectives of management in each case are to cure or minimize the confusional condition with the hope of maintaining as much independence as possible in the patient. This means, in both cases, a careful evaluation of possible treatable causes followed by the implementation of a suitable therapeutic regimen for them. There is also a need to establish living conditions that allow adequate supervision and care for the patient following the episode, either at home or in an institution.

ACUTE CONFUSIONAL STATES

The main clinical features of acute confusional states are clouding of consciousness, impairment of memory, disorientation, muddled thinking, perceptual disturbances with illusions or even hallucinations, delusional ideas, agitation, restlessness, insomnia, anorexia, and dehydration. It may be too readily assumed that an old, confused lady is suffering from dementia because she is arteriosclerotic and that little can be done except perhaps to provide placement. The truth is that while assessment of this common problem may prove difficult and complex, in some cases there is a rewarding response to appropriate treatment. In others, continuing, thoughtful, long-term care is required.

The characteristic feature of the acute confusional state is its sudden onset. One day the individual is sensible and in charge of the situation; the next, there is obvious disorientation and loss of control. This course of events is in marked contrast to the slow, almost imperceptible, development of amnestic features in the majority of cases of classic senile dementia.

ETIOLOGY

There are a great many conditions which may present as acute confusional states. A thorough examination and investigation should be made in the search for relevant diagnostic information (Table 5–1). In a multicenter study in Britain, pneumonia, cardiac failure, urinary infections, neoplasia, and depression were the five most common conditions responsible for acute confusional states (15). Kral (23) believes that the common denominator in all these widely disparate conditions is that each acts as a severe stress to the old person, whose resistance to such a phenomenon is greatly reduced.

Confusion is a good example of how diseases produce different symptoms in the very old person from those they produce in a young person. Each condition causes cerebral cell function to deteriorate because of the anoxic, toxic, or metabolic effects stemming from the condition. In the child, an acute infection may produce convulsions; in the adult, rigors; and in the old person, a confusional state.

Slowing in Sensory–Motor Link-Up

Introducing a speed factor in carrying out set tasks can ultimately cause the older person to fall far behind the younger in performance. The change in functioning of cerebral cells appears to slow the circuit from sensory stimulus to motor output. Sensory–motor link-up, which is fastest in the young and becomes progressively slower in old age, constitutes the most vulnerable part of neurologic function. In states of unsupportable stress, this link is likely to be the point at which cerebral function fails. This may be the case in acute confusion. Accepting this as a working hypothesis, it seems that treatment should be designed to slow down, simplify, and reinforce the sensory input in the hope of restoring intellectual control. This may seem highly theoretic, but there are some grounds for it.

TABLE 5–1. Causes of Acute Confusional States

Cause	Examples
Vascular accidents	Myocardial infarction
	Cerebral infarction
	Peripheral gangrene
	Pulmonary embolism
Infections	Pneumonia
	Urinary tract
	Osteomyelitis
Metabolic	Hypoglycemia
	Myxedema
	Hepatic failure
	B_{12} or folate deficiency
Circulatory	Congestive cardiac failure
	Tachyarrhythmia
	Heart block
Homeostatic failure	Postural hypotension
	Dehydration
	Electrolyte disturbance
	Fecal impaction
Drugs	Alcohol
	Hypnotic, tranquilizer
	Antihypertensive, antiParkinsonian
	Antidepressant and other drugs
Senile Epilepsy	
Anemia	Occult hemorrhage
	Uremia, chronic
	arthritis, or neoplasia
	Sideroblasts
Neoplasia	
Collagen disease	Giant cell arteritis
	Periarteritis nodosa
Trauma	Subdural hematoma
Surgery	Cataract enucleation
Psychosocial	Bereavement, retirement
Depression	

Lack of Communication

In Case Report 5–1 one of the factors which helped Mr. Brown was the line of communication between himself and the geriatrician. A major cause of Mr. Brown's confused and often belligerent attitude was his inability to understand, in detail, what was happening to him. The geriatrician explained the situation to him repeatedly and at length, answering all his questions. Slowly, the feeding in of consistent messages in addition to the correction of physical conditions strengthened Mr. Brown's return to normal thinking. Experience suggests that one cannot overemphasize the importance of this type of communication between physician and patient in situations where intellectual ability has been impaired.

Another illustration of this theory can be seen in the variability of nursing management of elderly confused patients. There are some nurses who almost instinctively manage such patients effectively with little or no use of restraints or drugs. They have a talent for establishing rapport with such individuals because they listen to them and understand and respond. These nurses provide sensory input which is recognized as friendly, even if not understood, by the muddled patient who therefore remains calmer. There are other nurses who, through no fault of their own, lack this capability and are uncomfortable and less efficient with an awkward confused patient. The practicing physician, too, must try to establish a similar link with the patient if the best results are to be obtained. This is not easy and may be impossible, but careful listening and intelligent responding can achieve a great deal. Although this involves time, a commodity that is often scarce, an extra 5–10 min at the outset may be an enormous saving in the long run. This is an area in which the gerontologist's research efforts to understand the nature of aging changes in cerebral function could be all-important.

Environmental Change

CASE REPORT 5–3

Shortly after a highly successful 90th birthday party attended by 150 people, Mr. Charles had to spend 2 months visiting various members of his family while the daughter and son-in-law with whom he lived had a much needed holiday. A day before their return, the old man, who had expressed his dissatisfaction and irritation with the arrangement on several occasions, quite suddenly became acutely confused. He never fully regained his senses, but settled into a stable routine when returned to his own home a day or two later.

Environmental change greatly affects elderly patients. For those who are already confused, the move may spell disaster and serious deterioration may develop; for those on the brink of intellectual failure, it may be the final straw. This is most likely to happen in those whose normal sensory input is reduced by poor vision or hearing or by long periods of complete recumbency.

INCIDENCE

It is difficult to compile reliable data for the number of episodes of acute confusion which might be expected in a known population of old people. There must be many mild incidents which are transient and are therefore not reported to any physician, while some of those that are reported may clear up under the family physician's care. There are no recent extensive reports from family medicine on this subject. There are a few reports from psychiatric hospitals over the past 25 years, one of the best being that of Roth (30). He studied 450 people aged 60 years or over who were admitted to a psychiatric hospital during the years 1934, 1936, 1948, and 1949, grouping their disorders under five headings: 1) affective psychosis (49%), 2) senile psychosis (25%), 3) paraphrenia (10%), 4) acute confusion (8%), and 5) dementia (8%). Kral (24) has (much more recently) confirmed the 8% incidence of acute confusional states occurring in a psychiatric hospital.

It is likely that these two series from psychiatric hospitals represent a group with more behavioral problems and less physical disease than a similar group which might be encountered in emergency departments of general hospitals. There are statistical reports on the incidence of mental disturbance in patients referred to or admitted to geriatric departments of hospitals in Britain, but there are so many variations in the way in which these cases are referred that they offer no indication of the true incidence of acute confusion. No physician familiar with the work of medical emergency departments would deny that old people with acute confusional states form an appreciable proportion of day-to-day arrivals. An unpublished study (32) of 61 individuals aged 70 and over admitted to one acute general hospital via the emergency department over a period of some months had an incidence of confusional states of 15%. The figures are small, but the study continues. It is likely that there will be 10%–20% of elderly patients in any unselected emergency series suffering from acute confusion.

EVALUATION AND EXAMINATION

Acute confusional states are a medical emergency. The individual is likely to be sent to the emergency department of the nearest community or general hospital at once. Some may reach psychiatric hospitals, depending on the local custom and the attitude of the family physician. The steps in the diagnostic procedure are the same whether the patient has been brought to an emergency department, is first seen at home, or is in a psychiatric hospital. The normal systematic procedure of history taking, physical examination, and investigation with appropriate tests is followed as with any medical problem.

History

It is important to establish as precisely as possible when and how the confusion developed, and one useful method of obtaining this information is to ask family or friends when the individual was last quite clear mentally. Inquire about other symptoms or signs which the individual may have complained of (such as pain, cough, or dysuria). Attempt to obtain a past history of illness in the patient and other members of the family. A clear chronologic account of events leading up to the mental breakdown is as important in this situation as in any other medical case. It is wise to ask for all bottles of medicines which are being or may have been taken.

Physical Examination

It is often extremely difficult to examine a confused patient, and it may take more than one visit to the patient's bedside. Subjects may exhibit a strained, haunted look, as though not knowing which way to turn. They may pace aimlessly about, be unwilling to sit down, listen, or talk, and be quite unable to concentrate on the physician's questions. They are apt to resent attempts at examination, and this procedure has to be carried out without their cooperation and even, at times, in the face of active hostility. In such situations, patience is mandatory.

The physician can make a reasoned informed guess at the state of hydration, observe respirations and their rate, check the pulse, look for peripheral edema, alteration in color, or evidence of injury, and feel for temperature with little physical interference with the patient. More direct intervention may stimulate a variably vigorous hostile reaction which will offer evidence of motor power. With the help of a nurse, relative, or colleague, it may be possible to undertake a quick auscultation of heart and lungs and a brief palpation of the abdomen. These maneuvers should be made with the express object of looking for pneumonia, obvious arrhythmia, full bladder, or evidence of an acute abdomen. Be content with a little progress at this stage, endeavor to introduce one or two basic treatments, such as administration of extra fluid and antibiotics if indicated, and plan to see the patient again in 2–3 hours. Ideally, all drugs, including sedatives, should be temporarily avoided to establish a satisfactory base line uncluttered by a variety of competing drug effects. There are few drugs which cannot be stopped in this way, but care is necessary with insulin or steroids, as sudden discontinuance might be dangerous.

A rectal examination should never be omitted. There are a number of reasons for this. The confused person is unlikely to maintain normal bowel habits, may not eat or drink enough, and quickly becomes constipated. Dehydration results in drying of the stool, which adds to the problem and may lead to impaction. The resulting discomfort or pain aggravates the condition by adding restlessness to the confusion. Whenever a patient wanders during the night hours, a degree of colonic stasis should be suspected. The clinical features of the constipation–dehydration syndrome so familiar to physicians in geriatric medicine are

1. Dry tongue
2. Sunken eyes
3. Abdominal tenderness (left iliac fossa)

4. Palpable colon
5. Impacted rectum
6. Urinary incontinence
7. Raised BUN
8. Nocturnal restlessness
9. Delirium

Investigations and Laboratory Tests

During this initial difficult phase, it is important to obtain a blood sample for immediate testing. Initial investigations should include a chest x-ray, full blood count, including erythrocyte sedimentation rate (ESR) and differential white count, electrolytes, blood urea nitrogen (BUN), creatinine, glucose, albumin, globulin, liver enzymes, calcium, phosphate, uric acid, electrocardiogram (ECG) and urine specimen, preferably taken by suprapubic aspiration or catheter. Estimations of any relevant drug serum levels, such as digoxin, diphenylhydantoin (Dilantin), or barbiturate should not be forgotten.

If routine tests fail to reveal a cause for the confusion, it may be necessary to use more elaborate measures to try and pinpoint the diagnosis. Brain scan, an electroencephalogram (EEG), angiography or even cerebral biopsy may be advisable, as well as a consultation with a neurologist. These procedures provide useful evidence, but should not be carried out until routine tests fail to shed adequate light on the problem.

While awaiting the results, the physician must complete a more thorough physical examination of the patient and complete the laborious business of clarifying and documenting the history. At this stage, the main objective is to establish, as quickly as possible, whether there is a treatable disease which may be responsible for the confusion.

CLINICAL MANAGEMENT

Throughout the initial examination and investigations of confused patients, the individual and relatives must be fully informed about the steps being taken to investigate and treat the condition.

The confusion may lessen from time to time, and it may be possible to establish contact with the patient during more lucid phases. Any reassurance and explanation which pierces the wall of disorientation helps to hasten the end of the episode. Patients in an acute confusional state should be seen frequently, and constant efforts should be made to understand the nature and cause of the confusion and to explain to them what is being done on their behalf. Particular care must be taken by attending physicians, nurses, or ancillary staff to avoid casual discouraging remarks, as such comments may do incalculable harm if overheard.

If the individual is restless, agitated, delirious, or manic, nurses, relatives, or friends will all have one concern: "Can't you give him something to settle him down?" The physician should try to resist this plea, at least until the cause of the episode is reasonably clear. The difficulties of managing patients who will not sit still for more than 2 min and who have no idea where they are but are determined to go home are considerable. Without a constant attendant, they may disappear from the ward. Others with a similar wanderlust, but who are already unsteady or weak, may fall repeatedly.

Restraints

CASE REPORT 5–4

Mrs. Dunn, an 85-year-old lady, was admitted to an acute medical ward suffering from mild congestive cardiac failure and mental confusion. After 3 weeks of treatment, her cardiac failure had been brought under control but not her confusion. The geriatrician was asked to see her with a view to expediting her transfer, which had already been requested, to a continuing care hospital. The message was received on a Tuesday afternoon, and the following day the geriatrician went to see her at midday. On arrival on the ward he learned that a bed had become available at the continuing care hospital that morning, and the ambulance crew was expected at any minute to transfer Mrs. Dunn. Although his services were now superfluous, he went in to see the patient. He found her lying in bed with crib sides up and a restraining binder on; she was whimpering with bewilderment and fear. Before anything could be done, the ambulance men arrived to take her off. Fifteen minutes after arrival at the new hospital, she died . . . scared to death!

It is easy to criticize the widespread use of a variety of restraints, binders, posies, or leather wrist straps which goes on in many hospital wards, but acute confusional states are serious clinical episodes which carry a considerable mortality and long-term disability risk. These devices are used to protect the patient from accidents or to allow necessary treatment to be given. It is fair to say, however, that the disturbing effect which they have on the patient in many cases defeats their purpose. Crib sides on beds arouse particular fears because they look like prison bars. Bemused, wandering patients require constant reassurance, comfort, and gentle encouragement. It is important to avoid confrontation or arguments with them. They are, for the moment, incapable of rational thought and can only be led, not driven.

If nurses who have developed great skill in this difficult area of patient management were provided with rooms furnished to accommodate their confused, elderly patients, the need for restraints would disappear. Beds of adjustable height, 15–42 in. above the floor, prevent serious accidents to restless patients. If patients can sit on the bed with their feet firmly planted on the floor, it is easier for them to balance themselves on standing up. If this type of bed is in a room which has wall-to-wall carpeting of a suitable robust type, the danger of significant injury from falls is reduced.

Patients in confusional states should be encouraged to get up, and suitable chairs are important. The standard geriatric chair equipped at times with a fixed tray table is useful. Some patients, however, do regard them as restraining, and resent them. The chairs can, of course, be used without the irritating tray. A second chair which has been found very helpful in a small but significant proportion of cases is the large, padded reclining chair. There the individual can be left in a comfortable, relaxed position from which it is very difficult to arise.

The most important need in any unit or ward which accommodates patients in acute confusional states is for extra staff who understand the problems.

Specific Treatment and Drug Therapy

Treatment is aimed at curing or alleviating the acute condition responsible for the confusion. Appropriate antibiotics for infections, adequate correction of metabolic disorders, use of digitalis and diuretics in heart failure, administration of fluids in dehydration, bowel clearance in fecal impaction, withdrawal of drugs in suspected iatrogenic states, and normal clinical management of vascular accidents should all be implemented as quickly as possible in order to offer the patient the best chance of a return to normal.

Drug treatment should be as simple and limited as possible. After establishing the current medicine regimen, the physician can discontinue some drugs before introducing new ones or even stop all treatment for 48 hours to clear the body of one potential cause of confusion. It may be necessary to immobilize the patient to achieve rehydration, and in some cases it is advisable to give an antipsychotic drug by the intramuscular route to this end. It is important to stress, however, that this should only be ordered when reassurance and persuasion have failed. The physician should review the prescription of any such drugs frequently and should not continue them unless it is absolutely necessary.

Chlorpromazine or thioridazine in a dose of 25–50 mg given in a once daily, usually nightly, dose or haloperidol 0.5–1.5 mg in the same way are the most effective antipsychotics. An intramuscular dose has a considerable hypnotic side-effect, but 24–48 hours deep sleep may help the return to normal sense in a few cases.

Drug treatment at this stage should be constantly monitored. Antidepressants may be helpful, but before resorting to them, consultation with a psychiatrist is advisable. Hypnotics may be required, but never barbiturates. Chloral, flurazepam or oxazepam are all effective. One old-fashioned and unpopular drug, paraldehyde, is very safe and can be given by mouth or per rectum. It is likely to cause muscle damage if used intramuscularly, however.

PROGNOSIS

The prognosis depends to a considerable extent on the severity of the underlying precipitating disease and how well and quickly it responds to treatment. In Hodkinson's series (15), 25% of his cases of toxic confusional states died, but 35% recovered to be discharged; the remainder were still in the hospital at the end of the study period. Preexisting dementia, defective hearing and vision, Parkinsonism, and advanced age were frequent predisposing factors; pneumonia, cardiac failure, urinary infection, carcinomatosis, and hypokalemia were the most common precipitating factors.

Kral (25) has described what became of individuals suffering from acute confusional states who were admitted to a psychiatric hospital. Half of his series recovered after treatment, sometimes prolonged, in the hospital; half of the remainder died within a relatively short time, and the final quarter remained permanently demented in long-term hospital care.

In both geriatric and psychiatric series, therefore, there was a considerable mortality—which emphasizes the serious nature of the condition. This is balanced by a real hope for full recovery in half of all cases, this being greater when prompt investigation and treatment is possible.

CHRONIC DEMENTING ILLNESS

Pearce and Miller (27) define dementia as "a symptom, arising from cerebral disease, often progressive, which is characterized by a decline of intellect and personality which reflect a disturbance of memory, orientation, the capacity for conceptual thought and often of affect." Its other consistent feature is its slow onset and gradual development. If one accepts this, it may be equally appropriate to use the term "dementing illness" to indicate all conditions which include dementia as one of their features. Such illness becomes increasingly common with advancing years and has been reported by one group to be present in as many as 22% of individuals over the age of 80.

Man owes his position as the dominant mammal to one factor: the vastly increased area of cerebral cortex with which his brain is equipped. If for any reason this area is impaired, man is reduced to the level of the weakest and most helpless of animals, unable to fend for himself or survive by his own efforts. Advanced dementia or cerebral failure therefore is a condition which is responsible for many potentially dangerous situations. Those who suffer from such illness continue to live in the community only at the cost of great mental and emotional strain on the part of relatives, neighbors, or friends. When one considers the vast sums of money that are poured annually into research on heart disease and cancer, it is surprising how relatively little attention has been paid to this common, severely debilitating condition. The great increase in the number of very old people in so many countries is at last changing this picture.

ETIOLOGY

As with acute confusional states, there is a multiplicity of causes for chronic dementing illness (Table 5–2). The majority of cases are caused by conditions in the primary group and first two categories of the secondary group (see section on Aging of the Brain in Ch. 4, Brain Failure). The importance of the other conditions is that there are cures available for many of them. They represent the small group of cases for whom adequate treatment may achieve cures.

Included in the group of dementing illness caused by vascular disease is an important subgroup, which has been well described by Adams and Hurwitz (2) —mental barriers to recovery from strokes. Inability to learn, for reasons which vary from clouding of consciousness to full-blown dementia, is the first major

TABLE 5–2. Causes of Chronic Dementing Illness

Type	Cause
Primary	Alzheimer (senile) dementia
(of unknown etiology)	Pick's disease
	Jakob-Creutzfeld disease
Secondary	Cerebrovascular disease
(due to recognized	Hypertensive lacunar disease
causes)	Trauma
	Parkinson's disease
	Huntington's chorea
	Giant cell arteritis
	Alcoholism
	Normal pressure hydrocephalus
	Cerebral tumor
	Myxedema
	Malnutrition
	Hypoglycemia
	Hypercalcemia
	Drug misuse
	Infection
	B_{12} or folate deficiency

barrier. Others are disturbed perception, disordered integrative action, and emotional upheavals. All three are also of particular relevance to mobility and posture.

INCIDENCE

As has already been stated, the incidence of senile and arteriosclerotic psychosis in Roth's 1955 series (30) was 33% of 450 cases over age 60 treated in a psychiatric hospital. Various other statements on the incidence of dementing illness in the general population have been made, but one of the most unequivocal came from a study reported in 1965 by Stokoe (34). He and his coworkers in Edinburgh examined a random sample of 200 people (91 men and 109 women) over the age of 65. Included in their program was a

semi-structured interview with brief psychological testing, incorporating the paired associate learning test described by Inglis in 1959. This helped to assess learning ability as distinct from intellectual ability and made the evaluation of the memory tests easier. The interview took about half an hour.

On the basis of this careful evaluation by a psychiatrist, 41 males and 53 females were judged to have mental disability, mostly of a mild degree. Of 29 men and 26 women thought to be demented, only 8 men and 8 women were considered to have a "moderate" or "severe" condition. An overall incidence of 8% for a group aged 65 and over is high. Sheldon (33) assessed a random sample of 369 individuals, again over the age of 65, and reported an incidence of 3.9%. Kay and his coworkers (21) in 1964 recorded a total incidence in those over 65 of 5.6%. None of these latter reports differentiate between the sexes, but Kral (25) draws attention to the fact that primary dementing illness is more common in women than men by a ratio of 3:2 or even 2:1. If one accepts a figure of 5% for the incidence of dementia in the population over the age of 65, then in a country such as the United States with 10% of its 200 million population in the relevant age group, one can conclude that there are 1 million witless, dependent dements. This number is likely to increase quickly because the population over the age of 80 is increasing faster than any other.

EVALUATION AND EXAMINATION

Clinical Features

The clinical features of chronic dementing illness are easily recognizable in the advanced case, but need careful evaluation by the questionnaire technique. Loss of memory is usually the first obvious feature. Kral (22) distinguishes between benign and malignant amnestic syndromes. In the former, details of an event being recounted (such as a person's name) are forgotten, but a clear picture of the total happening is retained; in the latter, the whole episode is completely forgotten. There is also a deterioration of the ability to reason and a tendency to perseverate and confabulate, the latter particularly in the early stages of the disorder.

Personality changes appear which are most obvious to the immediate family and friends. Often the cheerful individual tends to become very extroverted and euphoric, and the morose individual becomes totally withdrawn, silent, and apathetic. Less commonly the reverse occurs; for example, a tidy, neat person becomes uncharacteristically sloppy. In both cases, a point is reached where behavior goes well beyond the normally accepted bounds of decency. Clothes may be discarded, excretion may take place in public rooms, and eventually complete incontinence becomes established without any suggestion of embarrassment. In the early stages there may be symptoms of a depressive disorder or physical complaints of a vague nature, such as headaches. These inconclusive clinical features may not immediately suggest the onset of dementing illness, but such illness should always be suspected as a cause of apparently minor symptoms in the old.

Diagnosis of dementing illness is as important as in any other clinical condition. Even though at the present time there is no therapeutic answer, the physician must carefully establish the diagnosis in order to give both patient and family good advice. A valuable aid to the family physician is a joint clinic at which both psychiatrist and internist see and assess elderly patients. The expertise of both disciplines is valuable for patients with mental disturbances which may be caused by or be associated with organic physical disease.

As an illustration, one clinical feature of dementia in its more advanced stages is focal neurologic damage, which causes symptoms such as dysphasia or dyslexia. Testing the sensorium may become a major problem without adequate means of response from the patient. Apraxia and inappropriate actions, such as pouring milk into the coffee pot, eating with fingers, or being unable to use a knife and fork, represent further evidence of focal damage. These features do not indicate vascular lesions if there is no other reason to suspect their presence but are caused by the cerebral damage responsible for dementing illness. As the physician practicing geriatric medicine is primarily concerned with caring for the patient, the differentiation between vascular or degenerative neuronal loss is less important than an understanding of the concept of chronic dementing illness. There are excellent accounts available for those who wish to probe more deeply into diagnostic complexities, however (1, 3, 27).

Investigations

The difficulties of history taking and conducting a physical examination for a patient with dementing illness are much the same as those for patients with acute confusional states, although they are less dramatic for patients with slow onset disease. For the same patient, opportunist techniques have to be used. The emphasis again is to make certain that treatable conditions are spotted and dealt with. It is obvious that excluding all the major causes for secondary dementing illness (Table 5–2) is both time-consuming and costly. Before suggesting an investigational routine, one further relevant point should be made. The study, of which the Stokoe paper (34) formed a part, was an investigation into the unreported needs of old people at home (40). The 200 old people in the study were drawn from three practices; in each the physician was known to have a particular interest in his older patients. In spite of this, there were approximately twice as many morbid conditions present in the group as were known to the physicians. This particular study has been widely quoted as an indication of the "iceberg" phenomenon of disease in the old: 87% of the dementing illness was unknown to the physician (Fig. 5–2). Because of a common belief that every old person is likely to suffer disability from old age and no one can do anything about it, patients may not seek medical attention until months or even years after a condition has first appeared. The longer dementing illness has been present, the less effective therapeutic measures are likely to be.

It is also true that the duration of the dementia may rule out some conditions as its cause. Deficiency of vitamin B_{12}, for example, may produce cerebral manifestations before the deficiency itself is obvious, but sooner rather than later pernicious anemia develops. Therefore, if a patient who has been suffering from dementing illness for an extended period is not anemic, the dementia is not caused by a deficiency of vitamin B_{12}. The eventual pattern of investigation depends on the history, duration, and the most likely cause for the dementia.

In one-quarter to one-third of cases, there may be good evidence of earlier cerebrovascular accidents with or without hypertension. In these cases, a step-like process of deterioration can usually be established. When the history is one of a steady, slow, dementing process, it is more difficult to decide how far to go with investigation. Only knowledge and experience can help, but in some cases it is wise to undertake skull x-rays, brain scans, or even an occasional angiogram

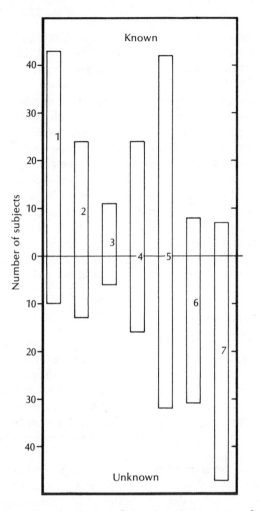

Fig. 5–2. "Iceberg" phenomenon of geriatric medicine. 1) respiratory system disability; 2) cardiovascular system disability; 3) central nervous system disability; 4) alimentary system disability; 5) locomotor system disability; 6) genitourinary system disability; 7) dementia (Composed from data of Williamson J, *et al.: Lancet* I:1117–1123, 1964)

to supplement the routine investigations. If even 2%–3% of these supplementary procedures revealed remediable conditions which were successfully treated, the cost of the 97% negative tests would soon be saved by the few not requiring long-term institutional care with all its costs. Even more rewarding, however, would be the rescue of those individuals who could recover.

The treatment and general care of old people suffering from chronic dementing illness is not easy. Frequently such morbidity goes unreported because relatives, friends, or neighbors accept the idea of "senility," and obviously the patient is unable to complain.

PREVENTION

In view of the iceberg phenomenon, an attempt should be made with the help of public health nurses and social agencies to discover cases early. Each family physician should set out to discover those of his practice who show any evidence of dementing illness. Investigation can establish those for whom active treatment may be possible. What about the others, who constitute the vast majority?

Psychologists now believe that, in the same way that nonmitotic muscle cells respond to exercise programs by becoming stronger, so nonmitotic neurons may function better when their level of stimulation is increased. The many ways this can be done hinge on bringing subjects into active contact with other people. Countering the sensory deprivation of loneliness and isolation is important. The success of clubs of all kinds for senior citizens is an indication of how valuable such organizations are. The individuality of the elderly may be a major deterrent, however, as some stubbornly refuse to be involved with "a lot of old people," disregarding the best advice of their physicians. Loss of adequate vision and/or hearing may also deprive the individual of adequate sensory stimulation, and special efforts need to be made with the blind and deaf.

Retirement Communities

In certain areas of the world, retirement villages or communities have been established in which the elderly live among contemporaries with similar experiences of major world events, the same exposure to difficult economic crises, and identical or closely related educational backgrounds. For many these communities offer social, emotional, and sensory stimulation that maintains cerebral functioning at an optimal level. On the other hand, it may be asking for trouble to commit the elderly to such ghettos where they can brood over the life that has passed.

In any event, social developments of this kind begin and flourish because they are almost certainly answering a community need. It would be of value to assess the comparative incidence of dementing illness in such a community with that of a matched sample continuing to live in their own homes amid a population of mixed age.

Day Hospitals

For those who are beginning to show evidence of amnesic disease and for others with progressing physical disability, geriatric day hospitals can play a vital supportive role. An essentially British innovation, the idea of combining physical treatment and consultative facilities with social and recreational activities in one center has a great deal to commend it. Brocklehurst (6) describes the British experience in some detail. It is not difficult to appreciate the theoretic desirability of an arrangement whereby an elderly lady who is suffering from moderately severe osteoarthrosis and living alone is transported to a modern, spacious, comfortable day hospital two or three times a week. Arriving there at midmorning, she receives appropriate physical therapy for her joints, with a good exercise component for her weakening muscles. Lunch in a cheerful social atmosphere is followed by a short relaxation or gossip half-hour; the afternoon may be spent playing bingo, checkers, dominos, cards, or even chess—according to taste. The lady returns home between 4 and 5 o'clock feeling stimulated, refreshed, and much more content. Two or three months of such day hospital therapy can go a long way to reestablish the lady's hope and confidence in her own ability to live and enjoy life in spite of her disabilities. For the patient with dementing illness, the sensory stimulation and reality orientation basis of the day clinic can help to maintain life at home.

CASE REPORT 5–5

An 85-year-old lady lived within 400 yards of a day hospital in Birmingham, England. She was alone and began to worry her neighbors because of increasing forgetfulness, leaving the gas turned on without lighting it, burning out kettles, and creating situations of potential danger to herself and others. Because of a chronic leg ulcer, she was referred to a geriatrician, who arranged for her to attend the day hospital. Because she was so near, the hospital nurse would go and fetch her, but after a few occasions she learned to go alone. She enjoyed her daily visits to the center and continued to live in her own home; for some months her dementing illness was arrested.

SURVIVAL

The day hospital is an important link between home and hospital, especially to the person with dementing illness for whom the prospect of leaving home is unthinkable. A feature of dementia is the remarkable talent for survival which is retained by the mindless person left in the familiar environment. Talking to such persons makes one wonder how they could survive for 2 days. Yet many not only survive, but manage to look after themselves reasonably well for months and even years. Their homes become as grubby and disheveled as they do themselves, but provided they are left in peace and can cling to routine, they soldier on.

There is a very delicate balance between failing cerebral function and the individual's ability to survive. The one thing which shatters this balance is the arrival of the geriatrician or psychiatrist, who takes one look and says, "Off to the hospital tomorrow!" When this happens, as inevitably it must, the hospital staff marvels that this particular old person has survived alone at home for so long. There are two reasons for this. In the first place, by reducing the range of activities from the larger neighborhood to the immediate neighborhood, to the house, and finally to one room, individuals reduce the demands that are made on the last little bit of functioning brain. The second factor is that friends, relatives, and neighbors, in spite of all the brickbats thrown at them, do rally round and help look after such failing old people. This is particularly true when he or she has been a popular member of the local community. One of the most difficult questions, therefore, is at what point should the person with dementing illness be moved from home to institution? Once made, the move can seldom be reversed. It is, therefore, all the more important to maintain support in the person's own home for as long as possible.

CASE REPORT 5–6

Miss Henson, aged 93, lived in an attractive bungalow in a group of about 30 similar dwellings built for senior citizens. An autocratic and independent person, she had maintained herself very well until 6 months before the geriatrician encountered her. Forgetfulness, disorientation, and personality changes had then become obvious. Thanks to a dedicated welfare department aide, she was kept nourished and clean, but the situation became desperate. When examined by the physician, she was ambulant with no evidence of cardiorespiratory dysfunction. Although unaware of the date or the time of day, she knew she was in her own home and refused to be moved. She did, however, agree to come to the day hospital with her aide. For a month, she came for 2 days each week. She remained incontinent at home and her dementing illness was no better. One afternoon at the day hospital she was yawning and seemed tired. It was suggested to her that she lie down for a while. She agreed, went willingly to a ward, and was put to bed. She never left the hospital, but settled happily, wandering about at will during the day.

CLINICAL MANAGEMENT

What can the physician do to help the forgetful, wandering old person whose thinking has gone and who is unable to offer any cooperation? The physician can cure only a small number of cases. The remaining large group is maintained at home by relatives, friends, or neighbors or is accommodated in institutions of varying kinds—some ideal, but many quite unsuitable. The contribution of the physician is then advisory and therapeutic. It is a highly significant role, however, and properly fulfilled can assist greatly in the general care of the patient.

Communication

In the process of examining and testing elderly patients the physician becomes the person with the fullest knowledge and understanding of them. He or she also knows from professional training the likely outcome in each case. The way in which these two distinct stores of information are used varies with the particular circumstances of the patient. The first objective is to attempt to make the patient understand the situation. Communication may be extremely difficult, and it often appears that nothing has been understood. In some cases, part of the message gets through; in others, not one word. For the sake of the former, the attempt should be made.

The relative or friend who has been taking the major responsibility for the patient should be present to hear what is said. It is the physician's duty to help everyone deeply involved in the situation to understand as fully as possible the nature of brain failure and its physical cause. Many people need reassurance that this is not something brought on by mental or moral weakness. It should be stated that, while some cases are due to arterial disease, the cause in the majority of cases is not known. Having established the nature of the condition, a necessary time-consuming business, the physician, the patient, and others involved must create a practical plan for the future.

Creating a Plan for Care

The most important person is the patient. An attempt must be made gently and slowly to discover what he or she would like. This may be a fruitful exercise at an early stage of dementing illness, but becomes less relevant in more advanced cases. Unfortunately, many cases are brought to the physician's attention only when a crisis has arisen. Miss Henson was a case in point. This is a major reason for programs of case finding. The crisis frequently precipitates the transfer of the patient from a domestic to an institutional environment. Since planned changes are least emotionally disturbing, every effort should be made to plan them. It is possible to persuade patients to accept what is obviously the best answer.

Cases of dementia can be divided into three groups. The first comprises old people who live in a reasonably secure domestic situation, for example, with some family member. There is no urgent fear for the nourishment or general care of this patient. The old person is forgetful, vague, and lost, may need prompting to come and eat or go to the bathroom, but presents no distressing behavioral problems. These patients often do well if the family has extra help to share the burden of care. Such help includes day care at a hospital or senior citizens' center and occasional periods of 2–3 weeks in a home or nursing home while relatives have a holiday. The 24-hour-a-day care of a witless wanderer, however sweet he or she may be, is quite a strain. A plan should also be established to cope with sudden illness or other catastrophe in the family support.

The second group has behavioral disorders which produce recurrent crisis situations, such as wandering off with or without clothes on, frequently in the late afternoon or early evening with the intention of "going home"! Others turn night into day, remaining placid and half asleep all day but waking up and wandering about at night. In either case, the abnormal behavior may be accompanied by belligerent outbursts which are very wearing on long-suffering families or friends. It is wise to admit such people to an institution at once for an initial careful assessment and an attempt at establishing a drug regimen that will help to control behavior.

The third group includes all old people with dementing illness who live alone, whether they exhibit behavioral problems or not. Again, the first reaction is to admit them to a hospital, but care should be taken as this may cause permanent loss of their last faint grip on reality. Early recognition and careful arrangement of support services may well maintain some of this group at home, as illustrated in Case Report 5–5.

Admission to Institutional Care

The first major decision after the diagnosis of chronic dementing illness has been confirmed is whether or not institutional care is needed. If so, what type, and if not, what support services are required at home? In this decision, the patient, the family, and other interested individuals should be involved. Since dementia is caused by organic physical changes, it is not recognized by some psychiatrists as properly lying within their field. It is perhaps best regarded as falling between the fields of psychiatrist and internist and is properly, therefore, the concern of both. Close cooperation between the two can certainly be of enormous value to the patient in the management of the condition. Certification of the demented person as one requiring compulsory admission to an institution is a decision best made jointly by physician and psychiatrist.

Behavior Modification

Once the decision for or against an institution has been made, the second problem is how to moderate behavior and keep the patient as content as possible. Individuals probably become restless for one or more of three basic reasons: 1) physical discomfort, 2) emotional upset, fear, anxiety, or bewilderment, and 3) vivid, nightmarish hallucinations or delusions.

Efforts to establish whether or not there is any physical discomfort should be carefully carried out by relatives, nurse, and physician. The individual's appetite and excretory pattern should be noted. Anorexia, constipation, dysuria, and frequency of micturition are all common, and a businesslike approach to them is important. The possibility of fecal impaction or urinary tract infection should be investigated and any necessary treatment given. Repeated examinations should be carried out to exclude the presence of developing boils, carbuncles, ulcers, or other lesions, such as chronic arthritis, which may be responsible for discomfort and restlessness.

Anxiety and fear may be more difficult to pinpoint. The best antidote is a secure, relaxed environment in which the patient feels safe. This ideal goal is often difficult to achieve in a domestic environment because few daughters, who usually bear the brunt of the responsibility for care, are able to detach themselves emotionally from the patient to offer dispassionate, yet watchful, attention. The availability of good "senior-sitters" may help enormously by allowing the family to organize itself adequately for what will always be a stressful task. Day hospital care can also be helpful.

CASE REPORT 5–7

Mrs. Clement lived with a married daughter who was devoted to her. She also had a second daughter who lived nearby. The old lady was 87 years old, and 9 years earlier she had had a partial colectomy for carcinoma of the colon. She had a severe degree of dementing illness that had developed over the preceding year or two, suffered from calcific valvular disease, and occasionally experienced bouts of congestive cardiac failure. The main dementing features were severe amnesia and marked feelings of insecurity. There were also episodes of fecal incontinence.

The insecurity caused Mrs. Clement to follow her daughter around the house with monotonous persistence, which drove the latter to distraction. It was agreed to try having the old lady spend 2–3 days a week in a continuing care hospital where attention could be given to her incontinence by enemas and suitable surveillance of her cardiac condition could be undertaken. At the same time, her daughter would have clear days to organize her own life. This arrangement proved very satisfactory for about 6 months, until it became obvious that it was beginning to bewilder Mrs. Clement more, and she was kept in the hospital altogether. Secure and content there by this time, she no longer followed people around. Her daughter visits frequently, and the optimal method of caring for the old lady has been achieved.

The hallucinatory, nightmarish fantasies represent a reasonable interpretation of the often paranoid and violent types of behavioral disturbance sometimes encountered. In this situation, phenothiazine drugs are the best answer and may have to be used parenterally in appreciable dosage. In some cases doses which cause heavy hypnosis for up to 48 hours, followed by a slow reduction or withdrawal, can be quite effective, but this technique may require support by intravenous infusions to maintain adequate fluid balance. Patients who are noisy, belligerent and uncooperative can be effectively handled in this way. Chlorpromazine given intramuscularly in a dose of 25 mg is adequate in most cases but the range of 12.5–50 mg may be required.

Specific Treatment and Drug Therapy

Every attempt should be made to manage the patient's condition without drugs, but there are occasions when drugs become essential. In such situations, the therapeutic aim must be clear. For the overactive, anxious wanderer, a phenothiazine is probably the most effective drug. Chlordiazepoxide and diazepam cause muscle relaxation and therefore weakness, possibly predisposing the patient to falls.

Night management is a real problem. The circadian rhythm of demented patients often goes awry, and after peacefully sleeping away the day hours, they come alive at dusk and ruin the sleep of their fellows during the night. A judicious blend of activities during the day, isolation at night with a tolerant attitude toward wandering, and a hot drink once or twice during the night can be most effective, but requires a lot of nursing time. Bowel care and honoring normal lavatory habits during the night are also important.

Chloral, flurazepam, nitrazepam, and dichloralphenazone are effective, fairly short-acting hypnotics. Barbiturates should be avoided at all costs, as their depressing effect on cerebral function is too much for the atrophied cortex; they often cause acute delirium.

Two other groups of drugs can be helpful: antidepressants and analgesics or narcotics. Depressive states may coexist with degrees of dementia, and the association is a further reason for involving the psychiatrist in the planning of management. Tricyclic antidepressants may work very well, but dosage should be modest. It is preferable to give the daily amount when the patient goes to bed in order to minimize the dangers of postural hypotension, which is associated with administration of this group of drugs. Analgesics or narcotics are seldom required, but when there appears to be some persistent discomfort they are worth considering.

The measures recommended for the clinical management of patients suffering from chronic dementing illness are an application of humane understanding of a tragic human situation. Attempts have been made (with little evidence of unequivocal success) to improve cerebral function by more direct means. It is impossible to make definitive judgments on these efforts because the evidence is incomplete. In my own experience of vitamin E, naftidrofuryl, Hydergine, and Parenterovite, no consistent benefit is gained from their use. Some of the preparations which have been advocated include Parenterovite, a high dose of a vitamin B and C preparation administered parenterally (26), ribonucleic acid (9), hyperbaric oxygen (16), cyclandelate (4, 41), Hydergine (5, 12, 13, 17, 36), and naftidrofuryl (10, 19, 29). It is claimed that all of these have some effect on cognitive function, but the reported results of psychologic test scores or activities of daily living assessments in small numbers of subjects are not convincing.

It is well to note that one study, at least, has shown somewhat similar results from a concentrated, individualized team approach (7). This approach underlies the concept of reality orientation, well described by Judd (18). Reality orientation is based on a definitive type of sensory stimulation with large print notices and clocks and calendars constantly reminding individuals of where they are, what the date and time is, and who they are. This idea is of great value in the depersonalized institution and should be encouraged.

From the drug point of view, however, there is still some way to go. Cerebral vasodilators or metabolism changers are valuable attempts to learn more of how the thinking part of the brain works. It is almost certainly the laboratory, where new advances in the understanding of neuronal function are made, that will eventually provide the physician with more effective therapeutic tools. These are certainly needed.

REFERENCES

1. Adams GF: Cerebrovascular Disability and the Ageing Brain. London, Chruchill-Livingstone, 1974
2. Adams GF, Hurwitz LJ: Mental barriers to recovery from strokes. Lancet II:533–537, 1963
3. Allison RS: The Senile Brain. London, Edward Arnold, 1962
4. Ball JAC, Taylor AR: Effect of cyclandelate on mental function and cerebral blood flow in elderly patients. Br Med J 3:525–528, 1967
5. Banen DM: An ergot preparation (Hydergine) for relief of symptoms of cerebrovascular insufficiency. J Am Geriatr Soc 20:22–24, 1972
6. Brocklehurst JC: The Geriatric Day Hospital. London, King Edward's Hospital Fund for London, 1970

7. Brody EM, Cole C, Moss M: Individualizing therapy for the mentally impaired aged. Social Casework: 54:453–461, 1973
8. Brown W: Practice in associating colour names with colours. Psychol Rev 22:51, 1915
9. Cameron DE, Solyom L: Effects of ribonucleic acid on memory. Geriatrics 16:74–81, 1961
10. Cox JR: A double blind evaluation of naftidrofuryl in treating elderly confused hospitalized patients. Gerontol Clin 17:160–167, 1975
11. Dixon JC: Cognitive structure in senile conditions with some suggestions for developing a brief screening test of mental status. J Gerontol 20:41–49, 1965
12. Emmenegger H, Meier-Ruge W: The actions of hydergine on the brain. Pharmacology I:65–78, 1968
13. Gerin J: Symptomatic treatment of cerebrovascular insufficiency with hydergine. Curr Ther Res II:539–546, 1969
14. Hodkinson HM: Evaluation of a mental test score for assessment of mental impairment in the elderly. Age Ageing I:233–238, 1972
15. Hodkinson HM: Mental impairment in the elderly. J R Coll Physicians Lond 7:305–317, 1973
16. Jacobs EA, Winter PM, Alvis HJ, Small SM: Hyperoxygenation effect on cognitive functioning in the aged. N Engl J Med 281:753–757, 1969
17. Jennings WG: An ergot alkaloid preparation (hydergine) versus placebo for treatment of symptoms of cerebrovascular insufficiency: double-blind study. J Am Geriatr Soc 20:407–412, 1972
18. Judd MW: Reality orientation. Added supplement to Why Bother, He's Old and Confused. Occupational Therapy Department, Winnipeg Municipal Hospital, Morley Avenue E, Winnipeg, Manitoba
19. Judge TG, Urquhart A: Naftidrofuryl—A double blind cross-over study in the elderly. Curr Med Res Opin I:166–172, 1972
20. Kahn RL, Goldfarb AI, Pollack M, Peck A: Brief objective measures for the determination of mental status in the aged. Am J Psychiatry 117:326–328, 1960
21. Kay DWK, Beamish P, Roth M: Old age mental disorders in Newcastle upon Tyne. I. A study of prevalence. Br J Psychiatry 110:146, 1964
22. Kral VA: The senile amnestic syndrome: diagnosis, prognosis, treatment. In Psychiatric Disorders in the Aged. Manchester, England, Geigy UK Ltd, 1965, pp 144–153
23. Kral VA: Stress reactions in old age. Laval Med 38:561–566, 1967
24. Kral VA: Psychiatric problems in the aged: a reconsideration. Can Med Assoc J 108:584–590, 1973
25. Kral VA: Psychiatric problems. In von Hahn HP (ed): Practical Geriatrics. Basel, S Karger, 1975, pp 259–283
26. Krawiecki JA, Couper L, Walton D: The efficacy of parenterovite in the treatment of a group of senile psychotics. J Ment Sci 103:601–605, 1957
27. Pearce J, Miller E: Clinical Aspects of Dementia. London, Bailliere Tindall, 1973
28. Pfeiffer E: A short portable mental status questionnaire for the assessment of organic brain deficit in elderly patients. J Am Geriatr Soc 23:433–441, 1975
29. Robinson K: A double-blind clinical trial of naftidrofuryl in cerebral vascular disorders. Medical Digest 17:50–52, 1972
30. Roth M: The natural history of mental disorder in old age. J Ment Sci 101:281–301, 1955
31. Roth M, Hopkins B: Psychological test performance in patients over sixty. 1. Senile psychosis and the affective disorders of old age. J Ment Sci 99:439–450, 1953
32. Seymour DG, Henschke PJ: Unpublished data, 1977
33. Sheldon JH: The Social Medicine of Old Age. London, Published for the Trustees of the Nuffield Foundation, 1948, pp 107–139
34. Stokoe IH: The physical and mental care of the elderly at home. In Psychiatric Disorders in the Aged. Manchester, England, Geigy UK Ltd, 1965, pp 237–246
35. Stroop JR: Studies of interference in serial and verbal reaction. J Exp Psychol 18:643–661, 1935
36. Szewczykowski J, Meyer JS, Kondo A, Nomura F, Teraura T: Effections of ergot alkaloids (hydergine) on cerebral haemodynamics and oxygen consumption in monkeys. J Neurol Sci 10:25–31, 1970
37. Welford AT: On changes of performance with age. Lancet I:335–339, 1962

38. Weed LL: Medical Records, Medical Education and Patient Care. Chicago, Year Book Medical, 1971
39. Weschler D: Standardized memory scale for clinical use. J Psychol 19:87–95, 1945
40. Williamson J, Stokoe IH, Gray S, Fisher M, Smith A, McGee A, Stephenson E: Old people at home, their unreported needs. Lancet I:1117–1123, 1964
41. Young J, Hall P, Blakemore C: Treatment of the cerebral manifestations of arteriosclerosis with cyclandelate. Br J Psychiatry 124:177–180, 1974

Chapter 6

FALLING

This is the state of man: to-day he puts forth
The tender leaves of hopes; to-morrow blossoms,
And bears his blushing honours thick upon him;
The third day comes a frost, a killing frost,
And, when he thinks, good easy man, full surely
His greatness is a-ripening, nips his root,
And then he falls, as I do.

And when he falls, he falls like Lucifer,
Never to hope again.

                    Shakespeare, Henry VIII

CASE REPORT 6–1

Mrs. Carroll an active 81-year-old lady, had run a boardinghouse since being widowed 25 years earlier. In the summer of 1975 she developed a tendency to fall and was advised to give up her business and home. Towards the end of the year, she followed this advice and moved in with a cousin.

In November 1976 she was admitted to a hospital and referred to the geriatrician. The history was one of recurrent falls, every 4–6 weeks during the preceding 18 months. Outwardly sensible and alert, she suffered at times from forgetfulness and a tendency to perseverate. The move to her cousin's house had clearly worked out well, and he was a frequent visitor while she was in hospital; the two were on excellent terms with one another. The ménage included a number of dogs and cats, and Mrs. Carroll was very fond of them. Apart from falling, her main medical problem had been a mildly elevated systolic blood pressure.

Physical examination was largely negative. Mrs. Carroll looked her age, but her cardiopulmonary function was satisfactory, with no evidence of congestive failure and no major problem with shortness of breath. Her only other complaint was of tiredness. Her heart action was slow, 50–60/min, and for this reason the possibility of a degree of heart block was suggested. An electrocardiogram showed no evidence of this, however.

At the beginning of December 1976, she had a severe, sudden fall during the course of which she was incontinent. She gave her back a nasty bruise and was considerably shaken for several days. The nursing staff recorded that from time to time she became confused and more difficult to manage. When seen by the geriatrician she was always very sweet and reasonable with little evidence of mental upset. Her general condition slowly improved, and as she recovered some of her confidence, she became anxious to return home. This she did shortly before Christmas.

After only 10 days at home, she was readmitted on December 28th, following further falls. The general features of her condition remained the same as during her earlier admission. Ostensibly sensible, she was never able to give a clear coherent account of what had been happening to her without gaps in her memory. It was difficult to assess her mental status. The problems were again listed: 1) Falling remained the most significant and serious problem which Mrs. Carroll faced. No sooner did her condition improve a little and did she begin to recover her mobility, than there was a further fall. The cause of these remained obscure. 2) Mrs. Carroll was now constantly complaining of tiredness and weakness. When seen on January 1st, a bath had "taken all the stuffing out of me." This was symptomatic of her general, hopeless attitude. 3) A new feature was epigastric pain which occurred from time to time when she was feeling anxious and tense.

Examination revealed little change in Mrs. Carroll's condition from a month earlier. There were the remains of two black eyes and a sizable bruise below the right knee, the result of the latest fall. Her abdomen was a little distended, and there was tenderness in the left iliac fossa suggestive of colonic stasis.

To recreate confidence was going to take considerable time. Admission was arranged to a continuing care hospital.

In examining the nature of falling in old people one is looking at much more than the actual fall. Falling precipitates loss of mobility, and to the old person mobility is as precious as life. Falling may lead to major injuries and fractures which, in the old, may result in prolonged periods of immobility followed by a long, difficult rehabilitation. Much more significant, however, is the gradual decline of the old person's confidence in his or her ability to stand erect. Loss of confidence in one's physical capabilities is the loss of a most precious asset. In Mrs. Carroll's case this resulted in becoming a permanent resident in a continuing care institution.

CONTROL OF POSTURE

The ability to stand, walk, and run in an upright position is a unique feature of man as a mammal. Man's erect posture is achieved by a complex series of messages fed into the brain and translated by the sensory and motor cortex, the basal ganglia, and the cerebellum into appropriate responses. The various sources of sensory input are illustrated in Figure 6–1. Visual stimuli are of particular importance, and conditions such as seasickness might be described as disharmony between messages received from the eyes on the one hand and the vestibule on the other. The effect of excessive stimulation of the vestibule can be illustrated by the individual who experiences aerobatics as a passenger for the first time. The combination of unusual visual impulses with the world spinning around and excessive gravity effects can be extremely damaging to postural control when terra firma is regained!

Sheldon (29) studied postural control in groups of young, middle-aged, and old subjects. He devised a light aluminum frame which fastened on the individual's shoulders and had, projecting forwards from it, a triangular piece; at the apex of the triangle there was a spring-loaded pencil. Wearing this device, the

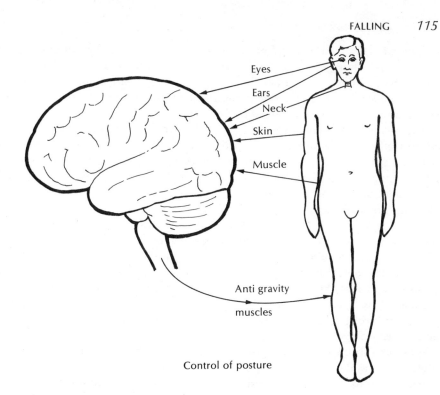

Eyes
Ears
Neck
Skin
Muscle
Anti gravity
muscles
Control of posture

Fig. 6–1. Sensory and motor pathways which control posture.

Fig. 6–2. Effect of age on sway as revealed by tracings in Sheldon's study. (Sheldon JH: Gerontol Clin [Basel] 5:129–138, 1963)

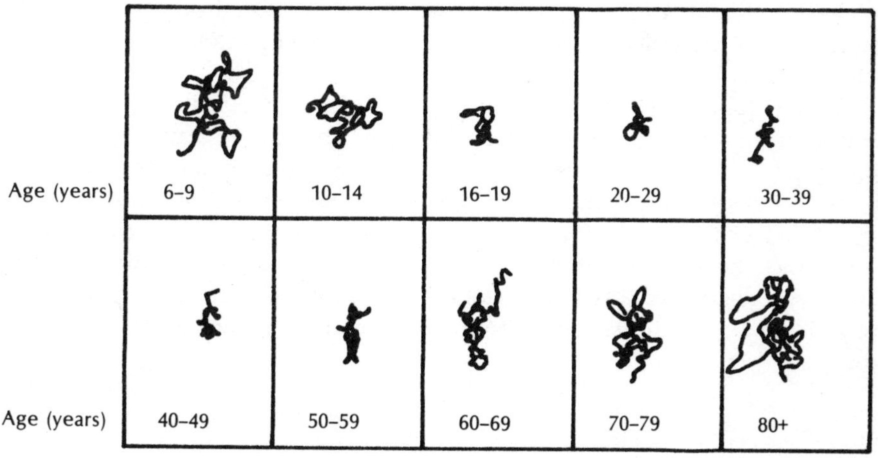

Age (years)
6–9
10–14
16–19
20–29
30–39
Age (years)
40–49
50–59
60–69
70–79
80+

individual was asked to stand with the pencil resting on a piece of graph paper at a suitable height. The object was to measure how far and how much the pencil would deviate from its original spot while the subject stood absolutely still for 1 min. Sheldon carried out this experiment with the subjects' eyes open and closed and with the feet apart and together.

The result of Sheldon's studies (Fig. 6–2) demonstrates clearly that postural control is a skill acquired in early life and is maintained through maturity between ages 16 and 60 but fails thereafter. By measuring the number of squares on the graph paper, Sheldon was able to make an approximate quantitative assessment of the degree of sway (Fig. 6–3). The lower of these two lines, with the subjects' eyes open, is used in Figure 4–9.

This simply constructed clinical test of postural control has been validated more recently by two other workers using much more sophisticated equipment. Hasselkus and Shambes (14) used a center of gravity apparatus in conjunction with two Hewlett Packard Calculators to estimate the area of sway. Their object was to investigate the effects of aging on postural control. They concluded, after comparing two groups of ten subjects each (21–30 and 73–80 years), that there was a significant difference in postural sway between the two groups. The older adults demonstrated a 50%–125% larger sway area.

Exton–Smith (8) used a Wright Ataxia Meter to study postural control. This meter is a simple device on which a person stands; a rod which projects from the platform measures the amount of sway in anterior and posterior directions. Exton–Smith observed not only that elderly people moved more than younger, but also that women were less able to hold their position than men. The degree of difference was quite striking, sway being up to twice as great in women. Another interesting finding of this study was that the degree of sway of those who fell because they tripped was not significantly greater than the mean for the age. On the other hand, individuals who had sustained drop-attacks or falls as a result of vertigo demonstrated a marked increase in anteroposterior movement.

Terekhov (30) has recently described another technique, called stabilometry, for measuring stability of postural equilibrium. The subject stands on an electronic platform which consists of square metal plates placed horizontally on top of each other. At each corner there is a load element which is constructed to record load changes in both sagittal and frontal planes. Linear tracings are recorded as the subject stands on the platform; they show variations in frequency and degree of sway which can then be measured. Increasing research in this field may contribute new information on the etiology of falling in the future.

BODY-ORIENTING REFLEXES

Body-orienting reflexes play an important role in preventing falls. Eyzaguirre and Fidone (10) describe labyrinthine, head-on-body, and body-on-head righting reflexes. The most complex arrangement is that in the labyrinth where the semicircular canals, filled with endolymph and lined at appropriate places by highly innervated mucosa, provide instant information about the position of the

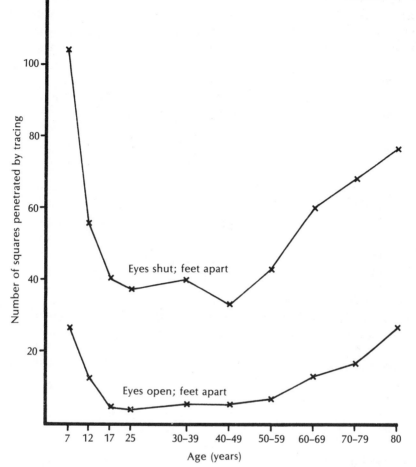

Fig. 6–3. Comparison of sway with eyes open and with eyes shut. (Sheldon JH: Gerontol Clin [Basel] 5:129–138, 1963)

head in space. The reaction of the body is to follow the head, thanks to the tonic neck reflexes. For example, when a cat falls, it first turns its head to face the ground, followed by its trunk; the animal lands on all four feet which are tensed to take the strain. The whole system works in a flash and is an excellent illustration of the sensitivity of the postural mechanism.

A similar system operates in man. The child is familiar with the sensation which may be induced by turning around and around very rapidly and the resulting fall to the ground with the world spinning. The child also knows how spinning in the reverse direction can counteract the original stimulus. This experience, which is enjoyable in childhood, becomes less so as one gets older. This is a simple illustration of the tendency for righting reflexes to become less effective with age.

The major function of the tonic neck reflexes is to enable the trunk to follow the position of the head. This is described as the head-on-body righting reflex, and it follows messages from neck proprioceptors to obey the position of the head. It has also been shown that a cat, if blindfolded and labyrinthectomized and lain on its side, will make attempts to right the position of its head. Such efforts are due to body surface receptors acting on neck muscles, the body-on-head righting reflex. The eyes control righting reflexes which require the visual cortex to be intact, one of the few body-orienting mechanisms not controlled by the brainstem. In general, however, the latter is the main site of postural control. The blood supply to this area comes from the vertebral circulation, a fact which may be relevant to drop-attacks.

PREDISPOSITION TO FALLING

The effect of age on postural control is to render it less effective. This is the single most important factor in the greatly increased number of accidents which the elderly have. Available studies also suggest that this predisposing factor is appreciably more common in women than in men. It is relevant to stress here that the incidence of falls in Sheldon's series (27) was twice as great at each age group in women than in men. Kral (17) draws attention to the fact that senile dementia is more common in women than in men in a similar proportion of 1.5:1 or even 2:1. Both the tendency to fall and dementia indicate deterioration in cerebral function which thus appears to occur more frequently in women. It should be emphasized that in neither case is the situation due to there being many more women in the older age groups. These figures are based on equal samples of men and women.

INCIDENCE OF FALLS

Because falling is common in old people, they usually accept it as an inevitable part of growing old and, surprisingly often, do not consult their physicians about the cause of the fall or what can be done about it. Sheldon (27) was one of the first to draw attention to this in his survey in Wolverhamptom. In his sample of the elderly population living at home in this English Midland city, 37% had sustained a fall within the previous few months. In a hospital study of 1000 cases (5) referred to a geriatric department the incidence of falling was 16%. The difference between the two series was that no attempt was made to question each individual directly about such episodes in the second one. The elderly person's failure to volunteer information about falls unless specifically asked to do so explains the much higher incidence in Sheldon's study, which included relevant questions.

CLASSIFICATION OF FALLS

Sheldon (28) and Clark (6) describe, in considerable detail, the natural history of falls in the elderly. Sheldon investigated 500 falls which were sustained by

TABLE 6–1. Age Distribution of Sheldon and Clark Series Compared With Cape Series

Series (date)	<60	60–69	70–79	80–89	Over 90	% Over 80
Sheldon (1960)	11	43	74	74	—	37%
Clark (1968)	· 8	85	156	174	27	45%
Cape (1968)	8	9	60	74	11	52%

TABLE 6–2. Classification of Falls

Cause	Sheldon (1960)	Clark (1968)
Accidental	224 (44%)	198 (46%)
Drop–attacks	125 (25%)	70 (16%)
Vertigo	37 (7%)	20 (4%)
Postural hypotension	18 (4%)	16 (4%)
CNS lesions	27 (5%)	76 (16%)
Miscellaneous	69 (15%)	70 (14%)

202 individuals, all of whom were living at home at the time of the inquiry. Of these subjects 86 were brought to the casualty department of the Royal Hospital, Wolverhampton; 59 were admitted to that hospital with a fractured femur. The names of another 57 old people who had sustained falls were provided by family physicians of the town. There were 34 men and 134 women in the 168 persons seen at home by Sheldon. Clark, on the other hand, was reporting on a personally observed series of 450 women, all of whom had sustained a fractured femur. Of Sheldon's cases 37% were over the age of 80, while 45% of Clark's subjects, who were all women, came into this age group (Table 6–1). The sex difference may explain the greater number who were older in the Clark series.

Both Clark and Sheldon classified the main causes of the falls which they described (Table 6–2). In any fall there are two major factors, the physical characteristics of the site at which it occurs and those of the subject who suffers it. By definition an accidental fall is precipitated by environmental factors, but others relate to the patient's condition. It seems logical therefore to follow Clark's example and divide falls into two main groups, those associated with environmental difficulties, the accidental ones, and those caused by patient factors which consist of a variety of problems. Inevitably there is a third category in which elements of both the first and second are implicated.

ACCIDENTAL FALLS

Almost half of the falls in each of the two series are accidental. Their particular importance is that steps can be taken to prevent many of them, a fact which was underlined by Clark. For example, a staircase which is badly lighted is inviting trouble. Loose rugs, low tables, stools, pets, and any object left casually on the floor may result in a trip. (Sheldon differentiated trips from accidental falls in his series, but in Table 6–2 they have been grouped together.) A sensible arrangement of the domestic environment can minimize the dangers of accidental falls due to these causes.

If it is essential for old people to go up and down stairs, rails should be placed on both sides so that two hands can be used instead of one. Old people sometimes miscalculate the number of steps or misjudge their position in relation to the next tread down. Although younger people also miscalculate or make such misjudgments, older people have a greater difficulty in regaining temporarily disturbed balance because of their impaired righting reflexes.

Slipping on greasy, wet, or icy surfaces may cause a fall. This seldom happens indoors, but fat may be spilled, wax may not be removed adequately from floors, etc. Outside the home, one does not need to emphasize the potential dangers in wintry conditions. Most accidents do occur indoors, however, either in the patient's own or adopted place of residence, be the latter a hospital, old age home, or nursing home. Clark found that 71 of the 450 falls he described happened outside but near to the home—in the backyard, by the front door, in the garden, or on steps. A further 71 or 16% occurred away from the domicile, most of those taking place on sidewalks, curbs, or roads.

DROP-ATTACKS

Drop-attacks are well described and recognizable happenings. The subject, in the course of normal routine, quite unexpectedly finds him- or herself on the floor or ground. The characteristics of the "drop" are its suddenness, its apparently complete lack of cause, and the inability of the person to describe what happened. If questioned about giddiness, loss of consciousness, or faintness to account for the sudden fall, the individual vehemently denies any such experience.

The second major feature of the drop-attack is the helplessness which is experienced on the ground. In some cases normal upright posture can be regained without any difficulty. Frequently, however, a state of paralysis of legs and trunk may make it impossible for the individual to move or resume the standing position. The drop-attack appears to be caused by a sudden failure of antigravity muscles which are then temporarily paralyzed until some nervous pathway is reestablished. If the subject is helped back to his or her feet, as soon as the feet touch the ground the nervous pathway is reconnected, and the victim may walk away as though nothing had happened. On other occasions, as was noted by Sheldon, patients have been able to reestablish the pathway by putting their feet against a wall or some solid object. They were then able to resume the upright position. Use of the arms may be possible; if there is a chair or other suitable object nearby, subjects may pull themselves to their knees and back to their feet. The transient paralysis affects the legs and some trunk muscles. This paralysis, which is flaccid in type, may persist for many hours if the individual is not helped. Cases have been reported in which unfortunate sufferers from a drop-attack have sustained serious burns because they fell close to a fire and were unable to move away from it.

Detailed histories of the falls were obtained in 96 of Sheldon's cases (28). Thirty-six occurred when patients were walking normally, 25 when they were turning round, 14 when standing, 8 when beginning to move, 8 when rising from sitting, 4 when throwing the head back, and 1 when getting out of bed. The circumstances are so variable that it is difficult to point to a single movement or action that might be responsible.

The most likely explanation for drop-attacks is that movements of the head and neck precipitate them. Such a suggestion can be easily understood if one considers the cervical spine and the course of the vertebral arteries. Many elderly people have a considerable degree of osteoarthritis of the cervical spine and some shortening of the neck from spondylosis. As a result, these arteries may pursue a serpentine course. If in addition to this there is less elasticity in the arterial wall because of significant arteriosclerotic change, sudden movements of the head and neck in almost any direction may precipitate momentary blood loss from vital reticular formations in the medulla. This could inhibit the function in the antigravity muscles. The hypothesis receives some support from the fact that the wearing of a simple cervical collar to restrict neck movements has quite often abolished these attacks.

Sheldon cites two cases in which the histories indicated that "the decisive factor in recovery of function lay in pressure on the soles of the feet." He goes on to comment that this was reminiscent of the "magnet response" or "positive supporting action" which according to Walsh (33) is "obtained most readily in decerebrate animals that have been subjected to a removal of the cerebellum." Pressure on the soles of the feet then produces extension of the limbs and bracing of the back. The blood supply to the cerebellum comes via the vertebral arteries, and Llinas describes how the proprioceptive nerve endings of the skeletal muscles end in the climbing fibers of the cerebellum (19). A sudden cut-off of the circulation to this part of the cerebellum might produce the "postural inhibition or sleep" which Sheldon postulates might cause the drop-attack.

VERTIGO

Giddiness or dizziness are vague symptoms which are quite common in the old. Vertigo, on the other hand, is a true rotatory movement which results in considerable inconvenience to the patient. The incidence of true vertigo in the elderly is much lower than that of giddiness or dizziness. Sheldon suggests that the reason why so few falls are caused by vertigo is that its nature warns the individual to grasp something or sit down as quickly as possible. Of the falls which are caused by vertigo, the most dangerous are those which occur when the individual is on stairs or looks down from a height.

The association of defective hearing and vertigo was noted in the Wolverhamptom survey. This was most marked in the oldest groups. Sheldon suggests that the results indicate a tendency for increasing degeneration to take place in both the cochlea and vestibule with increasing age. This is, unfortunately, a situation in which physicians remain helpless to do more than understand and sympathize.

POSTURAL HYPOTENSION

Over the past 20 years postural hypotension has been well recognized as a complication of antihypertensive therapy, and the risk of its occurrence increases with age (15). What is not so well known is that dehydration and a variety of drugs may cause orthostatic hypotension in the old. Apart from drugs (see Ch. 9, Iatrogenic Disorders), reduced efficiency of homeostatic mechanisms may lead to less efficient baroreceptor mechanisms and falls.

The possibility that postural hypotension is the cause of falling will be raised by the history. If episodes characteristically occur when the subject first arises from bed in the morning and there is an associated complaint of dizziness, one should suspect the diagnosis. Checking the blood pressure levels while the patient is lying down and then repeating this procedure after the patient has been sitting up or standing for 2 min. will confirm or refute the suspected diagnosis. A drop of at least 20 mm Hg in the systolic or 10 mm diastolic when the erect position is assumed is usually accepted as evidence of a significant orthostatic drop (see Ch. 8, Homeostatic Impairment). This condition causes a significant but not an excessive number of falls (Table 6–2).

CENTRAL NERVOUS SYSTEM LESIONS

There is some difference between the Clark and Sheldon series (Table 6–2) in the number of cases in which neurologic disease was implicated in the falls. This is perhaps more apparent than real, because Sheldon describes 500 falls in 202 individuals, of whom 20 had neurologic disease—subacute combined degeneration of the cord, paralysis agitans, cerebral thrombosis, and preexisting hemiplegia. It would be truer, therefore, to regard the proportion of Sheldon's subjects who had neurologic disease as 10%. Five percent represents the proportion of the 500 falls attributable to the neurologic cause.

Clark describes cerebrovascular disease, hemiplegia, Parkinson's disease, basilar insufficiency, and hypertensive cerebrovascular disease in 76 (17%) of his 450 cases. The probability of falls in association with these conditions needs no emphasis as there are obvious potential dangers in all the conditions mentioned.

MISCELLANEOUS

Extending the head backwards to look up at a shelf or a high cupboard is a common activity in everyday life. This may cause a fall through interference with the vertebrobasilar circulation. In Sheldon's series 20 falls occurred because of this movement. Weakness in the legs was described by Sheldon in 16 of his series of falls, but he found only a few falls out of bed or chair, 10 of 500 (2%). On the other hand, Clark described 29 bed and 28 chair accidents resulting in a fractured neck of the femur. He ascribed these to the absence of something for the individual to hold on to while standing, but the cause of such falls involves many factors. In Clark's experience, there was a high incidence of disease in such individuals.

These detailed and thoughtful studies of large numbers of falls in elderly people constitute the background information that is available to plan how to tackle the problem of falling. The predisposing feature common to all elderly subjects is reduced control of posture and movement, resulting from loss of neurons and deteriorating function of the surviving neurons. For the moment there is no possibility of altering the situation.

PRECIPITATING CAUSES OF FALLS

The precipitating causes of falls can be divided into three main groups (Table 6–3). The first are those which are pure accidents, the result of environmental hazards; medical falls result from disease in the patient. Of course, there are falls caused by a combination of these factors.

ARRHYTHMIAS

CASE REPORT 6–2

Mr. Archibald, aged 82, was out shopping with his wife in a large mall when, without any warning, he collapsed on the ground unconscious. An ambulance was quickly called, and on the way to the hospital he recovered his senses. There was evidence of a mild left hemiparesis and some disturbance of cognition. It was thought that he had sustained a transient ischemic attack, and he was treated for it. All went well for 36 hours. He was sitting in a chair by his bedside, having eaten his lunch, when he again collapsed suddenly. On this occasion, it was found that his blood pressure had fallen and was unrecordable and that he had a paroxysmal atrial tachycardia. For the following 3 days, Mr. Archibald's heart was monitored and the rate controlled by a combination of digoxin and propranolol. No further episodes of tachycardia occurred. After 10 days, during which he remained somewhat disoriented, he recovered completely both from the cardiac and cerebral point of view. He was discharged from the hospital at the end of 2 weeks.

TABLE 6–3. Precipitating Causes of Falls

Accidental*	Medical
Trips	Drop-attack†
Slips	Vertigo
Misjudging Steps	Postural hypotension†
Overreaching and	Tachyarrhythmia†
contributed to by	Carotid sinus syndrome
poor light on	Heart block†
stairs	Senile epilepsy†
Loose slip rugs	Central nervous system
Obstructions on	lesions
floor	Aortic valve disease
	Weakness†

*Some falls will result from a combination of accidental and medical factors
†Potentially treatable or preventable conditions

In this case a sudden tachyarrhythmia had caused a blackout and fall, and the transient loss of cardiac output was sufficient to cause damage to the brain. No precipitating cause for the tachycardia was found although a "silent" myocardial infarct was suspected but not confirmed by ECG examination or enzymes.

CASE REPORT 6–3

Mrs. Davis, aged 80, enjoyed good health until November 1976. She then developed a series of curious blackouts which caused a number of falls. She was found to have paroxysmal atrial tachycardia and was treated with digoxin. For 3 months she pursued a course of intermittent malaise, lethargy, and anorexia punctuated every few days by apparent improvement, but the improvement did not last. She was admitted to the hospital in March 1977 complaining of nausea, anorexia, and occasional vomiting. Serum digoxin proved to be 3.4 ng/ml; as the heart rate was 60/min, this was discontinued. Symptoms, however, did not clear and an upper gastrointestinal series revealed an ulcer in the cardiac end of the stomach and a sliding hiatus hernia. Gastroscopic examination confirmed the ulcer, and a biopsy excluded neoplasia. Ten days after admission symptoms began to clear but suddenly recurred in association with an attack of paroxysmal atrial tachycardia. Digoxin and propranolol were introduced, and a week later the patient was discharged in an improved state.

One week later she was back. It became obvious that the reason for her swings of condition were attributable to a sick sinus syndrome. Control of her tachycardia was not enough, and she had a demand pacemaker put in place to protect her from swings of abnormal bradycardia. Her progress thereafter was good, after a slow start.

This case illustrates the need for accurate diagnosis to elucidate the cause of what began as a series of falls. The occurrence of Adams–Stokes attacks needs no elaboration, the classic bradycardia of heart block being well recognized. It is now equally well treated by permanent pacemakers.

CAROTID SINUS SYNDROME

Simple vasovagal attacks do occur in the elderly, and a parallel condition is the oversensitive carotid sinus which, when accidentally rubbed against a firm collar, may produce enough vagal stimulation to cause the individual to faint.

CASE REPORT 6–4

Mr. Gordon, a very active 89-year-old man, was still accustomed to going into his business two or three times a week. His son, who was a family physician in England, asked the author to see Mr. Gordon because he was having blackouts. As was customary in the examination, the carotid sinus was gently massaged, and on this occasion the result was dramatic. The old man became unconscious and his heart almost stopped. He recovered quickly but the diagnosis was obvious. He suffered from a carotid sinus syndrome.

There is no clear action that one can take in this situation but, as my colleague remarked, they (the patient and his son) knew what was happening. Apart from advising the old gentleman to try and avoid hard collars, they were content to accept the occasional faint.

SENILE EPILEPSY

Another cause of unusual blackouts is senile epilepsy. It is common knowledge that jacksonian seizures may develop some months or years after a cerebral vascular accident. What is perhaps not so well recognized is that there are small numbers of people who develop a senile epileptic condition in old age for no very clear reason. Such people may simply lose consciousness transiently, may not actually convulse, may be incontinent, and may recover by lapsing into a type of postepileptic lethargy. Such cases have been described by Fine (12).

It can be useful to treat unexplained blackouts with diphenylhydantoin (Dilantin) for a period of some weeks to determine whether the blackouts and falls are prevented. Prior to this, an electroencephalogram (EEG) may confirm the diagnosis and should be carried out, but if this is difficult or the results are equivocal, a therapeutic trial is indicated.

WEAKNESS

Sheldon found that 12.1% of his 1948 sample suffered from weakness, with a greater incidence in women than in men. It seems likely that this explains why some individuals state that their legs gave way and down they went. In such cases an active rehabilitation program may help to prevent further falls.

EFFECTS OF FALLS

Falls can be divided into those which cause significant injury, such as fractures, and those which do not. Some patients remain remarkably unaffected by a series of falls over a period of weeks or months, but it is more usual for a slow loss of confidence to develop. The individual begins to fear the next fall and, rather than run any risk, begins to reduce activity.

The young child, who has equally unstable balance and is equally likely to fall, bounces up and regards it all as part of living. Apart from crying at the time of impact children are not affected and quickly recover. This reaction continues into young adulthood, particularly in those who practice vigorous sports in their third and fourth decades, but, falling becomes progressively more unpleasant as one moves into later years. The sequence of events for the old is falling, losing confidence, reducing activity, and becoming weaker; ultimately this path leads to immobility. Thus, even in individuals who do not sustain any significant injury, a fall is a serious matter. Every effort should be made to avoid recurrences.

FRACTURES IN THE ELDERLY

The results of any injury depend on two factors. The first of these is the nature of the trauma, and the second is the nature of the subject's bones.

Osteopenia

There is now ample evidence from the study of skeletal mass that there is a progressive loss of bone with increasing age (3, 9, 13, 24, 31). There are also data linking the incidence of fractures to this event (16, 25). Newton–John and Morgan (23) summarized present knowledge in 1968 by stating that the bone loss had five characteristics:

1. It begins earlier in women than men (usually in the fifth as opposed to the sixth or seventh decade).
2. The loss of bone follows a steady linear course in relation to age.
3. The rate of loss is about 10% per decade for women and rather less for men.
4. At each age the quantity of remaining bone follows a normal distribution.
5. The range of variation in bone density between different individuals does not alter with age. Those who have poor bones when young will develop osteoporosis when old; those with good dense bones when they reach maturity will lose bone at a similar rate but without becoming osteoporotic.

They represented their concept in a graph (Fig. 6–4). The authors based their hypothesis on a study of 30 papers, and there has been ample support for their view (2, 9, 24) since that time.

If osteopenia is accepted as part of the aging process, its clinical relevance hinges on its association with fractures. Much evidence of the incidence of fractures has accumulated in the past 20 years. Approximately 1 million fractures occur every year in women who are aged 45 or over and at least 700,000 of these are associated with osteopenia (25). Knowelden, Buhr, and Dunbar (16) describe the steeply rising incidence of femoral neck fractures beyond the age of 60. The incidence doubles every 5 years in women and every 7 years in men.

Albanese et al. (2) demonstrated bone loss using a carefully controlled radiologic technique and dental film. They compared the density of bone with that of an aluminum wedge which consisted of eight steps with increments of 1/20,-000 in. each. The authors commented that a step rather than a slope wedge was used to minimize errors of a linearity bias. They studied the second phalanx of the fifth finger using a recording photodensitometer, from the tracings of which results were read. Their whole technique meticulously controlled distance, kilovolts, amperage, film, time, temperature, age of developer, and densitometric measurements. Coefficient of bone density was measured in terms of 1000ths of an inch of aluminum (Fig. 6–5).

It can be seen that in both sexes bone loss is related to age. Bone loss is, however, greater in females than males at all ages, apart from childhood. From the age of 45, women lose calcium from their skeletons at a steady rate which continues throughout the rest of life. The process is speeded up by a loss of estrogens following the menopause. Males also lose bone, but to a lesser degree and from a later age. Two other studies working with the second metacarpal have shown similar results (9, 24).

Exton–Smith et al. (9) studied a total of 481 males and 483 females between

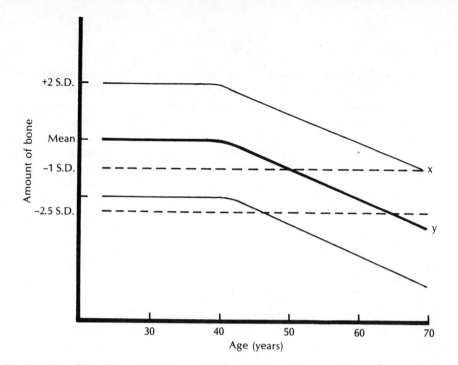

Fig. 6–4. Loss of bone from skeletal mass with age. The dotted lines x and y represent an amount of bone which, at age 30, is 1 standard deviation (SD) and 2.5 SD below the mean. (Newton–John HF, Morgan DB: Lancet I:232–233, 1968)

Fig. 6–5. Comparison of bone density at varying ages of males and females. Number of subjects shown by age and sex. (Adapted from Albanese AA *et al.:* J Am Geriatr Soc 17:142–154, 1969)

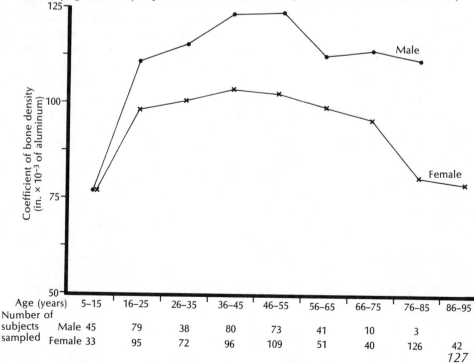

Age (years)	5–15	16–25	26–35	36–45	46–55	56–65	66–75	76–85	86–95
Number of subjects sampled Male	45	79	38	80	73	41	10	3	
Female	33	95	72	96	109	51	40	126	42

the ages of 5 and 90. They measured the external (D) and internal (d) diameters of the cortex and suggested that the cross-sectional area of the cortex ($D^2 - d^2$) was the best measure of bone density. Plotting these bone density figures against age produced a graph very similar in appearance to that in Figure 6–5. When they corrected for the larger skeletal size of males, the two lines came closer together but there was still a significantly higher degree of bone density in males at all but childhood ages. In their view, between the ages of 50 and 80 men lost 5% of bone per decade and women 7%. Similar findings have been reported by Nordin (24).

Incidence of Fractures

There are one or two interesting anomalies in the relationship between osteopenia and fractures. Albanese *et al.* (3) illustrate the high mortality rate of falls by age, race, and sex in the United States during the years 1959 to 1961 (Fig. 6–6). The incidence of death from falling in ages under 65 is about 20/100,000 of the population, but this rises steeply beyond the age of 65, particularly in white females. There is a striking difference in the mortality rate between white and nonwhite individuals and also between females and males.

There is also a striking difference in the incidence of fractured femora between males and females, which is emphasized by data on such cases in the City of Birmingham, England for the year 1975 (Table 6–4). In the younger age groups the incidence is very low, but beyond the age of 65 this climbs steeply with an increasing preponderance of elderly women.

There is an interesting difference in the incidence of fractured wrists and fractured femora in women. The former increases between the ages of 50 and 60 (Fig. 6–7) (25). This represents a sudden tenfold increase in late middle age, whereas the increase in femoral neck fractures comes later, between the ages of 65 and 90 (Table 6–4). Between the ages of 65 and 70, 30% of women are liable to fall, but by the time they are 85, almost half suffer such occurrences. This contrasts with the much lower figures for men of about 13% in the 65–70 age group, reaching a peak at 80–85, followed by a decrease. There is, therefore, plenty of evidence to indicate that falling becomes increasingly common with age. Women who are 90 or over have a one in four chance of sustaining a fractured neck of femur within the following year.

One interesting group described by Clark (6) was composed of 30 subjects with fractures who had sustained no or minimal trauma. Twenty-five of these people sustained their fracture indoors and five outdoors. One-third had steroid or senile osteoporosis, and three had osteomalacia without steatorrhea. Fractured neck of femur may thus occur without an obvious serious injury. This is an important point to remember. Any individuals who, for no good reason, suddenly discover that they cannot walk or who complain of pain in the hip or thigh should be x-rayed to exclude the possibility of such an atraumatic injury.

Age	Male		Female	
	Population	Fractured femora	Population	Fractured femora
0–44	329,460	35	305,635	11
45–54	65,315	13	66,165	22
55–64	60,995	28	63,360	56
65–74	33,475	46	47,670	130
75 and over	12,370	76(0.6%)	30,220	450(1.5%)
Total	501,615	198	513,055	669

(Wall M: Personal communication, 1976)

Fig. 6–6. Annual death rates for falls by age, race, and sex of persons aged 45 and over in the United States (1959–1961). (Albanese AA *et al.*: NY State J Med 75:326–336, 1975. Reprinted by permission from the New York State Journal of Medicine. Copyright by the Medical Society of the State of New York)

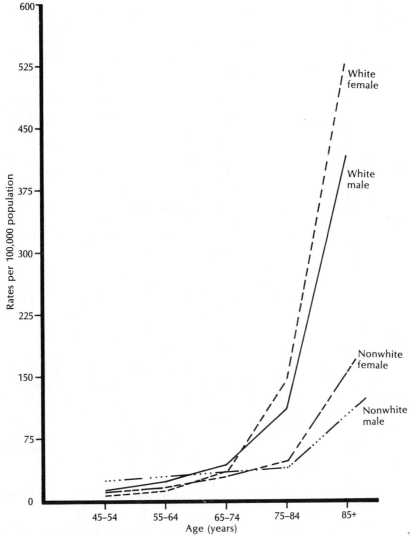

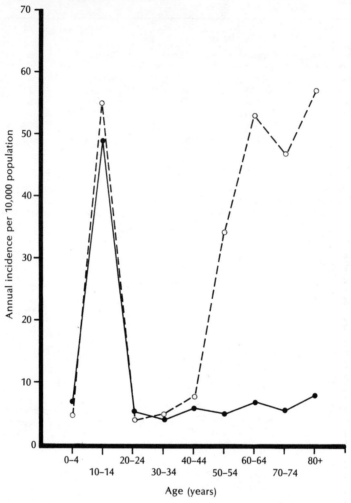

Fig. 6–7. Incidence of distal forearm fractures in relation to age. **o.** Females. **●.** Males. (Saville PD, Heaney RP: Osteoporosis. In von Hahn HP [ed]: Practical Geriatrics. Basel, S Karger, 1975)

CAUSE OF OSTEOPENIA

The rising incidence of both osteopenia and fractures with increasing age is associated with impairment of postural control. Many old people who fall, however, do not fracture bones; they presumably have lesser degrees of osteopenia. An ability to halt or reverse this process would be a notable medical advance which could greatly reduce the incidence of serious injury to the elderly. Since this text is not the place for a full review of a very complicated subject, the interested reader is directed to the detailed paper of Thomson and Frame (31).

There have been several recent studies of bone biopsy in cases of fracture.

Faccini, Exton–Smith, and Boyde (11) carefully examined specimens obtained from the iliac crest of cases of fractured neck of femur. The specimens were taken at the time of surgery, and 51 which contained both cortical plates were used in the final analysis. To act as controls 54 similar necropsy samples were taken from the same site in the iliac crest. The mean age of the fracture group was 80 years (58–96) and of the control group 76 (44–92). Quantimet 720, an image analyzing computer system, was used to measure the area of bone and osteoid. An eyepiece graticule was also used, and there was a good correlation between the results obtained by the two methods. The results indicated a significant relationship between the tendency to fracture and the proportion of osteoid rather than the proportion of either cortical or trabecular bone.

This study confirmed the findings of Aaron *et al.* (1) 2 years earlier which had suggested that osteomalacia in the elderly makes "an important contribution to the steep rise in femoral neck fractures with advancing age in the United Kingdom and that this is probably attributable to an absolute or relative deficiency of vitamin D." These authors also postulate that osteoporosis may be partly attributable to a degree of vitamin D deficiency, sufficient to cause malabsorption of calcium but not sufficient to produce osteomalacia. Obtaining bone biopsies at the time of surgery, they studied 125 cases of fracture of the proximal femur. Bone biopsies were also taken from the iliac crest, as were 83 control specimens taken during autopsies of individuals who died from acute disease with no known underlying condition that might have affected calcium metabolism. Their careful histologic study of the specimens showed an incidence of osteomalacia of 20%–30% in 102 females with fractures; the figure for 23 men was 40%.

In Denmark Lund, Sorensen, and Christensen (20) measured plasma 25-hydroxycholecalciferol levels in 67 consecutive cases of fracture of the proximal femur. The values found were not different from those in control groups taken at the same time of the year. They comment that oestomalacia is not uncommon among elderly people in Denmark but believe that it may depend more on a decline in the renal efficiency in converting 25-hydroxycholecalciferol to 1,25-dihydroxycholecalciferol than a low dietary intake of vitamin D. Renal function deteriorates steadily with age and in very old groups (75–100) is likely to be only 50% of what it was at age 30 (see Ch. 2, Physical Aspects of Aging). In many individuals it is appreciably less than this.

Lund and his coworkers (21) followed up their observations by treating seven patients, aged 65–81, suffering from "severe back pain and radiological signs of osteoporosis including two vertebral compression fractures" with 1α-hydroxycholecalciferol, the active metabolite of vitamin D. The results in this small but well-controlled trial indicated some reversal of the osteoporotic condition histologically, clinical improvement in six of the seven patients, and an increase in bone mineral content measured by photon absorptiometry. The method is not without risk as one patient developed a dramatic hypercalcemia which necessitated discontinuing the treatment. In this study there was no suggestion of increased levels of serum parathyroid hormone (PTH), which were measured by a radioimmune assay and were not affected by the treatment.

Vitamin D undergoes two changes after its absorption through the intestine. In the liver it is converted into 25-hydroxycholecalciferol, and this is converted in the kidney into 1,25-dihydroxycholecalciferol which is the biologically active metabolite. Because of reduced renal function this step may not be accomplished in the elderly person. The combination of a lower intake of vitamin D, less exposure to sunlight to convert skin ergosterol, and, most importantly, failing conversion in liver and kidney may lead to a deficiency of 1,25-dihydroxy-cholecalciferol. This might account for the mixed osteomalacic–osteoporotic situations in some cases of fracture.

Berylyne *et al.* (4) add a further complication. In comparing 10 young people (aged 18–19) with 16 old (aged 65–87, mean 76.8) they found creatinine clearance reduced in 7 of 9 old persons studied, serum PTH levels consistently raised, and thyrocalcitonin levels reduced. They suggest that parathyroid overactivity in response to chronic renal failure may be the cause of osteopenia in the old. To date, this work has not been confirmed and therefore its findings must be treated with caution.

A widely accepted explanation for the increased bone loss in postmenopausal women is lack of estrogen. Using a radiographic–densitometric examination of the proximal part of the radius, Meema *et al.* (22) demonstrated over a 4–10 year period prevention of bone loss in a group of women following the menopause by the use of estrogens. Lindsay *et al.* (18) conducted a more extensive study on 63 oophorectomized women treated with estrogen over a 5-year period, who were compared with a control group of 57 individuals given a placebo. They showed that in the first 3 years after removal of the ovaries there was a marked bone loss, but the rate of bone loss thereafter leveled off. In subjects who began estrogen treatment 3 or 6 years after the operation, some bone mass was regained.

Albanese *et al.* (3) in 1975, on the other hand, examined 50 normal, healthy postmenopausal women; some had received and some had not received long-term estrogen therapy. Their findings indicated that there was no difference in the incidence of bone loss in estrogen treated or untreated participants. On the other hand, when they used a calcium–vitamin D_2 combination, their results suggested that this was effective in all cases, whether the women were receiving estrogens or not. They did add, however, that the matter required further investigation.

The absorption of calcium occurs throughout the length of the small bowel. It is, however, mainly through the duodenum and jejunum rather than the ileum. Calcium is absorbed by passive ionic diffusion, facilitated diffusion, and by active transport. There is evidence that calcium absorption is reduced with age in both sexes, starting in the sixth decade for women and seventh for men. The reason for this change has not been clearly established but is almost certainly due to many factors. It is likely that changes in the mucosa of the intestine reduce the efficiency of active transport mechanisms. It is also likely that reduced renal function may impair the kidney's ability to produce 1,25-dihydroxycholecalciferol which also reduces the efficiency of absorption.

Different factors are involved in the absorption of calcium and the regulation of the levels of calcium in the body. There is evidence that the liver's ability to metabolize drugs is impaired with age (see Ch. 9, Iatrogenic Disorders), and the combination of reduced efficiency in the liver, intestine, and kidney may all contribute to the inability of the body to maintain its homeostasis of calcium adequately. The controlling mechanism lies in the parathyroid glands, and these are influenced by neuroendocrine control from the pituitary. One other factor in the absorption of calcium is the presence of bile and bile salts which are essential for the optimal digestion and absorption of fat. Reduction in these increases intestinal fatty acid content which decreases the amount of calcium available for absorption because the calcium is used by the fatty acids to form insoluble soaps. This whole subject is well reviewed by Wills (34).

TREATMENT OF OSTEOPOROSIS AND OSTEOMALACIA

The treatment of metabolic bone disease has gone through different fashions. Some years ago it was thought that the correct treatment for osteoporosis and backache, which is a frequent physical feature of the condition, was to give anabolic steroids. In women the use of estrogens has been widely advocated for years. It now appears that neither treatment has more than a temporary effect on the condition, and it is wise to avoid them. The purpose of therapy must be to improve the body's calcium status. The most effective method of doing this appears to be giving a combination of calcium and vitamin D_2. There is interesting evidence that whole bone extract may be a more efficient method of giving calcium than the more usual calcium gluconate. Windsor *et al.* (35) found that 15 old people (aged 70–98) absorbed almost twice as much calcium from such an extract as from calcium gluconate.

Osteoporosis may be asymptomatic or may cause a backache, usually located in the lumbar or sacral region. Osteomalacia is more often associated with pains, either localized or more generalized. A common feature of osteomalacia is myopathy with muscle weakness, usually proximal in site and frequently undiagnosed. Schott and Wills (26) cite a study from University College Hospital in London in which 20 of 45 cases of osteomalacia, caused by a variety of conditions, exhibited muscle weakness. On the other hand, of 91 patients with primary hyperparathyroidism only 6 had evidence of weakness. This type of myopathy can be associated with renal failure, a fact which is well recognized.

In elderly patients it is wise to remember that renal function may be seriously compromised by disease as well as age. This, combined with a diet poor in calcium, may lead to osteomalacia, increased osteopenia, and fractures.

The importance of metabolic bone disease in the etiology of fractures in old people cannot be denied. It is, therefore, of considerable importance to discover effective methods of minimizing senile osteoporosis or preventing osteomalacia in old people. This subject has been well reviewed by an editorial in the *Lancet* in 1976 (7).

MANAGEMENT FOR THE PROBLEM OF FALLING

Any old person who admits to falling should have this fact noted and added to his problem list. Careful notes of the sequence of events leading up to, and at the time of, the accident should be obtained. This may allow a confident diagnosis of a drop-attack to be made or may indicate that the fall was an accidental trip. The mechanisms involved should be carefully explained to the patient and associates. Using the suggestions given in Table 6–3 as a checklist, appropriate investigations can be made to define the cause of the fall, and appropriate measures can then be taken to control or prevent them. With this problem prevention is all important.

Clark (6) considered that one-quarter of the accidents in his series were preventable, one-half might have been prevented, and only the remaining one-quarter were inevitable. To elaborate his findings, 20% of the accidents in his study had an environmental cause with the patient in good health; in theory all of these could have been prevented. Forty-five percent had an environmental cause with additional patient factors such as osteoporosis, cerebrovascular degeneration, arthritis, poor vision, diabetes, etc. In these cases, prevention depended partly on the removal of environmental precipitants and partly on correction or adjustment of the patient's activities to allow for his or her disabilities. Even inefficient righting reflexes can be minimized by encouraging appropriate physical rehabilitation. In only 23% of the falls which Clark described were there patient factors that proved impossible to treat.

For drop-attacks a cervical collar should be tried. It should not be a rigid, metal affair but a simple light device that will be tolerated by a patient who may be alarmed by its appearance. Plastazote is a plastic material that is light and reasonably rigid. At 60°C it becomes soft and malleable. At this temperature a skilled occupational therapist can gently mold the substance to the old person's neck. Secured by simple Velcro fastenings it should be easy to put on each day. It is soon obvious whether it is of value. If falls are abolished, good; if not, one can throw away the collar and think again.

Arrhythmias may require monitoring, and in this situation the Holter Counter worn for 24 hours or more may be invaluable. Remember Mrs. Davis (Case Report 6–3) who had both tachy- and bradycardia with her sick sinus. A trial with diphenylhydantoin (Dilantin), a review of drugs which might cause hypotension, and treatment for parkinsonism can all be of value in appropriate cases. Weakness can be countered by a rehabilitation program.

It is essential that the physician's curiosity ferret out the cause of falls. If this proves difficult, a willingness to try to prevent recurrence combined with reassurance to patients will help to rebuild that vital confidence without which they are likely to lose heart and become immobile.

REFERENCES

1. Aaron JE, Gallagher JC, Anderson J, Stasiak L, Longton EB, Nordin BEC, Nickelson M: Frequency of osteomalacia and osteoporosis in fractures of the proximal femur. Lancet I:229–233, 1974

2. Albanese AA, Edelson AH, Lorenze EJ, Wein EH: Quantitative radiographic survey technique for detection of bone loss. J Am Geriatr Soc 17:142–154, 1969

3. Albanese AA, Edelson AH, Lorenze EJ, Woodhul ML, Wein EH: Problems of bone health in the elderly. NY State J Med 75:326–336, 1975

4. Berylyne GM, Gen-Ari J, Kushalevski A, Galinsky D, Hirsch M, Shainkin R, Alotnik M: The aetiology of senile osteoporosis: secondary hyperparathyroidism due to renal failure. Q J Med 44:505–521, 1975

5. Cape RDT: A Geriatric Service. Report to Birmingham, England, Regional Hospital Board, August 1968

6. Clark ANG: Factors in fracture of the female femur; clinical study of the environmental, physical, medical and preventive aspects of this injury. Gerontol Clin 10:257–270, 1968

7. (Editorial): Advances in osteoporosis? Lancet I:181–182, 1976

8. Exton-Smith AN: Lecture to Conference on Geriatric Medicine, University of Western Ontario, London, Canada, May 1976

9. Exton-Smith AN, Millard PH, Payne PR, Wheeler EF: Pattern of development and loss of bone with age. Lancet II:1154–1157, 1969

10. Eyzaguirre C, Fidone SJ: Physiology of the Nervous System, 2nd ed. Chicago, Year Book Medical, 1975, pp 233–248

11. Faccini JM, Exton-Smith AN, Boyde A: Disorders of bone and fractures of the femoral neck. Lancet I:1089–1092, 1976

12. Fine W: Epileptic syndromes in the elderly. Gerontol Clin 8:121–133, 1966

13. Gryfe CI, Exton-Smith AN, Payne PR, Wheeler EF: Pattern of development of bone in childhood and adolescence. Lancet I:523–526, 1971

14. Hasselkus BR, Shambes GM: Aging and postural sway in women. J Gerontol 30:661–667, 1975

15. Jackson G, Fierscianowski TA, Mahon W, Condon J: Inappropriate antihypertensive therapy in the elderly. Lancet III:1317–1318, 1976

16. Knowelden J, Buhr AJ, Dunbar O: Incidence of fractures in persons over 35 years of age. Br J Prev Soc Med 18:130–141, 1964

17. Kral VA: Psychiatric problems. In von Hahn HP (ed): Practical Geriatrics. Basel, S Karger, 1975, pp 259–283

18. Lindsay R, Aitken JM, Anderson JB, Hart DM, MacDonald EB, Clarke AC: Long-term prevention of postmenopausal osteoporosis by oestrogen. Lancet I:1038–1040, 1976

19. Llinas RR: The cortex of the cerebellum. Sci Am 323:56–71, 1975

20. Lund B, Kjaer I, Friis T, Hjorth L, Reimann I, Andersen RB, Sorensen OH: Treatment of osteoporosis of ageing with 1α–hydroxycholecalciferol. Lancet II:1168–1171, 1975

21. Lund B, Sorensen OH, Christensen AB: 25–Hydroxycholecalciferol and fractures of the proximal femur. Lancet II:300–302, 1975

22. Meema S, Bunker ML, Meema HE: Preventive effect of estrogen on postmenopausal bone loss. Arch Intern Med 135:1436–1440, 1975

23. Newton-John HF, Morgan DB: Osteoporosis: disease or senescence? Lancet I:232–233, 1968

24. Nordin BEC: Clinical significance and pathogenesis of osteoporosis. Br Med J 1:571–576, 1971

25. Saville PD, Heaney RP: Osteoporosis. In von Hahn HP (ed): Practical Geriatrics. Basel, S Karger, 1975, pp 367–380

26. Schott GD, Wills MR: Muscle weakness in osteomalacia. Lancet I:626–629, 1976

27. Sheldon JH: The Social Medicine of Old Age. London, Oxford University Press, 1948, pp 96–105

28. Sheldon JH: On the natural history of falls in old age. Br Med J II:1685–1690, 1960

29. Sheldon JH: The effect of age on the control of sway. Gerontol Clin 5:129–138, 1963

30. Terekhov Y: Stabilometry as a diagnostic tool in clinical medicine. Can Med Assoc J 115: 631–633, 1976

31. Thomson DL, Frame B: Involuntional osteopenia: current concepts. Ann Intern Med 85: 789–803, 1976
32. Wall M: Personal communication, 1976
33. Walsh EG: Physiology of the Nervous System. London, Longmans Green, 1957, p 125
34. Wills MR: Intestinal absorption of calcium. Lancet I:820–823, 1973
35. Windsor ACM, Misra DB, Loudon JM, Staddon GE: The effect whole bone extract on Ca_{47} in the elderly. Age Ageing 2:230–234, 1973

Chapter 7

INCONTINENCE

Yes, Life in youth-tide standeth still;
In Manhood streameth soft and slow;
See, as it nears th' abysmal goal
how fleet the waters flash and flow.

      Sir Richard Burton

THE NATURE OF INCONTINENCE

Incontinence means "wanting in self-restraint (esp. in regard to sexual appetite)" according to the *Concise Oxford Dictionary*. It adds: "unable to hold in something (of secrets, tongue, urine, etc.)." Yeates (36) defines urinary incontinence as "the passing of urine in an undesirable place" and adds that it is a complex and poorly understood phenomenon. It is certainly a common problem of elderly patients. Frequently concealed because of its embarrassing social consequences, it may be well established before it comes to the physician's attention. Williamson and his colleagues (29) emphasized the fact that urinary problems were among those most frequently hidden by elderly patients (Fig. 5–2). A tendency to leak urine is accepted as an unpleasant accompaniment of old age for which the physician can do nothing. This is unfortunate because the sooner it is known and investigated the better. Even in the most unlikely situations, some success may be achieved.

CASE REPORT 7–1

In August 1975, 81-year-old Mrs. Partridge, who had led a very active life both at home and in the community, was unable to respond to simple questions and was incapable of obeying a clear request to "put out your tongue" or "hold up your hand." She suffered from a severe degree of senile dementia which had been developing for 5 years. Each day she was lifted out of bed to sit in a chair for a few hours, during which time she stared in front of herself or at times slept. All four limbs were stiff, and the left arm exhibited cogwheel rigidity, commonly seen in parkinsonism. Her cardiorespiratory function was good with no shortness of breath or cyanosis. She was in a general hospital and because of urinary incontinence had an indwelling catheter.

 Mr. and Mrs. Partridge were a remarkable couple who had immigrated to Canada 50 years earlier. They had raised a large and very successful family and were devoted to one another. Mr. Partridge found it hard to understand or accept the sad condition of his wife, but it was obvious that she was going to require continuing care in an institution for the rest of her life. She was transferred to such a hospital towards the end of August.

Because of the suggestion of extrapyramidal disease a cautious trial with levodopa and later carbidopa was undertaken. This proved modestly successful for a period of 6 months. In November 1976, the catheter was removed and efforts were made to retrain her in bladder control. By this time she was talking freely to visitors and staff, but not making any sense. She was also walking with minimal assistance, and efforts at rehabilitation were continuing. She began a series of visits home to her husband, son, and his wife for a few hours at a time. On December 1st she went home for 6 hours and remained continent. On December 8th it was noted on her chart that she "can now walk unaided at times. Has gone several nights dry."

This, as it turned out, was her best time. She maintained the improvement with long spells of continence, particularly during the day, but occasional lapses at night. On May 15th, 1976, she fell off the commode and fractured her right femoral neck. The orthopedic surgeon favored conservative treatment for her. With immobility, the incontinence recurred. Fifteen months later, she was again continent during most of the day. There is hope in the most unpromising cases.

URINARY INCONTINENCE

INCIDENCE

In Sheldon's Wolverhampton survey (25) of 583 subjects he found only one case of "complete incontinence of urine." There were, however, 48 individuals who suffered from what Sheldon called "dribbling." The incidence of this rose with age from 5.9% of women between the ages of 60–64 to 27.2% of those 85 and over. Sheldon states that in the more severe cases and in older subjects frequency and urgency of micturition develops into the actual passage of urine, which is a very great burden in the lives of older women. Hobson and Pemberton (21) in their survey of 476 old people in Sheffield, England estimated that 44 women (15.5%) and 45 men (23.4%) had occasional incontinence of urine and that 21 women (7.4%) and 5 men (2.6%) had regular incontinence. They made no attempt to break down their subjects into different age groups.

The incidence of urinary incontinence rises among hospital patients, because they are likely to be in a poorer state of health than those in the general population. Of 928 cases referred to a geriatric department in Birmingham, England, 30% of both women and men showed some degree of urinary incontinence, either intermittent or persistent (13) (Table 7–1). A study of residents of institutions for continuing care in London, Ontario, in 1976 showed that 38% had some degree of urinary incontinence (15).

These figures are in broad agreement with other studies over the past 30 years. Affleck in 1947 (2), Brocklehurst in 1951 (5), Thompson in 1962 (27), and Brocklehurst again in 1964 (6) all confirm the frequency of urinary incontinence in old age. Milne (24) describes the prevalence as shown in hospital surveys, which demonstrated a variation of 21%–47% (women) and 18%–48% (men)

TABLE 7-1. Urinary Incontinence in 928 Patients Referred to Selly Oak Hospital Geriatric Service, 1960–1961

	Females	Males	Total
Continent	415	232	647
Intermittent incontinence	58 (10%)	24 (7%)	82
Persistent incontinence	120 (20%)	79 (23%)	199
Total	593	335	928

due to differences in the assessment of incontinence. In some surveys incontinence was noted on admission, while in others it was not noted until after a period of treatment. There were also varying interpretations of what constitutes incontinence. Such anomalies caused the differences between Sheldon's and Hobson and Pemberton's data from the community. Willington (30) found 33.6% of all elderly people admitted to a hospital incontinent, but this figure was reduced to 12.9% (women) and 15.8% (men), whose incontinence persisted after treatment.

CONTROL OF MICTURITION

Urine flows from the kidneys into the bladder in a steady trickle. The bladder is a muscular organ which stores the urine until it is convenient to void. Maintaining complete control of the act of micturition requires a complex series of neurologic centers and pathways.

In the wall of the bladder are a series of stretch receptors which respond to increasing volume of urine in the organ by stimulating the bladder center in the second, third, and fourth sacral segments of the spinal cord (Fig. 7–1). Contraction of bladder muscle and voiding follows. This reflex arrangement is the total controlling mechanism in newly born infants. As children develop, an afferent pathway is established from the sacral cord to a center in the brain which makes them aware of bladder filling. This center may be located in the anterior part of the cingulate gyrus and part of the superior frontal gyrus (3). When the social advantage of remaining dry and controlling the time of bladder emptying is recognized, young people develop a further center, probably in the frontal cortex and related to the motor control area of perineal structures, which enables them to inhibit the sacral reflex action.

The two components of this system of voluntary inhibition of micturition enable the individual to control the act and remain continent. The locations of the different components have not been clearly established, but there are clinical clues. Adams and Hurwitz (1) observed that urinary incontinence was more resistant to treatment in persons who developed "middle cerebral" strokes than those with vertebrobasilar insufficiency. Brocklehurst (6) cites two other studies, one involving frontal lobe tumors, 24% of which were associated with inconti-

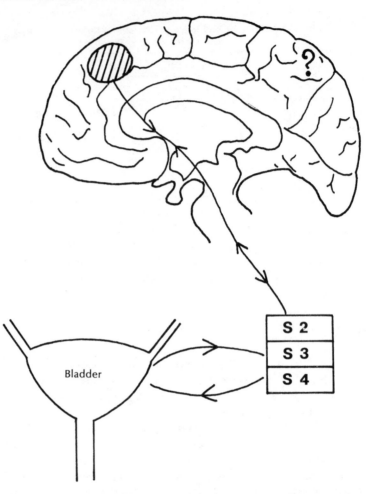

Fig. 7–1. Pathways and centers concerned with control of micturition. **S2, S3, S4.** Second, third, and fourth sacral segments of the spinal cord.

nence, and another involving an isolated case of a gunshot wound through a small portion of the right frontal lobe which caused persistent loss of urinary control.

Another important feature of urinary control has been shown in recent years by the study of intraurethral pressure profiles. Keston (22) has demonstrated that in normal individuals there is a zone 2–3 cm from the origin of the urethra at which the pressure is about 60 cm water. This maintains closure of the bladder outlet. Changes in this normal urethral pressure profile occur in a variety of conditions (Fig. 7–2). The results which Keston obtained in elderly individuals indicated lower maximum pressures and rather longer urethras than those described by Griffiths (19).

Garry (18) describes lamellated receptors, which resemble elongated pacinian

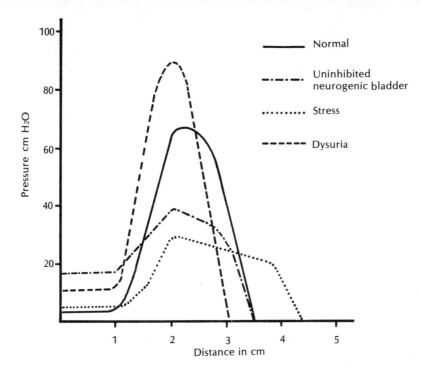

Fig. 7–2. Typical urethral pressure profiles under various conditions. (Keston M: In Cape RDT [ed]: Symposia of Geriatric Medicine, Vol. 3. Birmingham, West Midland Institute of Geriatric Medicine and Gerontology, 1974, p 86–90)

Fig. 7–3. Influence of age on maximal urethral pressures. Numbers in each group noted under means. (Composed from data of Malvern J: Br J Hosp Med 10:64, 1974)

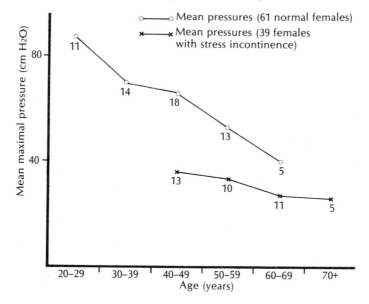

corpuscles, situated beneath the epithelium of the periurethral tissues. He expresses the view that muscle spindles lie in the external urethral sphincter, which is situated about the point where intraurethral pressure is greatest. Malvern (23) has demonstrated that in women between the ages of 20 and 29 the intraurethral pressure averaged 87 cm water but this declined steadily with age to 40 cm water for women between 60 and 69 (Fig. 7–3). Women with demonstrable stress incontinence had significantly lower urethral pressures.

Local nervous control is exerted by the autonomic nervous system. Afferent and efferent parasympathetic fibers from the second, third, and fourth sacral segments, play the major role. Midurethral pressure is controlled mainly by smooth muscles supplied by adrenergic fibers. Bladder functioning is affected by outflow obstruction and increases in intravesical pressure from external compression which may be temporary (coughing or sneezing) or more permanent (obesity or pelvic tumor). Pathology in the bladder itself, stones, papillomas, or carcinomas, may either cause increased intravesical pressure or may stimulate afferent receptors.

Andrew and Nathan (4) studied patients with lesions in the forebrain and hypothalamus. Their results suggest that the anterior part of the frontal lobe controls septal and hypothalamic nuclei which, in turn, regulate micturition and defecation. There appear to be two levels of central inhibition of afferent impulses, the first an automatic effect from the basal ganglia and the second a consciously exerted voluntary abolition of the reflex arc by the frontal lobe center. By keeping tension in the pelvic floor and maintaining the posterior urethrovesical angle, continence can be sustained. Relaxing the pelvic floor and adopting a suitable posture facilitates voiding of urine which is forcibly driven out by the detrusor muscle.

Cystometry

Cystometry consists of running sterile water into the bladder through a catheter at a slow steady speed. There are two common methods. Wilson (35) was one of the first to develop a simple but effective technique 30 years ago. In Wilson's method a steady infusion at a rate of 10 ml/min is run into the bladder. Brocklehurst and Dillane (8, 9) devised a method in which 50 ml are introduced every 5 min. One other method of obtaining a cystometrogram is to encourage the subject to drink plenty of water and give an intravenous dose of furosemide to fill the bladder quickly. Tsuji *et al.* (28) have demonstrated that when this technique is used bladder pressures tend to be lower and capacity larger than with the more standard experimental methods.

The results of the maneuver are plotted on a graph called a cystometrogram (Fig. 7–4) which gives a picture of the behavior of the bladder. Residual urine is measured when the catheter is first inserted, and pressures are recorded during filling and at the point when bladder contractions first spontaneously arise. The ability of the subject to prevent voiding in response to these contractions, any leaking around the catheter during the procedure, and the capacity of the bladder can all be noted.

The Normal Cystometrogram

Residual urine in a normal individual is 10–25 ml. There is no leakage around the catheter during the procedure, and while there is a transient pressure rise with each 50 ml inserted into the bladder (Fig. 7–4), there are no spontaneous contractions until 300–400 ml have been introduced. Micturition can usually be inhibited at this level, but with an additional 50–150 ml voiding becomes necessary. Bladder capacity ranges 400–600 ml in normal subjects.

Cystometrograms in Elderly Women

Brocklehurst and Dillane (8) studied the cystometrograms of a series of elderly women. First they examined 40 nonincontinent women who had suffered illness for which they were hospitalized, later they examined 100 incontinent women (9).

If one compares the groups (Table 7–2) with normal individuals (Fig. 7–4), both groups of elderly females have abnormal bladder function. The difference between the two groups is one of degree. The disturbance of function is considerably greater in the incontinent group than the other. The onset of the desire to empty the bladder is delayed or absent in both groups. This is an indication of a failing receptor system. Recognition of bladder filling must precede voluntary inhibition, and if this is delayed, the inhibiting process has less time to prove effective. The symptoms of a failing receptor mechanism are urgency and precipitancy of micturition, which may be the prelude to urinary incontinence in the old person.

Fig. 7–4. Normal cystometrogram using 2 techniques. **A** shows effect of 50 ml increments of sterile water at 5 minute intervals; **B** illustrates the method of continuous filling at 10 ml per minute. Both methods achieve same end-point at **C.**

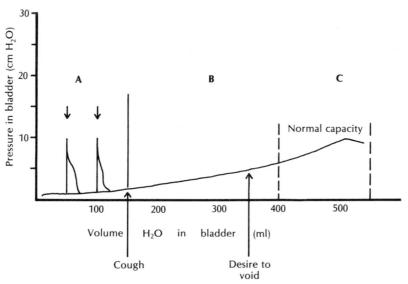

ETIOLOGY OF URINARY INCONTINENCE

If the controlling mechanism of micturition is the nervous pathway between the brain and the sacral micturition center, one can identify four different levels at which the mechanism may break down.

Uninhibited Neurogenic Bladder

The uninhibited neurogenic bladder is common to the majority of very old people and acts as the predisposing reason for the increase of incontinence at this age. The cortical cells in the frontal lobe responsible for the inhibition of bladder contractions may be damaged. Recognition of bladder filling is present, if usually late, but the ability to inhibit contraction by the bladder muscle is lost. There is marked precipitancy of micturition, which in the slow moving elderly person will almost certainly result in incontinence.

Cystometric examination of this type of bladder reveals a small to moderate volume of residual urine and an early desire to micturate. The time between desire to micturate and onset of contractions is short, there is leakage around the catheter, and the bladder muscle tends to become hypertonic and its capacity less than normal. In most cases, the patient's ability to prevent contractions or leakage is extremely limited. This situation may occur in patients following stroke and in those suffering from mental confusion, whether the confusion is acute or long-term (Table 7–3).

Loss of neurons and deterioration in global cerebral function (see Ch. 4, Brain Failure) result in a less reliable inhibiting mechanism in old people. Most suffer from some degree of uninhibited neurogenic bladder and thus have a predisposition to incontinence.

TABLE 7–2. Cystometrogram Findings in 40 Continent and 100 Incontinent Elderly Females

	Continent	Incontinent
Residual urine		
>100 ml	5 (12%)	29 (29%)
Bladder capacity		
<250 ml	9 (22%)	61 (61%)
Leakage around		
catheter	15 (38%)	83 (83%)
Uninhibited		
contractions		
during procedure	*11/24 (46%)	53 (53%)
Desire to		
void absent	2 (5%)	28 (28%)

*16 cases (7 previously incontinent and 9 with R. hemiplegia excluded because of abnormally high incidence of contractions 6/7, 7/9 respectively)

(Composed of data from Brocklehurst JC, Dillane JB: Gerontol clin 8: 285–319, 1966)

Reflex Neurogenic Bladder

In individuals with a reflex neurogenic bladder, control of bladder function reverts to that found in the infant. Because of severe cerebral disease or a lesion in the spinal cord, central pathways to and from the sacral bladder center have been destroyed. This is the bladder typical of the paraplegic. As the bladder fills, uninhibited contractions occur and at times voiding occurs involuntarily. The individual has no knowledge of bladder filling and is completely incontinent.

In such cases, cystometry reveals little or no residual urine and no desire to micturate. Spontaneous contractions occur almost at once from a hypertrophic bladder, which has a small volume.

Atonic Neurogenic Bladder

Loss of sacral posterior fibers or posterior nerve roots cuts off afferent stimuli from the bladder. The individual is totally unaware of bladder filling and the need to empty it and neglects to do so; the organ becomes overdistended because the reflex connection is broken. The picture is classically found in tabes dorsalis but may also be met in peripheral neuropathy such as that caused by diabetes mellitus. There is a constant dribbling overflow incontinence from a large distended bladder which is easily palpable in the lower abdomen.

Cystometry reveals a large volume of residual urine (400–600 ml), no desire to pass water during filling, spontaneous ineffective contractions, low intravesical pressure of only 10–20 cm water in the presence of a large, thin-walled organ with a capacity of 1 liter or more.

Autonomous Neurogenic Bladder

When the sacral segments of the cord are destroyed, the bladder becomes completely detached from external nervous control. This may happen in tumors of the cauda equina or in spina bifida. In this situation emptying the bladder depends on small axonal reflexes working through local ganglia. The mechanism is ineffective, and small amounts of urine are voided frequently with the patient unaware of it. There is thus a constant dribbling incontinence, usually associated with some urinary retention.

Cystometric findings are similar to those of individuals with an atonic neurogenic bladder, but dilatation of the bladder does not take place. Although

TABLE 7-3. Mental State and Persistent Urinary Incontinence

Mental State			Female	Male	Total
Normal		569 (58%)	46	35	81 (13%)
Mildly	} Abnormal	249 (26%)	34	23	57 (24%)
Severely		152 (16%)	30	18	48 (35%)

(Cape RDT: Mid Med Rev 8:33, 1972)

residual urine is considerable, it is less than in the tabetic situation. There are frequent contractions which never empty the organ but cause recurrent dribbling. Bladder capacity is normal or slightly reduced. There is no appreciation of filling by the subject.

Bladder Outlet Obstruction

In addition to the four neurogenic mechanisms, one physical feature is common in many cases of urinary incontinence, *viz.,* obstruction to the bladder outlet. This results in a dribbling incontinence similar to the overflow associated with an atonic neurogenic bladder. Most commonly seen in old men with enlarged prostates, it may also occur in women as a result of pelvic pathology; in both sexes it may occur as a result of chronic fecal impaction. Careful local examination reveals the nature of the obstruction. Chronic obstruction may result in chronic bladder distention. It is important to recognize this condition because prompt removal of the obstruction can restore bladder control to normal.

PRECIPITATING FACTORS IN URINARY INCONTINENCE

Control of the bladder is precarious for many elderly people. The determination to lead a normal life enables many with defective bladder control to maintain continence. Instinctively, appreciating the shortness of the time between the recognition of the desire to void and the need to avail themselves of washroom facilities, the elderly may plan their lives accordingly. Without drawing attention to the fact, they avoid becoming involved in social situations in which they do not know the site of the nearest lavatory. Of potentially more importance is a tendency to limit fluid intake in an attempt to reduce the possibility of embarrassment. It is important to recognize that many accept this restriction in the hope that it will allow them to continue to lead a normal life.

In such individuals a sudden breakdown of health, due to acute illness, may result in incontinence. Contrary to their fears, however, this need only be a transient episode; most regain control when the illness is treated. Admission to a hospital because of the illness may aggravate a tendency to lose control. Think of the unfortunate old person admitted to a hospital with pneumonia, put in bed with crib sides in position, given an unwanted sedative, and left until six in the morning. Almost inevitably, the sheets are wet. Many elderly patients who arrive in hospitals are accustomed to rising from bed one or more times each night to empty their bladders. Failure to appreciate this need results in episodes of bed wetting, and such patients may be given a label of incontinence for which they do not qualify. This is an example of how a sudden change in environment may upset the precarious control which the elderly person has over micturition.

One further precipitating factor is bed rest. For example, Mrs. Partridge (Case Report 7–1) was able to achieve continence during the hours spent out of bed much more easily than when she was in bed. Incontinence may become an acute problem for the old person who has had a myocardial infarction and who must spend a few days at complete bed rest. During this time it may be reasonable to use an indwelling catheter, but as soon as possible, it should be removed and every effort made to mobilize the individual. This encourages the restoration of micturition control.

ASSOCIATIONS WITH URINARY INCONTINENCE

Urinary incontinence is most strikingly associated with diminished mental capacity (Table 7–3). Brocklehurst (6) points out that "only one quarter of incontinence patients are without clinical evidence of pathological changes in the brain," which is further confirmation of the key role of deterioration in cerebral function.

Bacteriuria is a common finding in elderly women. In a series of 180 consecutive admissions to a female ward (14), 40 had colony counts > 100,000. Of these, 78% were incontinent. The same study examined the reliability of clean-catch midstream specimens of urine in determining the presence of bacteriuria. Specimens were collected on consecutive mornings from 54 female subjects, but in only 26 were the results the same, showing conclusively that such specimens are valueless. To determine the presence of bacteriuria in elderly females, it is necessary to catheterize them or obtain a specimen by suprapubic aspiration.

Bacteriuria and incontinence often coexist in females, but urinary tract infections are not significantly associated with the latter (11). In the Birmingham, England study (14), 37 subjects in a group of 40 with organisms in the urine were symptomless. In 31 (77%), however, there was urinary incontinence. Of the 140 subjects without bacteriuria, 73 (52%) were incontinent.

The relationship between bacteriuria and incontinence is, therefore, not clear. The Birmingham study, which involved only catheter specimens of urine in females, did suggest some association, but the results were obtained from a selected group of 180 subjects, 22% of whom were found to be bacteriuric on entry into the hospital. Brocklehurst *et al.* (11) found an incidence of infection of 20% in a representative sample of old people living at home, including 337 women aged 65–91. This incidence would almost certainly have been lower had the catheter technique been used.

The incidence of dysuria and frequency was low in both studies: 7% and 5% in the first, 9% and 13% respectively in the second. The significance of symptomless bacteriuria is doubtful. The Birmingham study showed how quickly resistance developed to sulphonamides, and the conclusion was reached that no symptomless bacteriuria should be treated in elderly women. It is likely that bacteriuria is more common in incontinent females because of contact with urine soaked clothes or sheets for appreciable periods. The chances of multiplication and ascending spread of organisms under such conditions must be high.

MEDICAL TREATMENT OF URINARY INCONTINENCE

Although it may appear that urinary incontinence is an irreversible condition for which little can be done, experience demonstrates that this is not so. For example, the incidence of urinary incontinence in individuals newly admitted to a hospital is greater than that of permanent incontinence. Treatment of the acute illness combined with a straightforward, encouraging rehabilitation program designed to restore the elderly person to their preillness state can reestablish continence. Control may be more precarious than it had been previously, but nevertheless, it is real and effective. One's presumption, therefore, on encountering an incontinent old lady with an acute illness should be that once the illness is under control and rehabilitation is under way, bladder control will quickly recover.

History

The first step in treatment is to determine how the condition developed, which may offer clues about its cause. This means careful elucidation of the history. Unfortunately, the early intermittent episodes of incontinence are likely to be concealed or forgotten, particularly if the patient lives alone. Relatives or friends may be able to provide useful detail, but they may be ill-informed. Points of importance in the history are any indication of frequency, dysuria, urgency or precipitancy of micturition preceding or accompanying the development of incontinence. Documentation of drug treatment and the introduction of diuretics should be noted. Information on the mental state of the patient is also of importance. Questions about nocturia, diurnal pattern of incontinence, and bowel function should also be asked.

Examination

Of particular relevance in the physical examination are cognitive function and neurologic state. Careful palpation of the abdomen for evidence of a full bladder should be part of the routine. Rectal examination is essential to check on the possibility of fecal impaction, which can cause bladder outlet obstruction and enlargement of the prostate in men. In women the introitus and vagina should be inspected for evidence of local infection or senile vaginitis. Vaginal examination excludes cystocele or rectocele formation and disease of the cervix or uterus.

Investigation

A specimen of urine collected by catheter or suprapubic aspiration should be examined routinely and sent for bacteriologic screening. Significant bacteriuria, if accompanied by symptoms, should be treated by the appropriate antibiotic.

Where facilities are available, cystometry provides useful additional information.

Treatment

The most effective way to improve cortical inhibition is to organize a general rehabilitation program. From the day of admission to a hospital or the beginning of management at home such a plan should be instituted. Emphasis should be placed on early mobilization.

This approach should be supplemented by attention to any local factors discovered in the rectum and pelvis. Any significant pathology which is amenable to treatment should be put right. Acute illnesses are likely to resolve quickly, and the chances of recovery of micturition control are good. The use of catheters in the acute phase of an illness may be of value to enable accurate records of fluid intake and output to be maintained. If catheters are used there should be closed drainage, and bladder wash-outs are best avoided. The catheter should be removed immediately when the need for it is over.

These measures will deal adequately with most cases of transient urinary incontinence caused by acute illness in elderly people. There is a larger group of cases, however, in whom the urinary incontinence preceded the acute illness or in whom it is established. Can anything be done for these individuals? Present methods are not very effective and consist largely of attempts to retrain the bladder to a regular pattern of emptying which will establish what might be called "supported continence."

The basis of this technique is a regular routine of sitting on the lavatory at 2-, 3-, or 4-hour intervals throughout the 24 hours. The hope is that the individual will slowly reestablish an inhibition capability, which will maintain continence most of the time. Efforts have been made to introduce this type of regime for subjects with indwelling catheters by clamping the catheter and releasing it at regular intervals. Evidence in favor of such a procedure is lacking, and there is a danger that it may increase the risk of bladder infections. It is mentioned because it seems reasonable, but in the author's hands it has seldom proved effective.

Willington (32) describes retraining of voluntary inhibition of micturition as the creation of a conditioned reflex. The act of voiding follows the stimulus of knowing that the bladder is full and occurs under normal circumstances when the person is relaxed, is in a comfortable appropriate position, and has privacy. When the initial stimulus is lost, Willington suggests that attempts be made to create a conditioned reflex which can take over from the lifelong natural one (Fig. 7–5). Success hinges on knowing the appropriate time to offer associated stimuli, and this can be established by accurate charting of incontinence episodes or by using a device designed for the purpose. Charting is usually adequate during the day, but more difficulty arises at night. The use of a time recorder which allows the time of voiding to be noted is described by Willington.

After the time at which incontinence has been established over a series of nights, it is then possible to awaken the patient and present the secondary stimuli at a time when the bladder is full. Willington's logical approach to this problem offers more hope of success than any other and is based on recognition of four major factors.

1. Voiding will occur only when the bladder is well filled. Presenting subsidiary stimuli at other times may not only be unsuccessful but may convert them into positive inhibiting forces. Here lies the danger of the 2-hour panning technique.
2. The individual's own habit pattern must be considered; not all will fit the

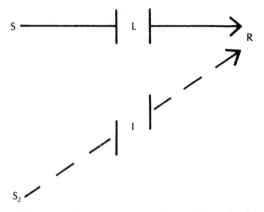

Fig. 7–5. Rationale of Willington's bladder retraining by conditioned reflexes. **S.** Stimulus (full bladder). **L.** Loss of stimulus. **R.** Response (voiding). **S₂.** Associated stimuli such as correct position, pressure on buttocks, privacy, absence of clothing. **I.** Inhibiting agents such as pain, wrong position, presence of clothing. **S₂** is offered to the patient when bladder is full. (Willington FL [ed]: Incontinence in the Elderly. London, Academic Press, 1976, p 185–201)

hospital ward routine. Careful documenting on an incontinence chart will provide information on patients' habits.

3. "It is a physiological feat, requiring considerable fortitude, concentration and discrimination to expect a patient to micturate or defecate lying on their back in bed," writes Willington. This should be remembered.

4. Attention to detail is important. Sitting the subject on a sanitary chair supplies the correct stimulus. Can the patient be expected to reject the stimulus for a vital few minutes while the chair is wheeled to the washroom and placed over the lavatory? The bedpan should be in position in the sanichair.

One technique, which was originally suggested by Wilson (34) in 1948, has received support more recently (17). Wilson noted that performing cystometries appeared to have a beneficial effect on the subjects. Dunn and his coworkers used a much more vigorous approach, forcibly distending the bladder for periods of 30 min. They claim to have greatly improved a number of cases who became continent and remained so for several months. This offers hope of a possible advance for the future and is an area in which more work needs to be done.

Anticholinergic drugs have been prescribed in efforts to obtain control of the uninhibited neurogenic bladder. Propantheline bromide, orphenadrine, emepronium bromide, and flavoxate hydrochloride have all been tried but without unequivocal success. (The last two are not available in the United States or Canada at the present time.) There is a very marginal benefit to be obtained by the use of these drugs in a true uninhibited bladder, but, in the person who retains some awareness of bladder filling, they can be useful. The individual who is continent during the day, but lapses at night may be helped to continence at night—but the results are often disappointing. The most effective combination reported is 15 mg propantheline and 50–100 mg orphenadrine (10) given t.i.d.

FECAL INCONTINENCE

In Sheldon's survey (25) there were only three instances of fecal incontinence in the 477 individuals for whom complete data were obtained. One of these was a woman of 60 who, bedridden with a stroke, had complete incontinence of both urine and feces. The other two subjects had no urinary troubles but suffered from intermittent lack of control over their bowels; one had undergone a major pelvic operation, and the other was a woman of 90 with dementia. The very low incidence of 0.6% was attributed by Sheldon to the fact that fecal incontinence almost always results in admission to an institution.

The Sheffield study (21) reported a similar situation with only three men and five women occasionally incontinent of feces and two additional women regularly so. Both of the latter had serious brain damage, one due to hemiplegia and the other to dementia. The three male cases were associated with enlargement or removal of the prostate gland.

A different situation prevailed in 873 patients referred to a geriatric department in 1960–1961. Of females, 5% suffered from intermittent and a further 12% from persistent fecal incontinence. The figures for men were 6% and 13%, respectively.

This incidence is, therefore, about half that of urinary incontinence.

CONTROL OF DEFECATION

Control of defecation is based on a mechanism similar to that of micturition. The stimulus to defecate is the entry of bulk into the rectum, resulting in dilatation of that organ which stimulates contraction of colonic and rectal muscles and evacuation through the anus. It seems likely that socially acceptable control of defecation is achieved by establishing a nervous control much like the control of micturition. It is well known that one can prevent or postpone defecation until a suitable moment. An unfortunate consequence of this is that, if repeated often enough, the individual's bowel function suffers. A regular habit is essential to maintain the best bowel function throughout life. Elderly people may suffer problems such as an atonic colon because of their own earlier misuse of bowel function.

Brocklehurst (7) compared his cystometrograms with similar pressure recordings from the rectum which were obtained by a balloon distention method. He inserted into the rectum a balloon which could be distended to 250 ml. In a group of 19 fecally incontinent elderly men he found that in seven it was impossible to distend the balloon beyond 150 ml. In each case, the passage of the balloon was preceded by involuntary contractions. Brocklehurst believed that the controlling mechanism for bowel evacuation was similar to that for the voiding of urine.

CAUSES OF FECAL INCONTINENCE

There are three groups of causes for fecal incontinence: 1) intestinal pathology, 2) fecal impaction, and 3) loss of nervous control.

Intestinal Pathology

A wide variety of conditions of the large bowel may be responsible for fecal incontinence. Examples are carcinomas, diverticulosis, papillomas of colon or rectum, and anal lesions such as hemorrhoids, fissures, rectal prolapse, or loss of the anal sphincter. These may all result in disturbance of bowel function with episodes of diarrhea and some loss of control. In every case of fecal incontinence, it is important to examine the lower bowel thoroughly, both manually and by sigmoidoscope, to ascertain if there is local bowel pathology.

Fecal Impaction

Fecal impaction is a common major problem associated with illness and debility in old people (see Ch. 5, Confusion). Changes take place in the gastrointestinal tract during aging, such as the tendency of digestive enzyme secretion to diminish in quantity with age (see Ch. 2, Physical Aspects of Aging). From an anatomic point of view, there appears to be little change in the appearance of the gut, but there is probably some loss of muscle cells and nervous tissue from the myenteric plexus. Brocklehurst and Khan (12) have demonstrated that transit time through the intestine is increased in older subjects. They gave four ambulant elderly people and eight long-stay geriatric patients radiopaque pellets to swallow and timed their passage through the gut. In five of the long-stay patients, the time taken was more than 2 weeks, and in two pellets were still present at the end of 3 weeks. Even in the ambulant subjects there was a considerable increase in the length of time the pellets took to pass through the bowel. In a younger group of adults described by Hinton *et al.* (20) 80% of markers were passed within 1 week and the majority within 3 days. Only one of the eight elderly long-stay patients of the Brocklehurst study passed all the markers within 1 week.

Increased intestinal transit time encourages the development of constipation. Added to misuse of laxatives and bad habits, it is a significant factor in colonic stasis. In this situation a large, solid mass of stool may form either in the rectum or in the sigmoid colon and act like a ball valve. Irritation of the surrounding mucous membrane causes inflammation and secretion of mucus-containing fluid which results in a frequent flow of stool colored fluid.

One of the essential parts of the physical assessment of an elderly patient is a rectal examination. This will reveal the presence of impaction, unless the blockage is beyond the reach of the finger in the sigmoid colon.

Loss of Nervous Control

Loss of nervous control over defecation is analogous to the condition of an uninhibited neurogenic bladder. The individual does not recognize that the rectum is filling and defecation is about to take place. Therefore no prevention occurs. This is less common than its urinary equivalent, although accurate figures are not available.

TREATMENT OF FECAL INCONTINENCE

If fecal incontinence is due to colonic, rectal, or anal pathology, that condition must be treated by standard medical or surgical means. Success in this may reestablish control; if not, other measures, such as those for loss of neurogenic control, must be tried. To treat fecal incontinence due to neurogenic causes is difficult, because those who suffer from this are quite unaware of rectal filling.

CASE REPORT 7–2

Mrs. Flowers, aged 73, had radiotherapy for a carcinoma of the cervix in 1970. In June 1977 she was seen at the Geriatric Policlinic in London, Ontario. There were two problems: fecal incontinence and a slowly developing dementia. The first had developed following the treatment for the cervical cancer and was described as a precipitancy in the need for defecation. If she could not reach the lavatory in 2–3 min, there was an accident. This situation began before the intellectual deterioration of the dementia, but it had worsened when the dementia became obvious.

The patient was admitted to the continuing care hospital and was encouraged to be up and dressed each morning and in general to lead a normally active life. She was given a regular diet and a combination of Kaopectate and codeine during the day to slow down colonic motility. She was encouraged to evacuate the colon first thing in the morning, which was her habit. On this simple regimen some improvement in her control was achieved.

The management of such cases involves the same Pavlovian principles used by Willington (32) for urinary incontinence. For the bowel, Willington stresses the importance of knowing when the rectum is full and suggests that this goal can be achieved by using constipating drugs as was done with Mrs. Flowers. He advocates kaolin to constipate followed by bisacodyl (Dulcolax) suppositories to secure evacuation. Such a routine can then be maintained on a daily or alternate day schedule. There is no indication of the degree of effectiveness of these measures, but the logic of the approach is appealing. It also offers a plan in which patient, relatives, and professional attendants can all cooperate.

MANAGEMENT OF BOWEL FUNCTION

The management of bowel function in the elderly, in particular those who are maintained in institutions, is difficult and requires careful attention. The recognition of the importance of bran as a source of fiber and a bulk producer has been a major advance. Its use by young people on a regular basis may go a long way to prevent the atonic colon which is so typical of old age. Even for the old, bran can be very helpful, and many patients will be cured of a tendency to constipation if they take 4 tablespoonfuls of powdered bran with their meals each day, 4 tablespoonfuls being the total daily amount. Some care, however, has to be used in introducing it into the diets of very old and debilitated patients. In a recent unpublished trial at a continuing care hospital, two elderly individuals became greatly distended as a result of bran and required careful measures to clear the gut. A gradual introduction is therefore important in such individuals.

Old people need to be constantly reminded of the need to take plenty of liquid. This is particularly true in hot weather because of the extra insensible loss of water from the body. If fluid intake is inadequate, water must be reabsorbed by the colon to maintain water balance. This dries out the stool, which is sufficient to cause an impaction in an adequate but sluggish bowel.

Fecal softeners in combination with a suitable stimulant such as Senokot, given daily in carefully adjusted doses, can resolve threatened impaction. The use of 2 tablets containing 374 mg standardized senna concentrate and 100 mg dioctyl sodium sulfosuccinate has been recommended by DeLuca (16) for the management of constipation in severely incapacitated aged nursing home patients. Smith (26), however, pointed out that excessive doses of senna may, in time, produce degeneration of the myenteric plexus in man and mouse. Unfortunately, there is no indication of the amount of senna given to the mice in her study. Nevertheless, one obviously has to bear in mind that stimulant laxatives are two-edged weapons.

PREVENTION OF SOILING

Incontinence poses grave social problems in a domestic setting. It can also permeate the atmosphere of any institution which accommodates elderly disabled persons. During the past two decades advances have been made in the design of incontinence pads and other devices to moderate the unpleasant nature of the condition. The main hope must lie in better methods of prevention, but in the foreseeable future there will be a need for pads, pants, and similar devices.

One of the few physicians to study this area of care is Willington (31), who has used basic physical principles and a study of materials to find a workable device. His concern has been to maintain the hopelessly incontinent individual in a comfortable and socially acceptable state. It is important, he says, that the patient not be harmed by the method chosen but is kept warm and dry in a manner "which causes no injury to his ego and odour is reduced to a minimum." The patient who is not confined to bed requires a garment which is inconspicuous but effective in order to preserve social independence.

Willington describes the principles of hydrodynamics which are important to the patient with urinary incontinence. Fluid travels along wood pulp or paper by surface tension and can soak upwards until the weight of the column of fluid and effects of gravity predominate. It accumulates at its most dependent point but spreads by surface tension (Fig. 7–6). The lowest point is the perineal region on which the subject sits. By concentrating on the physical laws involved, Willington designed a "marsupial pant" (Fig. 7–7). As he describes it, "a single piece of knitted hydrophobic material (100% polyester fibre) was made into a tailored pant, the urine was attracted outside a plasticized knitted pouch placed over the genital area, containing the absorptive materials." As a result of this arrangement, when urine is involuntarily voided it passes through the hydrophobic material into the incontinence pad, which absorbs the water and pre-

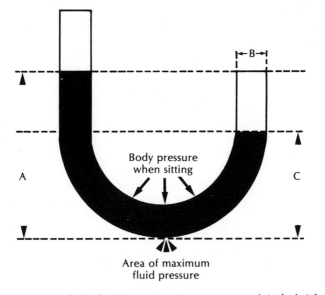

Fig. 7–6. Hydrostatic principles in devising an incontinence garment. **A** is the height of wetness in front. **B** is the thickness of pad. **C** is the height of wetness behind and upper posterior of pad. (Willington FL [ed]: Incontinence in the Elderly. London, Academic Press, © 1976, p 185–201. Reprinted by permission)

Fig. 7–7. Marsupial pants. (Willington FL [ed]: Incontinence in the Elderly. London, Academic Press, © 1976, p 185–201)

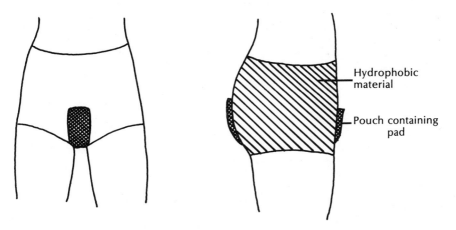

serves a dry genital area. Air can still circulate next to the skin. The pouch into which the incontinence pad is placed opens to the front so that the pad can be changed by the patient.

Willington recommends his garment in only two circumstances: 1) as a method of preserving social acceptability when all other attempts at rehabilitation have failed, and 2) as an aid to those receiving other treatment but who have not yet regained continence. In addition to these two indications, it is suggested that the atmosphere in many nursing homes and continuing care hospitals could be greatly improved by the use of such a simple yet well-designed garment to maintain cleanliness, freedom from unpleasant odors, and protection for the skin of the elderly patients.

Fecal incontinence is less easily managed. A major problem is the cleaning of the patient. Encouraging results have been achieved by the use of a nonionic detergent, derived from kerosene, which is used commercially as a gel to remove car grease (33). There is a new garment called the Doublet Pant which has been tried out in Europe. It is made of polyester with stretchable side panels and includes a panel of 10-ply creped absorbent paper backed by polythene. Willington recommends such a garment for patients in a defecation retraining program or those with intractable local lesions such as rectal prolapse, fistulas, or persistent fecal discharge.

REFERENCES

1. Adams GF, Hurwitz LJ: Mental barriers to recovery from strokes. Lancet II:533–537, 1963
2. Affleck JW: The chronic sick in hospital; a psychiatric approach. Lancet I:335–359, 1947
3. Andrew J, Nathan PW: Lesions of the anterior frontal lobes and disturbances of micturition and defaecation. Brain 87:233–262, 1964
4. Andrew J, Nathan PW: The cerebral control of micturition. Proc R Soc Med 58:553–555, 1965
5. Brocklehurst JC: Incontinence in Old People. Edinburgh, Livingston, 1951
6. Brocklehurst JC: The aetiology of urinary incontinence in the elderly. In Anderson WF, Isaacs B (eds): Current Achievements in Geriatrics. London, Cassell, 1964, pp 115–121
7. Brocklehurst JC: Bowel management in the neurologically disabled; The problems in Old Age. Proc R Soc Med 65:66–69, 1972
8. Brocklehurst JC, Dillane JB: Studies of the female bladder in old age. I. Cystometrograms in non-incontinent women. Gerontol Clin 8:285–305, 1966
9. Brocklehurst JC, Dillane JB: Studies of the female bladders in old age. II. Cystometrograms in 100 incontinent women. Gerontol Clin 8:306–319, 1966
10. Brocklehurst JC, Dillane JB: Studies of the female bladder in old age. IV. Drug effects in urinary incontinence. Gerontol Clin 9:182–191, 1967
11. Brocklehurst JC, Dillane JB, Griffiths L, Fry J: The prevalence and symptomatology of urinary infection in an aged population. Gerontol Clin 10:242–253, 1968
12. Brocklehurst JC, Khan MY: A study of fecal stasis in old age and the use of "dorbanex" in its prevention. Gerontol Clin 11:293–301, 1969
13. Cape RDT: A geriatric service. Midland Med Rev 8:21–44, 1972
14. Cape RDT, Ehtisham M, Zirk MH: Management of bacteriuria in the elderly female. In Urinary Tract Infection. London, Oxford University Press, 1973, pp 223–228
15. Cape RDT, Shorrock C, Tree R, Pablo R, Campbell AJ: Square pegs in round holes. Can Med Assoc J 117:1284–1287, 1977
16. DeLuca VA: The management of chronic functional constipation in the severely incapacitated aged nursing home patient. Medical Counterpoint 6:25–27, 1974

17. Dunn M, Smith JC, Ardran GM: Prolonged bladder distension as a treatment of urgency and urge incontinence of urine. Br J Urol 46:645–652, 1974

18. Garry RC: The control of the urinary bladder and urethra. In Anderson WF, Isaacs B (eds): Current Achievements in Geriatrics. London, Cassell, 1964, pp 97–104

19. Griffiths DJ: The mechanics of the urethra and of micturition. Br J Urol 45:497–507, 1973

20. Hinton JM, Lennard-Jones JE, Young AC: A new method for studying gut transit times using radiopaque markers. Gut 10:842–847, 1969

21. Hobson W, Pemberton J: The Health of the Elderly at Home. London, Butterworth and Co Ltd, 1955, pp 39–44

22. Keston M: Current research in urinary incontinence in geriatric female patients. Birmingham, England, In Cape RDT (ed): Symposia of Geriatric Medicine, Vol 3. West Midland Institute of Geriatric Medicine and Gerontology, 1974, pp 86–90

23. Malvern J: The control of micturition in the female. Br J Hosp Med 10:63–70, 1974

24. Milne JS: Prevalence of incontinence in the elderly age group. In Willington FL (ed): Incontinence in the Elderly. London, Academic Press, 1976, pp 9–21

25. Sheldon JH: The Social Medicine of Old Age. London, Oxford University Press, 1948, pp 74–75

26. Smith B: Affect of irritant perogatives on myenteric plexus in man and the mouse. Gut 9: 139–143, 1968

27. Thompson J: Incontinence in the elderly. In An Introduction to Geriatric Medicine. Glasgow, Forest Hall Hospital, 1962

28. Tsuji I, Kuroda K, Nakagima F: Excretory cystometry in paraplegic patients. Br J Urol 83: 839–844, 1960

29. Williamson J, Stokoe IH, Gray S, Fisher M, McGee A, Stephenson E: Old people at home, their unreported needs. Lancet I:1117–1120, 1964

30. Willington FL: Problems in urinary incontinence in the aged. Gerontol Clin II:330–356, 1969

31. Willington FL: The prevention of soiling in urinary incontinence. In Cape RDT (ed): Symposia of Geriatric Medicine, Vol 3. Birmingham, England, West Midland Institute of Geriatric Medicine and Gerontology, 1974, pp 91–95

32. Willington FL: The physiological basis of retraining for continence. In Willington FL (ed): Incontinence in the Elderly. London, Academic Press, 1976, pp 185–201

33. Willington FL: Hygenic methods in the management of incontinence. In Willington FL (ed): Incontinence in the Elderly. London, Academic Press, 1976, pp 227–244

34. Wilson TS: Incontinence of urine in the aged. Lancet II:374–377, 1948

35. Wilson TS: A practical approach to the treatment of incontinence of urine in the elderly. In Willington FL (ed): Incontinence in the Elderly. London, Academic Press, 1976, pp 85–95

36. Yeates WK: Normal and abnormal bladder function in incontinence of urine. In Willington FL (ed): Incontinence in the Elderly. London, Academic Press, 1976, pp 22–41

Chapter 8

HOMEOSTATIC IMPAIRMENT

*Youth longs and manhood strives
but age remembers,
Sits by the raked-up ashes of the past
Spreads its thin hands above the
whitening embers,
That warm its creeping life blood
till the last.*

> *Oliver Wendell Holmes*

HOMEOSTATIC CONTROL

Homeostasis can be defined as the body's need to maintain a constant internal environment despite external changes. In clinical terms this control governs body fluid and acid-base balance, blood pressure, temperature, appetite, thirst, and reaction to stress of all kinds. The center of homeostatic control is the hypothalamus, which acts in close association with the anterior pituitary. While much of the communication throughout the body is carried out by hormones, the whole system is under the control of the brain (Fig. 8–1).

The more efficient the individual's control of homeostasis, the greater the state of health. This ability to cope with any difficulties which the environment may present is characteristic of human beings. When we think of strength and good health, we are apt to think of people with great physical attributes. In fact, these are not necessarily the healthiest or strongest people. The assessment of health should be governed more by ability to adapt to stress than by pure physical prowess. One example is the ability of man to cope with marked changes of temperature. He can live in temperatures which range from +40°C to −40°C and not only survive but live an active life by using ingenuity. Good control of homeostasis means an ability to adapt or react to any stress.

If one considers an arrangement which controls temperature automatically in a room, a kettle, or a swimming pool, four essentials are required: 1) a thermometer to monitor the temperature, 2) a switch to control a heating mechanism, 3) the object to be heated, and 4) the means to heat the object. When the thermom-

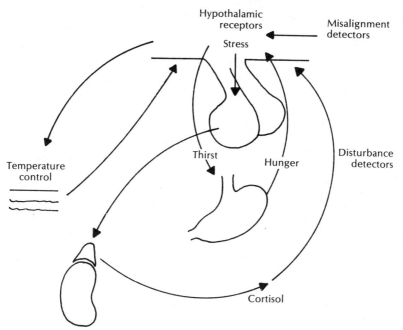

Fig. 8–1. A diagrammatic representative of some major homeostatic mechanisms which may become less efficient in old age.

eter goes above the desired temperature, the heating is switched off automatically; when the temperature falls below the required level, the switch is reversed. Horobin (11) emphasizes that, for such a system to operate successfully, the monitoring device (the thermometer) has to be placed within the object (room, kettle, or pool).

If the atmosphere outside the receptacle is cold, this acts as a disturbing influence to the temperature in it. Measuring the temperature outside indicates the need for a heating device but does not make it possible to maintain a constant, even heat. Assessing conditions within the area means that the combined effect of inside heating and outside cold are taken into account. This is the method adopted by biologic systems.

Body temperature is monitored by receptors located in the hypothalamus. Core temperature is that of the blood, and it is this which bathes the sensitive sensors. The body loses heat through the skin by flushing and dilating skin capillaries and increasing sweat formation which evaporates on the skin surface. The body retains heat by constricting the superficial blood vessels and shivering to create more heat. Extremes of heat or cold are first recognized by receptors in the skin which warn the hypothalamus of a need for action. These act as disturbance detectors which send signals to the centrally situated misalignment detector in the hypothalamus, which will in turn act to maintain the constancy of body temperature (11).

A similar arrangement governs hunger and thirst. These two sensations signal an urgent need for food or water to the individual experiencing them. Hunger is probably stimulated by subtle alterations in glucose and fat levels in the hypothalamic blood; thirst, by variations in ionic concentration of the circulation. The stomach acts as the disturbance detector by producing characteristic hunger pangs and signaling the brain. Once a few mouthfuls have been consumed or a glass of liquid imbibed, these feelings subside although it may take much longer for the appropriate levels in the blood to right themselves. The disturbance element provides the raw stimulus to take quick action, leaving the refined misalignment detector mechanism to maintain the necessary balance.

Many of the controlling systems of homeostasis are critical for the individual. One example is the brain's need for an ample supply of glucose. After a meal, blood glucose levels rise quickly and are efficiently controlled by the action of insulin in the healthy individual. If, however, the individual then plays a vigorous game of squash, increased supplies of glucose are expended. There are four methods by which levels can be quickly built up. These are by the action of cortisol and epinephrine from the cortex and medulla of the suprarenal gland, respectively, glucagon from the pancreas, and growth hormone from the pituitary (11).

A similar, more complicated system of fall-back arrangements governs the control of blood pressure. Under the primary control of receptors in the carotid arteries in the neck, there are subsidiary or supplementary sensors in the walls of other major arteries, such as the aorta, and these quickly take over should the sinus nerves be lost for any reason.

The importance of the hypothalamus as the major controlling factor in many homeostatic mechanisms is underlined by its role in producing corticotropin releasing factor (CRF) which passes via a direct arterial link to the anterior pituitary. This is the sole stimulus to the secretion of the adrenocorticotropic hormone which initiates the body's adaptation system to stress. Although the complexities of these and other arrangements are beyond the scope of this work, it can be said that homeostatic control is mediated through receptors in all parts of the body, including some in the brain itself, which relay information that is coordinated and processed by the neuroendocrine system.

Inevitably with loss of neurons and damage to those that survive into old age the complicated mechanisms of homeostasis become less efficient. Comfort (4) has suggested that old age is the point at which genetically determined differences appear. Human beings are born with great reserves for all physiologic functions. This reserve is gradually used up until in the ninth and tenth decades there are few reserves left. Each person follows an individual course in this inexorable process, with different systems being affected to different degrees. Homeostasis is the amalgam of functioning of different systems which enable the individual to withstand stress, to stand erect, and to survive in extremes of temperature. Altered presentation of disease, inability to adapt to low or high temperatures, instability of blood pressure control, and disturbances of gut motility are the main clinical features of homeostatic disorder in old age.

ALTERED PRESENTATION OF DISEASE

CASE REPORT 8–1

Mrs. Power, aged 90, had been completely demented and unable to look after herself for the past 2 years. She lived in a Home for the Aged and spent all her time either in bed or in a chair; she had to be lifted from one to the other. In June 1977, she collapsed and was brought into the emergency department of the local hospital. Examination revealed rapid breathing with a quick pulse but no fever and no gross evidence of systemic disturbance other than a mild degree of shock. Chest x-ray showed that the right lung was almost completely solid. She was treated with a course of ampicillin, and her condition quickly improved to her usual state. She returned to the Home after 1 week in the hospital when a second x-ray showing some clearing of the consolidation.

With her severely damaged brain the old lady did not respond to her infection in a typical manner with chest pain, fever, or cough. Collapse, tachypnea, and cyanosis were the only clues. This is an extreme case, but similar, less dramatic differences in presentation regularly occur in elderly patients.

All diseases are attacks on the individual which are resisted by the homeostatic mechanisms. In response to a pneumonic infection, for example, the body normally reacts by a series of systemic events which include temperature rise and increased heart and respiratory rate. In the child, the systemic reaction is swifter and more severe than at any other age, with convulsions often accompanying the rapid rise of temperature. The heart rate increases considerably, and the respiratory rate is likely to double or treble. Blood pressure may drop if the infection is severe enough to produce shock. In the mature adult, the rapid rise of temperature may be accompanied by rigors, but not convulsions. In both the young and middle-aged groups there may be episodes of delirium in severe cases. This vigorous systemic reaction exemplifies the mobilization of the body's defense mechanisms which, with the help of antibiotics, clear the infecting organism from the lungs. Even the local reactions may be of value, *i.e.,* coughing helps to clear infective material from the chest.

In the elderly person, however, resistance is less effective, the systemic reactions may be mild or absent, and the infection may quickly gain the upper hand. One of the more common symptoms encountered is mental confusion (see Ch. 5, Confusion), which parallels convulsions in children. There are many cases when infections declare themselves with the characteristic features seen in younger patients, but the physician must be alert to recognize latent infectious diseases in difficult, indeterminate situations. Pneumonia and cystitis are the two common ones, but any infection, from cellulitis to meningitis, may turn up with very little warning.

Another recurring situation is the so-called "silent coronary." There are many elderly coronary patients who have chest pain and a reasonably clear picture of infarction, but there are others in whom pain is absent and physical findings may be difficult to interpret. Unexplained sudden development of congestive heart failure or onset of confusion are clues, and physicians must cultivate a high level of suspicion.

ORTHOSTATIC HYPOTENSION

CASE REPORT 8–2

At the age of 72, Mr. Sweet, now 77, had developed attacks of dizziness which were not true vertigo. If he was out when he developed such an episode, the only thing to do was have himself driven home and then sit or lie down until the symptom passed. The dizziness would last 1–2 hours at a time. He was investigated fully at Hamilton, Ontario, in April 1974; an angiographic study of his cerebral vessels was made at that time. Apart from an aberrant left vertebral artery, the angiograms were normal. At that time, a serum cortisol estimation was noted at 3 mcg/100 ml, below the accepted normal level, but unfortunately confirmation of this isolated finding was lacking. Treatment was introduced with steroids, ephedrine, diphenylhydantoin (Dilantin), and perphenazine, but there was no record of their effectiveness. A diagnosis of postural hypotension was included in the discharge list.

In September 1974, the patient was admitted to the Westminster Hospital in London, Ontario. The same findings were present, and angiographic studies were not repeated. He was transferred to the geriatric wing of this Veteran's Hospital.

During 1975 his symptoms became more dramatic. There were three blackouts at the beginning of August 1975, one occurring when he was walking, one when in bed, and one when sitting.

The patient, seen on August 7th, was a slim man who looked his stated age, was sensible if a little lethargic, and inclined to misunderstand questions because of deafness in his left ear. He was most cooperative throughout the examination. He had a pigeon chest deformity with a mild degree of senile emphysema associated with it. His heart sounds were normal, and his resting blood pressure in bed was 90/60, the same in both arms. When he stood up, the systolic pressure on the right arm dropped below 60 mm Hg, he became faint, and he had to lie back in the bed at once. All his leg reflexes were brisk and both plantar responses were extensor. The remainder of his examination was within normal limits.

His systolic blood pressure levels were taken over a period of 4 weeks in August and September 1975 (Fig. 8–2). Serum cortisol levels on August 14th were 11.2 mcg/100 ml in the morning and 3.2 mcg/100 ml in the afternoon. After adrenocorticotropic hormone (ACTH) stimulation on August 18th, however, 8.2 mcg/100 ml pre-ACTH rose to 34.6 mcg/100 ml, which is a reasonable response. Empirical treatment with 0.5 mg ACTH twice weekly was continued for some months with reasonable effectiveness. In 1976, however, his more dramatic blackouts recurred.

Postural hypotension is common in patients receiving large doses of antihypertensive medications (see Ch. 9, Iatrogenic Disorders). In more recent years, with improved titration of dosage and better drugs this situation has become easier to manage. It is still not uncommon in old people, however. A state of mild dehydration with reduced blood volume, reduced activity, and the taking of a variety of medications all predispose patients to the condition. The resulting symptoms are vague, usually described by patients as dizziness or some such term indicating a feeling of lightheadedness without specific rotatory vertigo. If such a symptom is associated with the patient standing up and beginning to walk about or is most frequently encountered in the early part of the day, shortly after getting out of bed, then postural hypotension should be suspected.

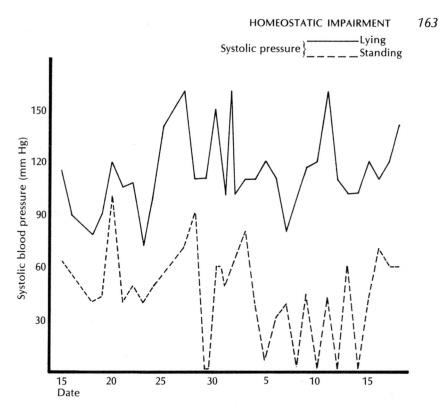

Fig. 8–2. Case Report 8–2: lying and standing systolic blood pressure recorded daily over a 4-week period.

Fig. 8–3. Incidence of orthostatic hypotension by age and sex. Subjects were divided into groups whose systolic pressure fell on standing by 20–29 mm Hg (**a**), 30–39 mm Hg (**b**), and 40+ mm Hg (**c**). (Adapted from data of Caird FI *et al.:* Br Heart J 35:527–530, 1973)

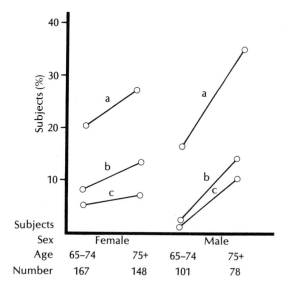

General deterioration of cerebral function may give rise to orthostatic hypotension *per se* as in Case Report 8–2. Blood pressure is maintained by baroreceptor mechanisms mediated through the autonomic nervous system. Any condition which upsets proper functioning of this system may create a danger of postural hypotension. Apart from central damage, peripheral neuropathy due to diabetes or alcoholism are two other factors of importance which are common in elderly patients and may cause hypotensive problems.

Caird, Andrews, and Kennedy (3) examined 494 elderly people in and around Glasgow, Scotland, and demonstrated a fall in systolic pressure in the erect position of 20 mm Hg or more in 24% of their subjects. When grouped by age, above or below 75, the incidence was 16% between 65 and 74 and 30% for the 75+ group (Fig. 8–3). These authors examined various conditions which have been associated with hypotension to assess which was of greatest significance in the development of hypotension. They noted organic brain disease, heart disease, absent ankle jerks, varicose veins, drugs, anemia, bacteriuria, hyponatremia, and combinations of two or more of these conditions. Their results indicated that there was no significant association of hypotension with any individual item but a combination of two or more increased the likelihood of the subject having a postural drop in blood pressure level.

Johnson *et al.* (13) carried out a similar study of 100 patients in a geriatric unit. The incidence of significant postural hypotension was greater when readings were taken after standing for 2 min than they were when position was changed from lying to sitting for 5 min. Their results are consistent with those of the Glasgow group who measured the pressures after standing for only 1 min. A substantial proportion of the geriatric patients felt dizzy when they first assumed an upright position. Johnson and Spalding (14) emphasize that abnormal falls in blood pressure may harm the brain and, for this reason alone, it is important to recognize the condition. There is also the danger of falls and broken bones (see Ch. 6, Falling).

Thomas and Schirger (24) noted the principal somatic–neurologic manifestations associated with hypotension (Table 8–1). The age range of the 57 subjects was 42–76 years (mean 60). There was evidence of involvement of the corticobulbar and corticospinal tracts, basal ganglia, and cerebellum. Their findings were usually bilateral, and 34 presented a picture resembling parkinsonism. The authors concluded that the cause of the idiopathic orthostatic hypotension in their cases was a primary disease of the nervous system.

These were carefully selected subjects with a striking drop in systolic blood pressure of at least 50 mm Hg on standing up. The authors acknowledge their bias towards cases with neurologic involvement and emphasize the association of this condition with disorders in the spinal cord and the brain. The main disturbance lies in control of blood pressure levels through appropriate circulatory reflexes.

Ziegler *et al.* (25) have recently reported on a group of ten patients suffering from orthostatic hypotension. All were tired and suffered from a variety of autonomic disturbances, including urinary incontinence (8), anhidrosis (6), constipation (6), heat intolerance (5), and fecal incontinence (2); 6 showed evidence

TABLE 8–1. Somatic–Neurologic Deficits in 57 Patients with Idiopathic Orthostatic Hypotension

System	Manifestations	Number
Corticobulbar– corticospinal	Hyperreflexia	48
	Extensor plantars	29
	Dysarthria	17
	Sucking reflex	13
Extrapyramidal	Masking of face	33
	Rigidity ±	
	Cogwheeling	29
	Monotony of voice	18
	Tremor at rest	16
Cerebellar	Intention tremor	23
	Ataxia of gait	22
	Ataxic–dysarthric	
	speech	2
Miscellaneous	Horner's syndrome	
	Anisocoria	
	Diminished ankle	
	jerks	
	Intellectual impairment	28

(Composed from data of Thomas JE, Schirger A: Arch Neurol 22: 289–293, 1970)

of parkinsonism with cogwheel rigidity, bradykinesia, and a shuffling gait; 5 of the 6 had an extensor plantar response; 5 had tremor; and 5, hyperreflexia. The picture was the same as that described 14 years earlier by Thomas and Schirger (23). Ziegler and his colleagues were able to go one step further and divided their ten cases into six with and four without central nervous system deficit. Estimation of norepinephrine levels confirmed the difference between the two subgroups (Fig. 8–4).

Hickler (9) In commenting on this work, points out that "there is, characteristically, an associated loss of cholinergic as well as adrenergic function"—hence anhidrosis and constipation. He also concludes that "after prolonged bed rest, patients, particularly the elderly, who have no intrinsic defect in their sympathetic nervous system will have a degree of postural hypotension owing to a conditioned obtundation of the adrenergic reflex mechanism." It seems likely that, in addition, they may also have some damage to the autonomic system from neuronal loss or damage to cells.

CLINICAL FEATURES OF POSTURAL HYPOTENSION

By the nature of orthostatic hypotension the symptoms appear when patients assume the erect posture after lying or sitting for some time. Dizziness or faintness are the most common complaints; they were present in all 30 cases of one series (23). Other features noted were blurring of vision, general weakness, slurring of speech, ataxia, and headache. Headache occurred in only one of their subjects, but all the other symptoms occurred in at least one-third. If such

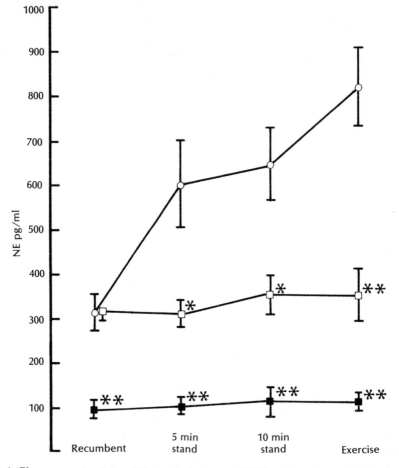

Fig. 8–4. Plasma norepinephrine (NE) levels (mean $+$ S.E.M.) while subjects were recumbent, standing for 5 and 10 minutes and while they were exercising. NE concentrations are shown for 10 control subjects (○), 6 patients with normal plasma norepinephrine levels while recumbent (□), who also had diffuse neurologic signs (Shy-Drager Syndrome), and 4 patients with low plasma norepinephrine levels while recumbent (■), who did not have diffuse neurologic signs (idiopathic orthostatic hypotension). (Ziegler MG *et al.* N Engl J Med 296:294, 1977. Reprinted by permission)
*Different from control subjects (P < 0.01 by student's t-test)
**(P < 0.001)

symptoms appear when the individual assumes an erect position, postural hypotension should be suspected. Diagnosis is quickly confirmed by measuring the blood pressure in the lying position and taking it after the patient has sat up or stood for 2 min. The fall in the blood pressure level should be at least 20 mm Hg for the systolic and 10 mm for diastolic pressures before a diagnosis of orthostatic hypotension is made. Because of orthostatic hypotension, some individuals have trouble during the night when they get out of bed to empty the bladder; they become dizzy and fall.

TREATMENT OF ORTHOSTATIC HYPOTENSION

A series of well-recorded blood pressure readings to confirm the suspected diagnosis is the first step in an attempt to correct or ameliorate orthostatic hypotension. Review of the current program of medications follows, with particular attention to antihypertensive, diuretic, phenothiazine, antidepressant, anticholinergic, benzodiazepine, and barbiturate drugs. Reorganization of the treatment may be all that is necessary to cure the complaint, but unfortunately it is seldom as easy as that. The physician is usually facing a common therapeutic dilemma in managing illness in the elderly. Is it more advantageous for a patient to continue to take a diuretic and be maintained free of cardiac failure, or should it be stopped or reduced in the hope of relieving the dizziness of postural hypotension? No general rules can be given, but it is mandatory that the physician carefully consider the patient's medication program and be ready to take action on possible culpable drugs.

The second major feature of management is communication with the patient. Physicians are notoriously bad at informing patients of their diagnoses and what must be done about them. In the case of postural hypotension, however, the dizzy spells associated with arising from bed or chair may alarm the patient and make an explanation even more important. A clear explanation with advice to move out of bed slowly and deliberately may reassure and encourage the alarmed individual.

Having dealt with the drug regimen and offered a reassuring explanation, the physician can make two other suggestions. Without responsive baroreceptors, the blood follows gravity when the subject stands up and pools in the calf venous plexus. This pooling cannot be prevented, but its volume can be reduced by the use of a strong elastic supporting garment. In some cases this may be all that is needed. Certainly it should be tried. The need is for a full-length pressure garment, not a pair of elastic stockings that reach only halfway up the thigh. The garment must be pulled on before the legs are put over the side of the bed if it is to be helpful. The final measure is to consider drugs that may help to maintain the blood pressure level or even increase it. In Case Report 8–2, ACTH proved of some value, and that or similar compounds which increase mineralocorticoid levels are theoretically potentially helpful. Before resorting to such measures it is important to review every aspect of the case to clarify any obscure factors in the situation. The empirical use of such drugs can then be assessed on a firmer basis.

CONTROL OF BODY TEMPERATURE

The ability to function in markedly different environmental temperatures depends on a delicate balancing mechanism in the hypothalamus. The present view is that the posterior hypothalamus controls what Johnson and Spalding (14) call "the set point" for temperature regulation, and this depends on "the constancy of the intrinsic ratio between sodium and calcium ions." The anterior hypothalamus is the site of central thermal sensors which provide the information on which the controlling posterior portion of the area functions.

Adjustments in temperature are made through a variety of mechanisms (Table 8–2). The efficiency of the mechanisms which are mediated through the autonomic nervous system decreases with advancing age. As a result, the very old, in common with the very young, are particularly susceptible to both hot and cold extremes of temperature. Hey (8) has shown that babies have difficulty in maintaining deep body temperature during the first days of life. This is an interesting phenomenon as it suggests that, in common with micturition and postural control, temperature control is established shortly after birth. The effectiveness of temperature control is well maintained throughout life but deteriorates in old age. This is one more indication of the significance of global cerebral failure (see Ch. 4, Brain Failure).

HYPOTHERMIA

The most common condition due to faulty heat regulation in the elderly is accidental hypothermia, which is caused by the exposure to low environmental temperatures of a subject unable to take any precautionary measures against it. There are a number of situations which may precipitate accidental hypothermia. An old person who lives alone may fall and be unable to get up or attract anyone's attention; a demented individual may wander, lost, for hours in freezing conditions; an alcoholic may collapse, drunk, by the side of the road. Accidental hypothermia is an interesting condition from an epidemiologic standpoint. While the incidence in Great Britain is appreciable, it is relatively uncommon in North America. Taylor (22) in Somerset, England, estimated that as many as 20,000–100,000 elderly people die each year from diseases associated with hypothermia.

Mills (18) points out that the condition was thought to be uncommon until about 20 years ago, but since then it has been reported on a number of occasions and has been increasingly recognized with the more widespread use of low

TABLE 8–2. Control of Body Temperature

Heat gain	Heat loss
Ingestion of food	To atmosphere
Through skin and lungs	Lack of clothing
Basal metabolism	Unavoidable loss
Exercise	Respiration
Involuntary	Skin
Shivering	Urine and feces
	Involuntary mechanism
	Skin vessels
	Sweating

(Johnson RH, Spalding JMK: Disorders of the Autonomic Nervous System. Great Britain, Blackwell Scientific Publications, 1974)

reading thermometers. In 1964 two series from London, England, involved a total of 47 subjects. Rosin and Exton–Smith (19) reported on 25 women and 7 men, 16 of whom had been seen in the previous winter, which was a very cold one in Britain, while McNicol and Smith (17) described 15 patients admitted to the Central Middlesex Hospital during the same winter.

The main reason for the appreciable number of hypothermia cases in Britain is the average household temperature. Fox and his colleagues (7) carried out an

Fig. 8–5. Change in central (ear) temperature on exposure to cold. (MacMillan AL *et al.*: Lancet II:165–169, 1967)

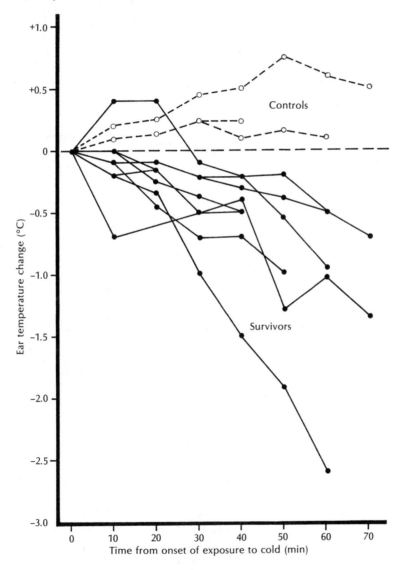

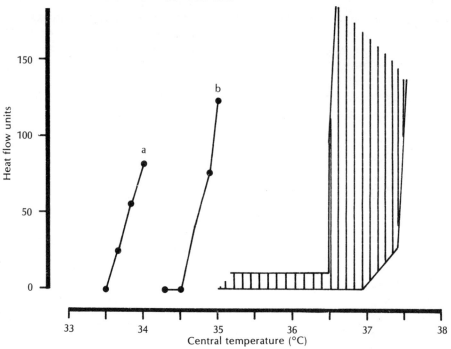

Fig. 8–6. Central (ear) temperature and heat elimination, indicated in arbitrary units by heat flow disks on the finger pulp, in two survivors (**a** and **b**) from accidental hypothermia in the elderly. The central temperature was that with which they presented for examination. When radiant heat was applied to the trunk, the survivors show brisk reflex vasodilatation, although their central temperature is well below that which normally inhibits this reflex. The shaded area indicated findings in normal subjects. (Johnson RH, Spalding JMK: Disorders of the Autonomic Nervous System. Philadelphia, Blackwell Scientific Publications, 1974, p 158)

extensive survey in 1973 and found that 75% of 1000 homes of elderly subjects were at or below 21.8°C (70°F), which was the minimum level recommended for old people by the Department of Health and Social Security. Perhaps more significant than that was the fact that more than half had room temperatures below 16°C. Most series of cases of accidental hypothermia contain a significant proportion of people who have fallen and remained on the floor, exposed to subnormal room temperatures; 10 of Rosen and Exton–Smith's cases and 27 of 40 patients described by Mills were found in this way.

MacMillan *et al.* (16) have demonstrated that liability to accidental hypothermia is not necessarily part of the aging process but is due to central temperature regulation becoming faulty. Eight survivors from a hypothermic episode quickly became cold, with markedly reduced temperatures, following exposure to cold air. Three normal control subjects submitted to the same cooling procedure reacted by a sustained rise of central temperature. All three controls shivered vigorously but only two of the eight survivors showed slight and inconstant shivering (Fig. 8–5).

Individuals who are liable to hypothermia also show an abnormal re-

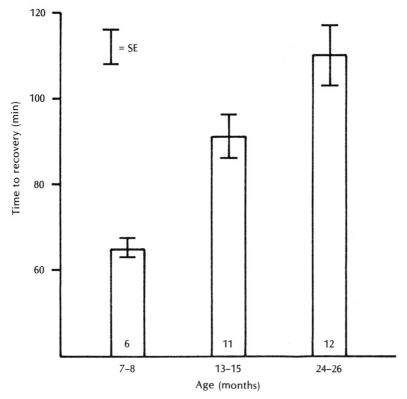

Fig. 8–7. Age related differences in recovery time of rats following 3-min whole body ice water immersion. Number of animals in each group noted in the lower part of box. (Composed from data of Segall PE, Timiras PS: Fed Proc 34:83–85, 1975. Reprinted from Federal Proceedings)

sponse to rewarming when core temperature is low. Johnson and Spalding (14) demonstrated this by comparing the effects of this process on 2 survivors from episodes of accidental hypothermia (Fig. 8–6). These two subjects showed prompt reflex vasodilatation before their central temperature, measured in the ear, had returned to normal. That behavior is in marked contrast to that of a group of normal (*i.e.,* not liable to hypothermia) elderly individuals whose mean values are illustrated in the hatched part of the diagram. The significance of the two observations is that the mechanism which normally inhibits vasodilatation and increases metabolism, while central temperature is low, has ceased to operate. That behavior is in marked contrast to that of a group of normal elderly individuals (Fig. 8–6). The significance of the two observations is that the mechanism which normally inhibits vasodilatation and increases metabolism while central temperature is low has ceased to operate.

There is experimental evidence in rats which suggests that, apart from pathologic states, aging *per se* may reduce the efficiency of temperature control. Segall and Timiras (20) studied 29 rats, who were immersed in ice water for 3 min. There were three groups, aged 7–8 months, 13–15 months, and 24–26 months, respectively (Fig. 8–7). The oldest group of rats took almost twice as long to recover as the youngest.

CASE REPORT 8–3

Mrs. Kirk, aged 72, had been widowed in the spring of 1975. The loss of her husband was a severe blow to her, and her loneliness led her to seek solace in alcohol. For 3 years she had suffered from occasional falls, and she was recieving monthly shots of vitamin B_{12} for pernicious anemia. Her only other physical complaint was of some dysuria and frequency of micturition during the winter of 1975–1976, and she continued to have nocturia (two or three times/night).

In the summer of 1976 following a bout of drinking she spent a month in the psychiatric ward at Victoria Hospital, London, Ontario. During this time she was seen by the geriatrician, who agreed to assist with follow-up supervision. Discharged home in July 1976, Mrs. Kirk came under the care of an excellent Public Health Nurse who not only visited her daily for some weeks but kept careful records of her progress.

All went well throughout August and September. When seen on September 3rd her thyroid function was checked and proved to be just within normal limits but at the hypothyroid end of the scale: $T_4 = 4.0\mu g\%$ and thyroid-stimulating hormone (TSH) 8.8 $\mu u/ml$. Mrs. Kirk was seen again in October and was well, but when brought to the clinic on December 3rd she showed marked deterioration.

She was disheveled and somewhat bloated, had gained 12 lbs, and looked myxedematous with a puffy face and croaking voice. Her temperature taken rectally did not record on a normal thermometer (*i.e.,* it was less than 35°C). Lack of a low reading thermometer prevented an accurate temperature recording, but there was no doubt that she was hypothermic. Admitted to the hospital, she warmed up to normal temperatures within 12 hours, the diagnosis of myxedema was confirmed, and she steadily improved after being treated with thyroxine. She was discharged on December 20th and, with her devoted Public Health Nurse, was still managing at home 8 months later.

A combination of loneliness, depression, alcoholism, and myxedema led to Mrs. Kirk becoming hypothermic. Both the last two conditions were mild in degree; her drinking was episodic and recurrent rather than intense and continuing; and her thyroid function was only mildly abnormal (TSH 11.6 $\mu u/ml$). She demonstrates a combination of circumstances that are not uncommon in North America.

It is important that every hospital emergency department be equipped with the low reading thermometers without which hypothermia cannot be diagnosed. Bristow (1) has pointed out that the elderly patient "complaining of a variety of nonspecific things," often confused and forgetful, may be hypothermic. He claims that low body temperatures may be as important as high ones. The association of hypothermia with drugs or alcohol ingestion or both is also noted, along with the possibility that hypothermia can sneak up on even the healthy who do not pay enough heed to the dangers of severe subzero temperatures. To date, there have not been many cases recognized in North America. To be sure that none are missed, more physicians should use low reading thermometers.

Clinical Features of Accidental Hypothermia

Hypothermia occurs when the deep body temperature is reduced to 35°C or lower. The equivalent on the Fahrenheit scale is 95°. To make accurate observations it is necessary to use a special thermometer which records temperatures from 24°C (75°F) upwards. The temperature should be taken rectally, and the thermometer should be left in the rectum for 5 min.

Rosin and Exton–Smith (19) describe the clinical features in their 32 subjects, who were between the ages of 60 and 92. Eleven subjects had temperatures 32.2°–35°C (90°–95°F). Of this group, six died in the hypothermic state: three from bronchopneumonia, one from a myocardial infarct, one from confusional state and chlorpromazine, and one from myxedema. Three other cases with bronchopneumonia died later, after recovering normal temperatures, and two recovered completely. There were 16 cases whose original temperature was 26.7°–31.7°C (80°–89°F); of this group 13 died without regaining normal temperature, and 2 other subjects died several weeks after restoration of normal temperature. The remaining one recovered. Five cases suffered from bronchopneumonia, four from cerebral hemorrhage, two from myxedema, and one each from acute confusion, pulmonary abscess, renal abscess, coronary ischemia, and dehydration. Five cases had initial temperatures below 26.7°C (80°F). Four of these died without regaining normal temperature, but one made a full recovery. Two cases suffered from acute pancreatitis with coronary thrombosis, and the other three cases suffered from transient cerebral vascular accident, bronchopneumonia, and fractured skull, respectively.

Recognizing that it is difficult to differentiate between features of accompanying disease and hypothermia, these authors suggest that consciousness becomes clouded below 32.2°C (90°F). Pallor and edema of the facial skin give the individual a myxedematous appearance; slow cerebration and a croaking voice were other features noted. The body is characteristically very cold, and placing a hand on the anterior abdominal wall under a layer of blankets to find that the area is stone cold is a clinical feature which, once experienced, is never forgotten. At temperatures below 32.2°C (90°F) there is a tendency to increased muscular rigidity with hyperreflexia in some cases, but in more than half deep reflexes become sluggish. The heart rate is reduced to 40–50/min; blood pressure is usually low. In Rosin and Exton–Smith's series, two cases developed gangrene of the toes.

Respiration is slow and sighing, but it becomes stertorous and rapid when pneumonia develops. Poor respiration leads to a variable degree of hypoxia, carbon dioxide retention, and respiratory acidosis. Because of this assisted respiration may be necessary (18). Pancreatitis is a known accompaniment and probably a result of hypothermia, and these authors were able to demonstrate its presence in two of their cases. There was, however, no abdominal pain or shock, the only positive findings being a vague tenderness in the epigastrium. A raised serum amylase was, however, found in 9 of their 11 cases.

The characteristic feature of the electrocardiograph is the presence of J waves, which occur at the junction of the QRS complex and the ST segment. T waves are usually flat or inverted, and there may be conduction defects. Hemoglobin and hematocit values may be raised during the hypothermic period but usually return to normal on rehydration. A concurrent raised BUN with oliguria and proteinuria may be slower to resolve, and it has been suggested that the kidneys may suffer damage from the low temperature.

Treatment of Hypothermia

There has been controversy over the speed at which rewarming should be undertaken. Core temperature is that of structures deep to the superficial shell through which most rewarming measures take place. Reheating the shell may result in a further drop in deep core temperature. There are, however, methods of directly heating the core by warm infusions or peritoneal dialysis. Current opinion is that patients who are severely hypothermic should be treated in intensive care units where oxygen is available and intermittent positive pressure ventilation can be used. A central venous catheter can be put in position for the measurement of pressure and the administration of warm fluid into the core. Dehydration and metabolic acidosis should be corrected as quickly as possible and a broad spectrum antibiotic given because of the danger of bronchopneumonia. Throughout there should be continuous or frequent monitoring of core temperature.

Mills (18) describes a more modest procedure which he has adopted in the absence of intensive care facilities. The mortality rate of his series was 50%, which compares favorably with other series reported in 1973. His procedure is to place the patient on a large cell ripple air mattress to prevent pressure sores, with a bed cage keeping the weight of blankets off the patient's feet. The room temperature is set at 26.7°C (80°F) which, Mills reports raises deep body temperature by 0.5°C/hour. Pulse and blood pressure are monitored, and if there is any suggestion of a drop in blood pressure, the patient is recooled by lowering room temperature and removing blankets. It may take several attempts at rewarming before the patient responds. Most of Mills' subjects recovered normal temperature within 12 hours in the hospital, and he felt that the more conservative approach produced good results in elderly patients.

Prevention of Hypothermia

Present experience suggests that hypothermia is a problem mainly in temperature climates where household heating arrangements may be inadequate. At risk groups are the elderly, those given to taking alcohol or drugs to excess, and foolhardy individuals who disregard the potential dangers of subzero temperatures. It is likely that, with the increasing age of the population, hypothermia may become more widely recognized in North America. Low reading thermometers should be available in all emergency departments so that ill elderly people arriving there may have an accurate deep core temperature recorded. In surveying at risk populations it is important to measure core temperature. This can be effectively done by measuring that of freshly voided urine (6), a technique which makes it unnecessary to place a thermometer in the rectum.

With the widespread use of central heating most of the elderly people of North America are well protected against cold conditions. Because of the possibility of power failures, however, the need for adequate alternative sources of warmth in apartment blocks for senior citizens and in every institution which cares for disabled old people cannot be overemphasized.

HYPERPYREXIA

If heat regulation is unsatisfactory in preventing hypothermia in certain old people, it is logical to anticipate that hyperpyrexia may also become a problem. Howell (12) has reported that "10 of 20 residents of a private nursing home, in Palm Beach County, Florida had a sudden onset of fever (greater than 100.6°F) in the period August 9–13, 1976. Five residents, whose temperatures ranged from 103°–106.4°F (mean 105.1°F) died." Howell described the steps which were taken to exclude other diseases and pointed out that during the period in question, when weather records indicated temperatures between 87°–90°F each day, the air conditioning system in the nursing home concerned had been shut down for repairs. In his view, the working diagnosis was heat stroke/hyperpyrexia secondary to environmental conditions.

The same year, Lyster (15) wrote that for the weeks ended July 2nd and July 9th there was a considerable increase in mortality in Greater London and the Southeast of England during a time when the temperatures were between 22.8°–23.9°C. Mortality increases when mean temperatures rise above 20°C and are lowest when they are about 17°–18°C.

Hyperpyrexia constitutes an emergency and rapid treatment is important. Active cooling with fans and wet sheets or ice, possibly assisted by sympatholytic drugs, such as chlorpromazine, should be used. The aim should be to reduce the body temperature to 37°–38.3°C (98.6°–101°F).

During the hot humid days of summer other less dramatic but equally significant problems may arise. Confusional states may be provoked by dehydration in such conditions, and it is important to remind older patients to drink an extra pint of fluid a day, or more, during hot weather. Extra salt is also valuable, particularly for those who have been warned off the condiment because of hypertension, because a significant amount of salt is lost through perspiration.

LARGE INTESTINAL FUNCTION

The colon carries out three functions: 1) storage of excreta, 2) a zone for reabsorption of water, and 3) a home for a large colony of bacteria. The latter may be important sources of vitamins of the B group, especially folic acid (11). In the normal individual the colon may be emptied once or twice daily, or as little as two or three times per week. There is no advantage in more frequent actions, but a regular habit is important (see Ch. 7, Incontinence). There is a common belief that the colon of the old person is more sluggish than that of younger people.

Brocklehurst and Khan (2) demonstrated that the intestinal transit time of radiopaque pellets in long-stay geriatric patients was increased (see Ch. 7, Incontinence). That this is an abnormal situation for elderly people was demonstrated by Eastwood (5), who examined two groups, each consisting of 10 men and 20 women aged 65–92. The control group (mean age 78) were ambulant, sensible, continent volunteers who had recently been in a geriatric hospital and whose bowel function was regarded as normal; the second group (mean age 79) were similarly ambulant, sensible, and continent but complained of having fewer than three bowel movements per week. The same method of following intestinal transit was used as in the Brocklehurst and Khan study (Fig. 8–8).

Within 5 days 80% of the pellets had been passed by the normal control group, which is what would be expected in a younger population (10). The group with delayed transit were suffering from disease. This study does not give any indication of the frequency of reduced intestinal motility in the old, which appears high to the practicing geriatrician. The association between bowel motility and homeostatic mechanisms is well illustrated by the following case.

CASE REPORT 8–4

Mrs. Ball, aged 95, had sustained a fractured femur 2 years earlier. At the time of that injury her progress had been complicated by the development of a severe degree of fecal impaction and colonic stasis. In May 1977, she had another fall which caused some bruising and local pain but no fracture. She was considerably shaken by it and 2 days later became confused and was admitted to the hospital.

X-rays revealed no further bony injury, but it was noted that the patient was very confused and dehydrated, with a distended abdomen. Because of the possibility of intestinal obstruction she was admitted.

After rehydration her confusion cleared and she was able to reveal the story of her

Fig. 8–8. Intestinal transit time of radiopaque pellets in two groups of elderly subjects, one constipated (fewer than three bowel movements per week) and the other normal. (Adapted from Eastwood HDH: Gerontol Clin [Basel] 14:154–159, 1972)

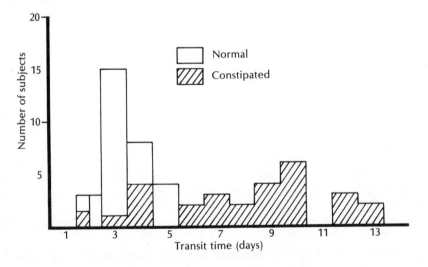

difficulties with impaction at the time of her earlier fracture. Rectal examination proved that there was no fecal mass present but her abdomen was grossly distended and was very quiet on auscultation. She was not in pain.

During the ensuing 5 days, a series of oil retention and soapsuds enemas, fecal softener, and Senokot were given at the respective ends of the alimentary canal. In spite of these little happened until the 6th day after admission. She then produced an enormous stool which required two pans for collection. Thereafter, she made a quick recovery and was able to return to the Old People's Home from which she had been admitted.

It would seem that this old lady sustained a kind of autonomic shock as a result of her fall which triggered off atony of the colon. This was an indication of a breakdown in homeostatic mechanisms.

INFLUENCE OF STRESS

"Stress is the nonspecific response of the body to any demand made upon it." Selye (21) goes on to explain that almost every activity is a stress in that it demands increased effort from the heart, lungs, brain, muscles, and glands. These may be unpleasant or pleasant but in both cases will have the same effect on body systems.

Some stresses, by stimulating the function of the suprarenal cortex, may play a role in prolonging life. Paradoxically, therefore, a certain level of stress is beneficial at a time in life when failing cerebral function is imperiling the ability of the body to react to it. Selye's (21) general adaptation syndrome concept is that, if the stress is within the capacity of the individual to contain, the stage of resistance raises the level of functioning for an indeterminate period (Fig. 8–9). Can this idea be related to practical policy for the elderly patient?

Fig. 8–9. The three phases of the general adaptation syndrome. (**a**). Alarm reaction. The body shows the changes characteristic of the first exposure to a stressor. At the same time, its resistance is diminished and, if the stressor is sufficiently strong, death may result. (**b**). Stage of resistance. Resistance ensues if continued exposure to the stressor is compatible with adaptation. (**c**). Stage of exhaustion. The signs of the alarm reaction reappear, but now they are irreversible and the individual dies. (Selye H: Stress without Distress. Scarborough, Ontario, New American Library of Canada, 1975, p 148)

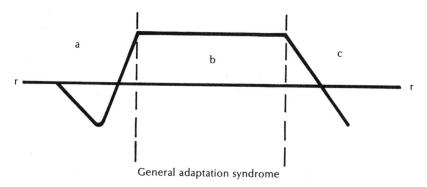

General adaptation syndrome

It is my belief that we do infinite damage to our old folk by not allowing them to struggle. There are many occasions when it is clear that shopping, weeding the yard, pruning the trees, cleaning the windows, or doing any number of chores, is difficult and challenging to the elderly householder. The function of physicians in these circumstances is to examine the task and decide whether it is difficult but possible in a reasonably safe way or impractical, with needless exposure to danger. Too often we are apt to take the easy way out and declare, "Don't you dare get up that ladder again to clean the windows!"

A succession of such remarks from the person on whose judgment the individual relies will quickly destroy initiative, effort, and the very will to live. Some stress is needed in spite of failing biologic mechanisms to cope with it. Physical exercise helps to maintain muscular strength, and thought-provoking and reality orientation programs encourage the sensorium; for the homeostatic system the elderly need regular exposure to a variety of stresses which should tax but not overwhelm them.

REFERENCES

1. Bristow G: On hypothermia. Reported in the Medical Post, May 24, 1977, Winnipeg, Manitoba
2. Brocklehurst JC, Khan MY: A study of fecal stasis in old age and the use of "dorbanex" in its prevention. Gerontol Clin II:293–301, 1969
3. Caird FI, Andrews GR, Kennedy RD: Affect of posture on blood pressure in the elderly. Br Heart J 35:527–530, 1973
4. Comfort A: Physiology, homoeostasis and ageing. Gerontology 14:224–234, 1968
5. Eastwood HDH: Bowel transit studies in the elderly. Radio-opaque markers investigation of constipation. Gerontol Clin 14:154–159, 1972
6. Fox RH, MacGibbon R, Davies L, Woodward PM: Problem of the old and the cold. Br Med J I:21–24, 1973
7. Fox RH, Woodward PM, Exton-Smith AN, Green MF, Donnison DV, Wicks MH: Body temperatures in the elderly. A national study of physiological, social and environmental conditions. Br Med J I:200–206, 1973
8. Hey EN: Thermal regulation in the new born. Br J Hosp Med 8:51–64, 1972
9. Hickler RB: Orthostatic hypotension and syncope. N Engl J Med 296:336–337, 1977
10. Hinton JM, Lennard-Jones JE, Young AC: A new method for studying gut transit times using radio-opaque markers. Gut 10:842–847, 1969
11. Horobin DF: An Introduction to Human Physiology. Lancaster, England, MTP Co Ltd, 1973, pp 7–20;142
12. Howell JT: Personal communication, 1976
13. Johnson RH, Smith AC, Spalding JMK, Wollner L: Effect of posture on blood pressure in elderly patients. Lancet I:731–733, 1965
14. Johnson RH, Spalding JMK: Disorders of the Autonomic Nervous System. Great Britain, Blackwell Scientific Publications, 1974, pp 79–152
15. Lyster WR: Death in summer. Lancet II:469, 1976
16. MacMillan AL, Corbett JL, Johnson RH, Smith AC, Spaldin JMK, Wollner L: Temperature regulation in survivors of accidental hypothermia of the elderly. Lancet II:165–169, 1967
17. McNicol MW, Smith R: Accidental hypothermia. Br Med J I:19–21, 1964
18. Mills GL: Accidental hypothermia in the elderly. Br J Hosp Med 7:691–699, 1973
19. Rosin AJ, Exton-Smith AN: Clinical features of accidental hypothermia with some observations on thyroid function. Br Med J I:16–19, 1964

20. Segall PE, Timiras PS: Age related changes in thermal regulatory capacity of triptiphan deficient rats. Fed Proc 34:83–85, 1975
21. Selye H: Stress without Distress. Toronto, McClelland and Stewart Ltd, 1974, p 148
22. Taylor G: The problem of hypothermia in the elderly. Practitioner 193:761–767, 1964
23. Thomas JE, Schirger A: Neurologic manifestations in idiopathic orthostatic hypotension. Arch Neurol 8:204–208, 1963
24. Thomas JE, Schirger A: Idiopathic orthostatic hypotension. Arch Neurol 22:289–293, 1970
25. Ziegler MG, Lake CR, Kopin IJ: The sympathetic-nervous-system defect in primary orthostatic hypotension. N Engl J Med 296:293–297, 1977

Chapter 9

IATROGENIC DISORDERS

What a drag it is getting old!

Life's just much too hard today
I hear every mother say
The pursuit of happiness
Just seems a bore
And if you take more of those
You will get an overdose

No more running for the shelter
Of her mother's little helper
They've just helped you on your way
Through your busy dying day.

M. Jagger

TOO MANY DRUGS!

In the United States in 1967 there were nearly three times as many prescriptions obtained by patients over 65 (11.4 per person) as under (4 per person) (49). In Britain, 30% of the Health Service drug bill is for the 12% of the population over 65. The pharmacist at my continuing care hospital (Parkwood Hospital) reported in October 1975 that 30 of the 186 patients in the hospital were consuming daily a total of 360 tablets, pills, or potions containing 93 different drugs (Fig. 9–1). Vitamins, hypnotics, psychotropics, diuretics, and laxatives were the five most common types of drugs, in that order. Although they are generally regarded as highly unsuitable for older patients, 10 of the 23 hynotics were barbiturates.

The reports of the Boston Collaborative Drug Surveillance Program indicate that this is characteristic of prescribing habits in North American hospitals for the chronically ill. Borda *et al.* (5) reported in 1967 that, in one such hospital in the Boston program, 644 drug orders were written in the first 10 days for 78 patients, an average of 8 per patient. The following is a list of drugs which an unfortunate 79-year-old spinster spilled onto my office desk, complaining not surprisingly, that they were doing her no good:

1. Ferrous Sulphate, 300 mg, t.i.d.
2. Danthron (Dorbane) for constipation, 75 mg, qhs

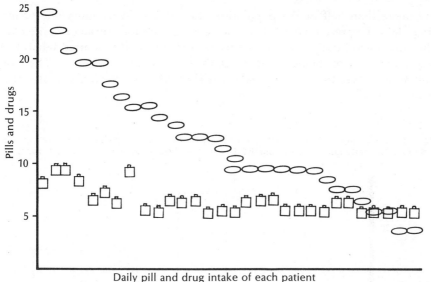

Daily pill and drug intake of each patient

Fig. 9–1. Daily drug and pill intake of 30 hospital patients. Subjects were receiving six or more medications on a regular basis. Oral = number of pills; bottle = number of drugs.

3. Spironolactone (Aldactone); 25 mg, t.i.d.
4. Furosemide, 40 mg, o.d.
5. Diazepam, 5 mg, t.i.d.
6. Digoxin, 0.25 mg, o.d.
7. Allopurinol, 100 mg, t.i.d.
8. Slow K, Tabs II, b.i.d.
9. Tetracycline, 250 mg, q6h (on last day)
10. Methyprylon (Noludar, hypnotic), 300 mg, qhs
11. Dimenhydrinate (antiemetic), 50 mg, b.i.d.
12. Oxeladin citrate for cough, (Pectamol) 20 mg, q.i.d.
13. Trimipramine, (Surmontil) 25 mg, qhs
14. Darvon N, 1, q4h
15. Nitroglycerine, as directed
16. Vitamin E, 200 units, t.i.d.

These were prescribed by no fewer than five different physicians!

Before attaching all the blame to the medical profession, however, a study by Fish and MacDonnell (15) should be considered. A stratified random sample of the Winnipeg population over the age of 65 was studied. The sample consisted of 484 residents, and each was asked about drug taking in the 3 days prior to the interview. The mean total number consumed by each individual was 3.2— and many of this group were presumably in good health! The interesting feature of this work was that almost half the drugs were self-prescribed and could not be blamed on the physician! Matthews and Feather (35) confirm this study when they report that, on the average, one drug is consumed by every Canadian every day; more than half of the population studied were consuming one or more drugs daily. Unprescribed medicines were more commonly used in a ratio of 5:4. The authors add that "Canadians surveyed in this study reported what seems excessive use of medicines, both prescribed and nonprescribed . . . The North American areas in the international study showed by far the highest rates of use of medicines."

Fig. 9–2. Drug taking of 731 residents in institutions for the elderly and chronically sick in London, Ontario. (Originally published in Cape RDT *et al.:* Can Med Assoc J 117:1284–1287, 1977)

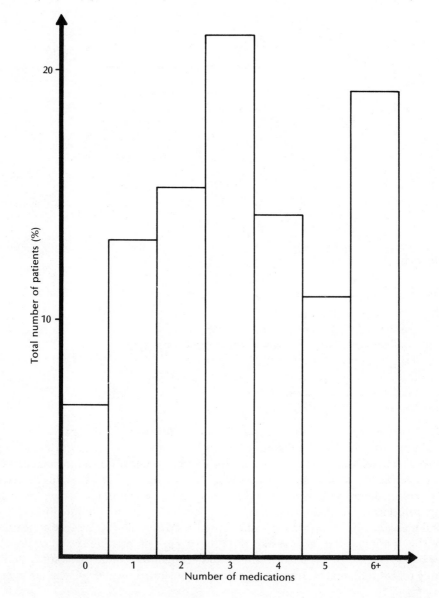

In London, Ontario (population 244,000), there are 2350 beds available in a variety of institutions for the elderly and chronically sick, mainly the former (90%). A survey of a one-in-three random sample of the occupants of these beds was carried out in 1976 (6) to study drug taking in the 731 individuals included in the study (Fig. 9–2). Two-thirds were having three or more drugs a day on a regular basis.

It is, therefore, fair to claim that polypharmacy is rife among old people in North America and probably in much of Europe and Australasia. The presence of multiple pathology leads to overprescribing and is compounded by the old person's tendency to add favorite remedies to the drug cupboard. Is this dangerous or undesirable? To answer that question, one must examine the way in which the elderly handle the drugs poured into them.

PHARMACOKINETICS IN THE ELDERLY

There have been a number of excellent reviews of pharmacokinetics in the elderly published in recent years by Bender (3), Gorrod (18), Crooks *et al.* (10), Triggs *et al.* (47), and Trounce (48). All agree on the main features (Fig. 9–3). From a practical point of view, the most important feature is the effect of the drug on the target tissues. The dose of drug given depends on the amount which is going to be available at this site. Absorption, metabolism, tissue and protein binding, and rate of excretion all affect the amount of drug which is available in the bloodstream to exert its clinical effect. The general effect of age on these various functions is to increase free drug in the bloodstream by reducing metabolism, having less protein or tissue available for binding, and slowing excretion. For all three reasons more of the active principle of the drug is available to exert its pharmacologic action. Elderly patients require less of most drugs for these to exert their optimal effect.

ABSORPTION

A few drugs are absorbed through the stomach, but most are absorbed by passive diffusion through the mucous membrane of the intestine. Rawlins (41) suggests that the speed of absorption increases greatly when the drug enters the small bowel. Food, a low gastric pH, pain, and nausea reduce gastric emptying, which delays absorption. The elderly produce less acid in their stomachs than younger people, and therefore passage through the organ is slower. Another factor of importance in the gastrointestinal tract is that old people have fewer secreting cells in the mucous membrane. As a result, the absorption of certain foods or drugs such as fat, glucose, thiamine, iron, and xylose may be reduced (3).

Most absorption takes place in the duodenum and jejunum by passive absorption, and the process is as efficient in the old as in the young. Some drugs, however, require active transport across the intestinal mucous membrane, and the assistance of catalytic agents may be needed. An example is the absorption

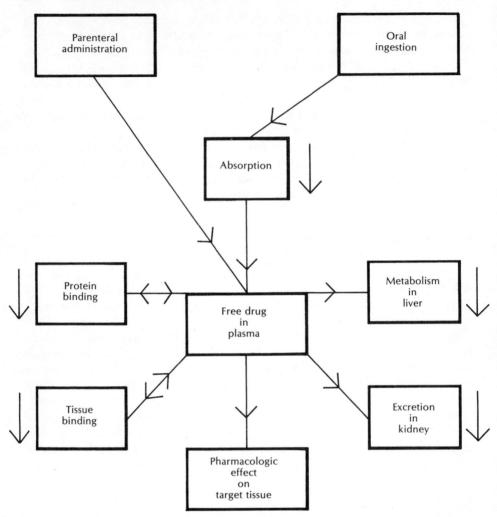

Fig. 9–3. Drug pharmacokinetics. Reduced activity of some functions in the elderly (**arrows**) affect drug dosage. (Adapted from Crooks J *et al.:* Health Bull [Edinb] 33:222–227, 1975)

of calcium, which only takes place in the presence of vitamin D in the form of its most active metabolite 1,25-dihydroxycholecalciferol (see Ch. 6, Falling).

The rate of passage through the bowel is also important. If any malabsorption is present, the rate of passage of the intestinal contents is speeded up. Another not uncommon occurrence in elderly people is the presence of one or more diverticuli in the duodenum or upper small bowel. By creating areas of stagnation, these may alter the intestinal flora which may, in turn, affect absorption. No good studies of this aspect of the aging upper alimentary tract have so far been carried out, although such diverticuli are seen quite frequently in old people. All available evidence, however, suggests that the majority of active drugs are absorbed effectively in the elderly.

After the drug reaches the bloodstream, the succeeding steps of its passage through the body varies with the individual drug (Fig. 9–3). Some are immediately metabolized in the liver, others are bound to protein or tissues, others are deposited in fatty stores, and finally some proceed straight to the kidney to begin being excreted via the urine.

METABOLISM

Drugs which are lipid-soluble compounds are metabolized by the liver. Two metabolic routes are involved: oxidation and acetylation (41). Drugs which undergo oxidation include barbiturates, tricyclic antidepressants, all anticoagulants, phenothiazines, diphenylhydantoin, phenylbutazone, warfarin, and diazepam while isoniazid, sulphonamides, and phenelzine sulfate are subject to the latter.

There appear to be some genetic differences in the rate and manner in which individuals oxidize drugs. Unfortunately the same individual may not metabolize all drugs at the same pace. It is known, however, that certain drugs stimulate the production of enzymes required for oxidation and increase the rate of oxidation of any other drug that may be given concurrently. One of the best known stimulators of drug oxidation in the liver is phenobarbital. This is important when phenobarbital and diphenylhydantoin (Dilantin) are being given jointly to epileptic patients. Oxidation may also be inhibited, for example, by coumarin anticoagulants or isoniazid. Concurrent administration of isoniazid or coumarins may reduce the required dose of diphenylhydantoin by blocking its metabolism and leaving more of it available in the bloodstream.

There is an interesting division of the population into quick or slow acetylators of drugs. This appears to be decided at conception by the genes. The individual who acetylates one drug slowly does the same for all other drugs. The adverse effects of isoniazid, hydralazine hydrochloride or phenelzine sulfate are more common among slow acetylators because of the persistence of higher plasma drug levels in such individuals. This property is unrelated to aging. Whether there is any impairment of the liver's ability to synthesize any necessary enzymes for the acetylation process with age is not yet known.

There is experimental evidence in both animals and humans that the production of enzymes necessary for oxidation in the liver is reduced in old age. Gorrod (18) reviews at some length the work of Kato and his colleagues in Japan who studied drug oxidation in female Wistar rats. The data of Kato and Takanaka quoted by Gorrod illustrate the changes in various parameters at different ages (Fig. 9–4). The implication is that the slower metabolism of aminopyrine, and hexobarbital in older rats is related to the reduced microsomal protein and cytochrome P–450 that is available.

This work has been substantiated by three studies in humans. The rate at which aminophenazone disappeared from the plasma of subjects who had taken 600 mg by mouth was higher in 8 young (25–30 years) people than in 40 old (65–85 years) people (29). Irvine *et al.* (27) demonstrated that same phenomenon when giving a single dose of 200 mg amobarbital to two

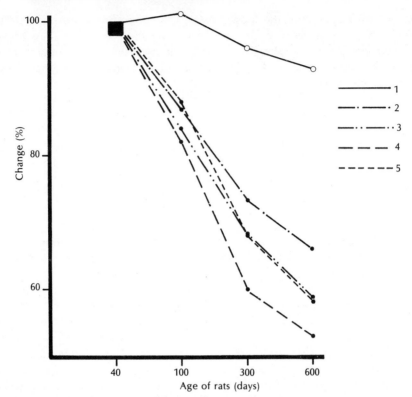

Fig. 9–4. Influence of age on 1) microsomal protein (mg/g liver), 2) liver weight (g/100g body weight), 3) cytochrome P.450 (nmol/mg), 4) aminopyrine N-demethylation (nmol/mg/30 min), 5) hexobarbital hydroxylation (nmol/mg/30 min) in female Wistar rats. (Composed from data of Gorrod JW: Gerontol Clin [Basel] 16:35, 1974)

groups of young (20–40 years) and old (over 65 years) subjects (Fig. 9–5). Earlier evidence of reduced liver metabolism due to smaller levels of enzyme production had come from geriatric patients in Dundee, Scotland. The mean plasma half-life values of antipyrine and phenylbutazone were 45% and 29% greater, respectively, in these patients than in young controls (38). Similar findings have been demonstrated for propranolol, a drug which is also metabolized by the liver (7).

PROTEIN BINDING

Some drugs in the bloodstream are in simple solution. The majority, however, are bound or attached to other constituents of the blood, such as albumin, globulin, and red cells. Most become bound to albumin and form protein–drug complexes which circulate in the blood. These linked particles affect serum levels of the substance but exert no pharmacologic action. For this reason any alteration in the extent of protein binding has considerable importance from a

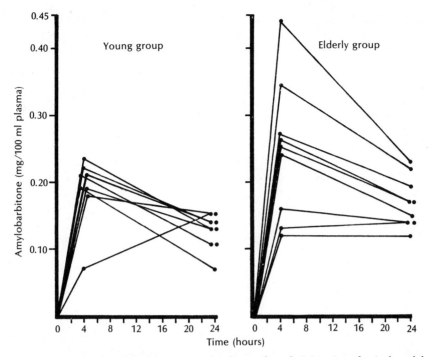

Fig. 9–5. Plasma levels of amylobarbitone at 4 and 24 hours after administration of a single oral dose of 200 mg amylobarbitone to a group of young and elderly subjects. The difference in the plasma levels at 24 hours is significant at the 5% level. (Irvine RE *et al.:* Br J Clin Pharmacol I:41–43, 1974)

therapeutic point of view. The albumin–drug complex becomes a "circulating drug reservoir that releases more drug as free drug is biotransformed or excreted (32)."

The extent of this process varies from drug to drug but many are more than 80% bound to protein. Examples include warfarin (3% free in serum), phenylbutazone (1%), salicylic acid (16%), diazoxide (9%), diazepam (1%), chlorpromazine (4%), and diphenylhydantoin (9%). Most of these drugs are used to treat elderly patients.

If a drug is extensively bound to albumin, it is protected from hepatic biotransformation. This applies to coumarin anticoagulants, phenylbutazone, and certain sulphonamides. These substances enter liver cells by a simple diffusion process or become concentrated in hepatic cells by active transport mechanisms. In the latter cases albumin binding may not prevent biotransformation. The combination of protein binding and diminished hepatic biotransformation may result in excessive prolongation of the half-life of some drugs.

To complicate the situation even further, the giving of two drugs which form complexes with protein may result in competition for binding sites. Koch–Weser and Sellers (32) describe the clinically important displacement interactions between drugs (Table 9–1). The use of anticoagulants in very old patients is hazardous under any circumstances and must be even more carefully evaluated if other drugs are used at the same time. Attention must also be drawn to the work of Hewick *et al.* (23), who found a highly significant difference between young and old subjects in the synthesis rate for clotting factors for the same plasma concentration of warfarin. They speculated that this might be due to a relative deficiency of vitamin K in old people.

One final important feature in this aspect of drug metabolism is the amount of albumin that is available for binding. Hypoalbuminemia may lead to a doubling of the amount of a drug free in the serum. Low albumin levels are common in elderly people, 3 g/100 ml being not unusual. This can lead to doubling of, for example, serum levels of diphenylhydantoin from a therapeutic to a toxic level. The main factors, therefore, in deciding dosage of drugs which bind to protein are hypoalbuminemia, hepatic or renal disease, and concomitant administration of displacing drugs. All of these factors are likely to arise in the elderly patient.

BINDING TO RED CELLS

Chan *et al.* (8) found plasma pethidine hydrochloride (meperidine hydrochloride) levels were higher in an old group of subjects (over 70) than in a young group (under 30). Each was given 1.5 mg/kg body wt of meperidine hydrochloride intramuscularly. Red cell binding of meperidine hydrochloride by the young group was much greater than by the old. If the difference in drug binding applied to other tissues, the authors felt that this would explain the high serum levels in the old and the resulting increased incidence of side-effects. These include hypotension, nausea, and confusion, but the frequency and severity of such reactions is often difficult to determine in clinical practice because the drug is given only to patients who are already ill. Chan and his colleagues examined the rate of protein binding but found that there was no significant difference with this drug between young and old. There is no doubt, in the author's

TABLE 9–1. Clinically Important Displacement Interactions between Drugs

Displaced drug	Displacing drug	Possible clinical consequences
Warfarin and other highly albumin-bound coumarins	Clofibrate Ethacrynic acid Mefenamic acid Nalidixic acid Oxyphenbutazone Phenylbutazone Trichloroacetic acid (metabolite of chloral hydrate)	Excessive hypoprothrombinemia Hemorrhages
Tolbutamide	Phenylbutazone Salicylates Sulfaphenazole	Hypoglycemia

(Koch-Weser J, Sellers EM: N Engl J Med 294: 311–316, 426–531, 1976)

experience, that meperidine hydrochloride (Demerol) is poorly tolerated by elderly patients. The reason for this lies in the increased quantity of free drug circulating because of its inability to bind with the old person's red cells.

RENAL EXCRETION

Renal function deteriorates between the ages of 30 and 90 (see Ch. 2, Physical Aspects of Aging). In individuals with no renal or hypertensive disease the glomerular filtration rate is reduced to 50–70 ml/hour by age 90. Drugs which are mainly eliminated by excretion through the kidneys therefore have a longer half-life in old people. Such drugs include digoxin (14), penicillin (21), sulfamethizole (47), methotrexate (33) and practolol (7). Some of these drugs are excreted partly by filtration through the glomeruli and partly by active secretion by the tubules. For this reason it is seldom possible to correlate creatinine clearance levels with the probable excretion rates of the drugs. In elderly people one has also to watch for associated renal disease. Not only kidney disease but dehydration, congestive heart failure, pneumonia, or urinary tract infections may all reduce elimination by this organ and prolong the half-lives of drugs excreted by this route.

Drugs which are excreted through the kidneys and are highly protein-bound are excreted very slowly. This slowness is aggravated if renal function is poor. Thus the deteriorating glomerular filtration rate of the older person results in very slow elimination of protein-bound drugs. This increases the half-life to a considerable extent. An example is diazoxide, which is 91% bound to serum albumin and eliminated by renal excretion. If the rate of renal filtration is reduced by one-half, the process becomes extremely slow and has an obvious effect on drug dosage.

Drugs which are eliminated by the renal tubules are not affected in this way. Active tubular secretion decreases the serum concentration of free drug, which is quickly replaced because there is a constant equilibrium between bound drug and free drug. As a result, as soon as free drug is excreted, a fresh supply is released from the protein-bound fraction. Certain penicillins are 90% or more bound to serum albumin but are excreted through the renal tubules. At each passage through the kidneys most of the free drug is removed, and thus elimination proceeds at a normal pace.

SIGNIFICANCE FOR THERAPEUTICS

Dosage schedules for elderly patients should be carefully assessed. In the majority a smaller dose than that given a younger patient will prove adequate. In addition, if the half-life of a drug is greatly increased, it may be possible to give it less frequently. For example, varying degrees of renal failure alter the appropriate dosage interval for antibiotics (Table 9–2) (4). The practical implications of alteration of pharmacokinetics in the elderly are therefore very considerable, all the more so because the elderly receive a great many drugs.

TABLE 9-2. Adjustment of Drug Dosage for Failing Renal Function

Drug	Glomerular filtration rate (ml/min) >50	10–50 Intervals between doses	<10 (hours)
Amoxicillin	8	12	16
Ampicillin	6	9	12–15
Tetracycline	9–12	12–24	Avoid use
Cloxacillin	6	6	6
Acetaminophen	4–6	6	8
Acetylsalicylic acid	4	4–6	Avoid use
Kanamycin	24	24–92	72–96
Procainamide	4	6–12	8–24
Allopurinol	8	8–12	12–24
Gentamicin	8–12	12–24	24–48
Cephalexin	6	6	6–12
Lincomycin	6	12	24

(Bennet WM, Singer I, Golper T et al.: Ann Intern Med 86: 754–783, 1977)

While the body's ability to metabolize, bind, or excrete drugs is being reduced by age, other relevant changes are occurring in the body (see Ch. 2, Physical Aspects of Aging). Lean body mass of muscle, liver, and brain is reduced (Figs. 2–2, 2–3, 2–4), and fat is increased. Ruedy (43) emphasizes how these changes affect dosage levels in the old. He also describes how, because of falling cardiac output (Fig. 2–5), which at age 80 is 58% of what it was at age 20, an intravenous bolus may achieve a much higher blood concentration in the old person. He cites lidocaine as an example; if 100 mgm is given intravenously to a 25-year-old, the approximate peak serum level will be 14.9 mg/ml; in an 80-year-old it will be 25 mg/ml. The cardiac output of the former would be 6.7 liters/min, which would have fallen to 3.9 liters/min by age 80.

ADVERSE REACTIONS TO DRUGS

Accidental overdosage or intentional attempts at suicide are not common in the elderly. Petersen and Thomas (40) report on acute drug reactions arriving in the emergency department of the Jackson Memorial Hospital in Miami, Florida during 1972. There were 1128 cases admitted and, of those, 60 (5.4%) were aged 50 or over, with a mean age of 59. The most frequently misused drugs were diazepam, Tuinal (sodium secobarbital and sodium amobarbital), phenobarbital, and propoxyphene. Nine of ten cases involved these tranquilizers, sedatives, or analgesics.

More common but more difficult to recognize are the many adverse drug reactions which occur in response to what are intended to be therapeutic doses. It is difficult to know how many such reactions occur in domiciliary care. There are now, however, a number of excellent studies giving details of adverse reactions to drugs which have occurred in hospitals. The Boston Collaborative Drug Surveillance Program has been one of the largest and most comprehensive

TABLE 9–3. Age Distribution of Patients with an Adverse Drug Reaction

Category	No. patients in category	No. patients with adverse reaction	% patients with adverse reactions among all patients in category
0–35	1875	381	20.32
36–45	1578	400	25.4
46–55	2292	621	27.1
56–65	2384	759	31.8
66–75	2016	661	32.8
76–85	1163	353	30.4
86–	218	65	29.8

(Adapted from Miller RR: Pharmaceutisch Weekblad 109: 461–481, 1974)

TABLE 9–4. Age and Adverse Reactions

Age of patients (years)	Number of given drugs	Number with reactions	Rate (%)
<60	667	42	6.3
60–69	252	27	10.7
70–79	178	38	21.3
80–89	59	11	18.6
90–99	4	0	0

(Adapted from Hurwitz N, Wade OL: Br Med J I: 531–536, 1969)

TABLE 9–5. Number of Drugs Taken by Patients with Adverse Reactions

	Number of patients given drugs	1–5 drugs		6+ drugs	
		No.	%	No.	%
No reactions	1042	654	62.8	388	37.2
Reactions	118	22	18.6	96	81.4

(Hurwitz N: Br Med J I: 536–539, 1969)

efforts to monitor drug prescribing ever undertaken. Miller (36) has given details of the age distribution of patients with adverse reactions (Table 9–3). It shows that the peak incidence in this large study of 11,526 patients came in the age group 66–75 when almost 33% of patients suffered such a reaction.

These findings were greater than those reported from Belfast, Northern Ireland, in 1969 (26). Hurwitz and Wade studied 1160 patients who received a total of over 6000 drugs while in hospitals; the overall incidence of drug reactions was 10.2%; but this became 21.3% for patients over the age of 70 (Table 9–4). One is likely, therefore, to encounter an adverse reaction to a drug in every third or fourth case in people of this age.

Hurwitz (25) in seeking predisposing factors, examined the total number of drugs which were being given to the adversely affected patients. Her results indicate that those who received six or more drugs had a much greater chance of developing adverse reactions than those who had fewer (Table 9–5). The majority of reactions were related to the gastrointestinal tract, nausea and vomiting being at the head of the list (26). The second most common type were neuromuscular disturbances, ranging from disorientation and excessive wakefulness to tremulousness, muscular twitching, epilepsy, myopathy and parkinsonism.

The severity of the adverse effect varies. Of Miller's cases (36) 50% were mild, but 10.5% were classified as major. No indication of the age of the subjects with severe reactions is given, but 1.2% of the total series died from their adverse reaction. In the Belfast study only 4 of 129 reactions were classified as severe, but it should be noted that the ages of the 4 were 61, 65, 68, and 75 (26). There were no deaths.

It is important to maintain a reasonable perspective in considering this problem. There are more potent drugs available than ever before, and much benefit can be derived from them. Potency means, however, toxicity. If there is to be an incidence of adverse reactions of 30% in our elderly patients, 1% of whom will die as a result, therapeutic enthusiasm must clearly be tempered with caution.

COMPLIANCE OF PATIENTS IN TAKING MEDICATION

It is easy to write a prescription with meticulous directions and hand it to a patient. It does not follow that the patient will obey the instructions given or even interpret them correctly. This is especially true with old people in whom forgetfulness and poor vision are problems.

In the United Kingdom geriatricians frequently visit patients in their own homes when they have first been referred to their department. In Glasgow, between August 1966 and August 1967, Gibson and O'Hare (17) made 273 such visits and studied compliance of these patients in taking the drugs which had been prescribed for them. These patients were taking 692 drugs. The general practitioner concerned had prescribed 640 of them; only 31 were self-prescribed. The remaining 21 were old medicines that had been in the house for some time. This is in marked contrast to the experience of Fish and MacDonnell (15) in Winnipeg (see Too Many Drugs!). Another notable difference was in the number of medications being consumed by each individual. Only 15 of the 273 were taking six or more (Fig. 9–6, see Fig. 9–2).

Gibson and O'Hare divided their patients into two groups; safe and unsafe. Those who were in the first group were taking not more than three drugs daily and had good supervision from relatives, neighbors, or friends. In this group of 188 cases, 19 (11%) were not taking their drugs as the physician had ordered and believed they were being taken. In the group of 85 subjects classed as unsafe because they had inadequate supervision and because they were taking four or more drugs the number not taking these as they were ordered was 36 (42%).

There is no certain way of insuring that a forgetful old person faithfully takes tablets exactly as they are prescribed. One can, however, reduce the chance of serious errors in four ways:

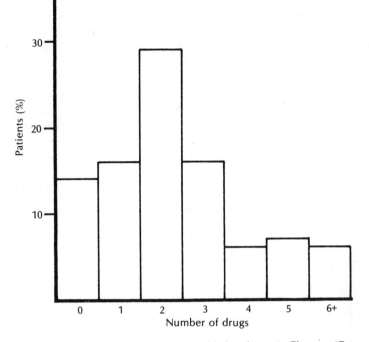

Fig. 9–6. Number of medications being taken by 273 elderly subjects in Glasgow. (Composed from data of Gibson IJM, O'Hare MM: Gerontol Clin 10:272, 1968)

1. Use as few drugs as possible.
2. Give one dose each day unless it is imperative to use a divided dose schedule.
3. Have instructions clearly printed in large letters on the bottle.
4. Find a relative, neighbor, friend, or public health nurse to take on the task of supervising the medication.

THERAPEUTICS IN GERIATRIC MEDICINE

CARDIOVASCULAR DRUGS

Cardiovascular disease predominates in old age, and its treatment demands the use of a number of drugs, often in combination.

Digitalis

One of the first studies of adverse drug reactions during hospitalization was carried out in Montreal (37). Of 731 patients admitted to one ward of the

Montreal General Hospital during the year from July 1, 1965 to June 30, 1966 18% suffered from such reactions. One of the most significant parts of this work was an appendix reporting the case histories of 12 persons who died as a result of digitalis intoxication. There were a total of 41 adverse reactions to the drug, all but 6 classed as of moderate or major severity. The mean age of persons with moderate reactions was 64.5; with major, life-threatening reactions, 66.7; and with fatal reactions, 68.1. Those who had minor reactions had a mean age of 51.1.

Two years later the Boston Comprehensive Drug Surveillance program (45) reported on 441 subjects who were given digoxin, and there was an incidence of 17% with side-effects. Of these, 16 (3.7% of the total sample) developed a major reaction, but no deaths were attributed to the drug. There was no signifi-

Fig. 9–7. Concentration of digoxin in μg/liter blood/70 kg body wt at intervals after the injection of tritiated digoxin. P values were less than 0.1 during the first 24 hours, but less than 0.01 thereafter. (Ewy GH *et al.*: Circulation 39:449–453, 1969. Used with permission of the American Heart Association, Inc.)

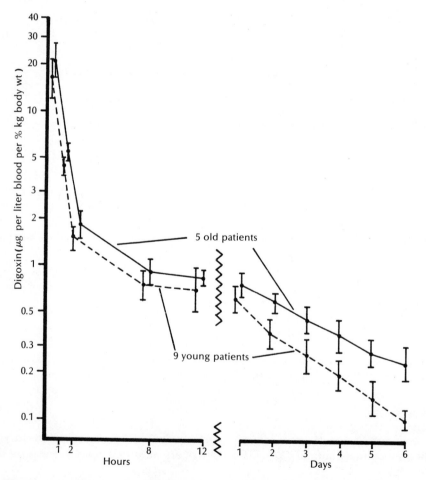

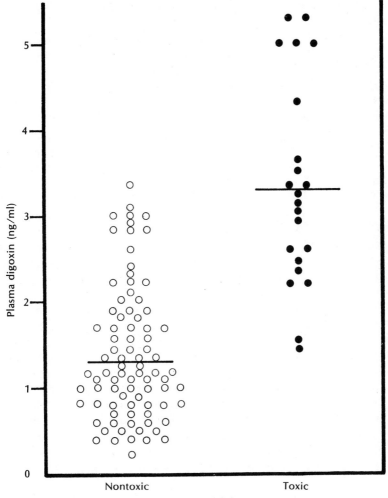

Fig. 9–8. Plasma digoxin concentrations in subjects with and without toxicity. Mean values represented by horizontal bars. (Evered DC, Chapman C: Br Heart J 33:540–545, 1971)

cant difference between the mean age of those who had or did not have a reaction. Since then, a considerable literature has built up on digoxin metabolism in the elderly and the incidence and reasons for intoxication by the drug. After a single intravenous dose, concentrations of digoxin and its metabolites were measured in a group of five elderly and nine younger subjects. Measurements of serum levels were taken daily for 8 days (Fig. 9–7). Ewy et al. (14) showed that the mean half-life of digoxin was 73 hours in the elderly and 51 hours in normal younger people. Creatinine clearance was reduced by one-half in the old group and digoxin clearance by more than one-third. Ewy and his coworkers maintained that the same dose of the drug given to young and old individuals could result in twice the effect in the older group because of the alteration of renal excretion.

Two years later Evered and Chapman (13) reported on routine oral maintenance digoxin therapy in 108 subjects. Twenty-two of those were found to have evidence of digoxin toxicity. The range of digoxin plasma concentration was 1.38 ± 0.77 ng/ml in the whole group, but those with evidence of toxicity had significantly higher levels (3.36 ± 1.2 ng/ml). There was, however, some overlap between the groups (Fig. 9–8). Evidence of digoxin toxicity in the 22 subjects included ventricular premature contractions (8); nausea, anorexia, and vomiting (7); first degree heart block (7); second degree heart block (1); nodal ectopic beats (1); and paroxysmal atrial tachycardia with block (1). The authors point out that "the most striking difference between toxic and nontoxic subjects studied is in respect to the age of the two groups." They consider that this is independent of diminished renal function and suggest that tolerance to cardiac glycosides is reduced with age. They do agree that a greater proportion of the subjects with toxic symptoms had high blood urea than of those with no toxic symptoms. There was no significant difference in plasma potassium concentrations between the two groups, although an association between hypokalemia and digitalis-induced arrhythmias has been emphasized.

Baylis *et al.* (1) confirmed that there is a reduced creatinine clearance in old people when they examined a group of 31 elderly patients who were adequately digitalized and free from toxic symptoms in a domiciliary practice. They found only four in whom plasma digoxin levels were above 2 ng/ml; none were hypokalemic and few showed any electrolyte disturbance. Plasma specimens for the estimations were taken at varying times after administration of the drug, while the individual was fasting. There was a poor correlation between plasma urea concentrations and those of digoxin and no linear relationship between digoxin and creatinine clearances. In spite of this, the latter indicated whether renal function was poor or not, which was useful in deciding a dosage schedule. The authors found the investigation helpful and practicable, even in a scattered rural general practice.

More recently Roberts and Caird (42) have taken this idea one stage further in studying "steady-state kinetics" of digoxin in the elderly. They determined the renal and biliary clearances of the drug and assessed the agreement of measured and predicted serum concentrations. The predictions were based on elaborate equations which used clearance data. The authors concluded that when the renal clearance of digoxin is 50 ml/min or greater there is little need to take into consideration hepatic function. Below that level biliary clearance assumes greater importance. They also emphasize the fact that any reduction in the glomerular filtration rate, whether it results from renal disease or other factors such as dehydration, myocardial or pulmonary infarction, or hypotensive therapy, may result in accumulation of digoxin in the blood and therefore in toxic effects.

Certain general principles, therefore, regarding the use of digoxin in elderly subjects can be stated on the basis of these and other studies. The drug should never be used unless there is a good indication for it, such as congestive heart failure or arrhythmias. With the first, there is little room for argument. After the congestive heart failure has cleared, however, it may not be necessary to continue digoxin administration although this is frequently done. One cardinal rule of geriatric therapeutics is that drug treatment should be constantly monitored, and if there is any evidence that a drug may no longer be necessary, its use should be discontinued. A second rule, of particular relevance to digitalis, is that the efficiency of renal function must be considered in deciding dosage. This is particularly important in arranging maintenance therapy. The individual who is dehydrated when admitted to the hospital for the first time is more sensitive to the effects of digoxin, and care must be taken with loading doses. The ease of obtaining serum digoxin levels makes avoiding toxic states much less difficult than in the past. Even with this information, however, it is possible to run into trouble.

CASE REPORT 9–1

Mrs. Ellis, aged 74, was admitted to the hospital on September 22, 1975, suffering from extreme lethargy. She had heavy drooping eyelids, shortness of breath, bilateral pleural effusions, and weakness of her legs. She had a left bundle branch block and was in sinus rhythm (see Case Report 10–1).

Fig. 9–9. Case Report 9–1. Four short episodes in the history of a 74-year-old female with chronic renal failure who illustrates difficulty of maintaining appropriate digoxin level.

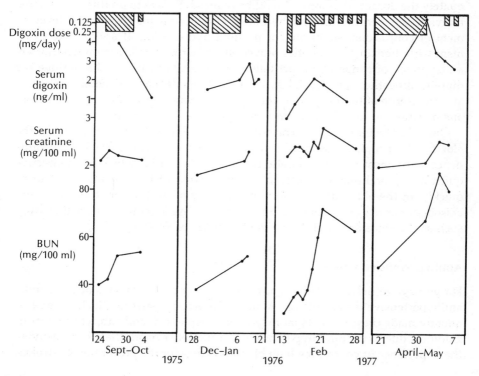

Serum digoxin proved to be 3.7 ng/ml and the drug was discontinued on September 29th. By October 3rd the level had fallen to 1.2 ng/ml. indicating the difficulties of maintaining a stable digoxin level in a patient with chronic renal failure (creatinine clearance 33 ml/min) (Fig. 9–9). The drug was later reintroduced with a lower dose but in May 1977, through an oversight, her dose was doubled with immediate increase in the serum level followed by slow return to normal. On this occasion she had marked anorexia, nausea, and vomiting and became obtunded. It took almost a week for the digoxin level to return to normal.

Extreme weariness and lethargy can be a reaction to digoxin toxicity, in addition to the common features of gastric upset or arrhythmias.

Diuretics

Diuretics are also used in the treatment of cardiovascular disease. Elderly patients respond to these drugs as well as people in younger age groups; there is no evidence to suggest that the quantity required to treat congestive heart failure is altered by age. Congestive cardiac failure is a condition which is cleared by treatment, but preventing recurrence is a matter of concern. It is widely accepted that, because diuretics are necessary for the treatment of heart failure, they form an essential part of maintenance therapy. In elderly patients, this may not be true. Some old patients may have problems if they continue such therapy on a maintenance basis, and the need for it should be constantly reassessed.

Once edema has cleared and the cardiovascular system is functioning adequately the dosage of diuretic should be reduced. Failure to do this causes some individuals to become mildly dehydrated. This, in turn, may lead to the development of confusional states and/or postural hypotension. If appropriate treatment with digoxin and diuretics proves effective for the old person who suffers a first attack of congestive heart failure, it may be possible to discontinue the diuretic altogether. The feasibility of such a step depends on whether there is any recurrence of failure. The features of overdosage with diuretics are lethargy and dizziness on standing, at times accompanied by confusion.

One other factor should be considered in deciding on diuretic therapy for the elderly. Old people are susceptible to incontinence of urine (see Ch. 7, Incontinence). The most favored diuretic is furosemide (Lasix) which is an effective quick-acting oral one. It results in the production of large quantities of urine quickly. In the old individual with precipitancy of micturition, this may cause episodes of urinary incontinence. For this reason use of more slowly acting drugs such as the thiazides or chlorthalidone may be preferable.

Antihypertensive Drugs

For years geriatricians in Britain have been aware of the dangers of prescribing antihypertensive drugs such as Aldomet to elderly patients. Such drugs frequently made these patients more lethargic, depressed, and subject to bouts of giddiness due to postural hypotension. On the other hand, there is no denying the importance of controlling high blood pressure for the prevention of strokes.

Recent work from Victoria Hospital in London, Ontario (46) suggests that one main reason for the difficulties of antihypertensive treatment in the elderly lies in obtaining accurate measurements of blood pressure levels (see Ch. 2, Physical Aspects of Aging). An understanding of the problem and a cautious approach to therapy are the only guidelines available at this time. Further work on this important topic is needed to resolve its present complexities. It is tempting to compromise by using a diuretic but the danger of dehydration, particularly in hot weather, has to be remembered.

To manage disease of the elderly cardiovascular system requires, therefore, not only clinical skill and knowledge but an awareness of the possible toxic effects of the available drugs. Constant monitoring of the situation to prevent overdosage and adverse reactions is essential. Iatrogenic effects are easy to cure by discontinuing the culpable drug, but they must first be recognized.

PSYCHOTROPIC DRUGS

Drugs which are designed to tranquilize, hypnotize, or stimulate the brain of old patients are frequently prescribed. They offer useful therapy in many situations, but at times they constitute pharmaceutic restraints which are the equivalent of physical ones (see Ch. 5, Confusion). To make the best use of these drugs demands understanding of their action and the circumstances in which each is likely to be effective.

Unfortunately, psychotropic drugs are used frequently without adequate thought. Learoyd (34) describes how 37 (16%) of 236 patients who were taking psychotropic drugs were admitted to a psychogeriatric unit in New South Wales because they were suffering from adverse reactions to the drugs. These consisted of simple drug intoxication with lethargy, confusion and disorientation, secondary effects such as postural hypotension, and disinhibition reactions such as restlessness, agitation, paranoia, and aggression. The diagnosis was made when the clinical features abated after the drugs were discontinued. The author of this straightforward practical account points out how deterioration of the patient's condition frequently was associated with an increase in the dosage or variety of drugs given. The mean number consumed by the 37 patients was 2.7 per person.

In a different setting, one long-term psychiatric hospital in Britain was able to decrease or stop psychotropic drugs successfully in 71% of a group of long-stay patients (16). These had been in the hospital for at least a year; in most cases, for 5–15 years. Of 200 randomly selected patients, 148 were receiving psychotropic drugs, and of these 117 were judged to need adjustment of their dose. The dosage was increased for 7 patients and decreased or stopped for 110. These patients were not all elderly, no indication of age being given. It is, however, likely that the majority were over 65.

Phenothiazines

First introduced in 1952, phenothiazines have maintained their position as antipsychotic agents and major tranquilizers. When first administered they have a sedative effect. For the grossly disturbed psychotic individual they are used frequently in large dosage in psychiatric institutions. For the elderly patient who is belligerent, awkward, or difficult they can be most useful. They may justifiably be used to buy a little time during which the reasons for acute confusional states or behavioral disturbances can be found. As with all drugs, however, one should be clear about the object of the treatment.

Like all potent drugs, phenothiazines do have side-effects which can be difficult to avoid and may be difficult to cure. Chlorpromazine was the first to be introduced 25 years ago, and it remains one of the most effective. It may produce jaundice due to a cholestatic process, or it may cause extrapyramidal signs which can be difficult to manage, such as a parkinsonian syndrome, dystonia or dyskinesia with facial grimacing, and akathisia in which the individual becomes unable to sit still and has a strong urge to move about (28). Tardive dyskinesia has been well described (31) as consisting of

involuntary and repetitive movements that especially affect the orofacial structures . . . . . . Characteristically, these movements include tongue protrusion, with licking of the lips, smacking and sucking lip movements, chewing and jaw deviations, facial grimacing, grunting and other peculiar sounds, furrowing of the forehead and eye-blinking.

There are other less frequent side-effects such as an abnormal reaction to sunlight. All the phenothiazines can produce postural hypotension, a significant reduction in temperature, some sedation, and anticholinergic effects which may cause constipation.

The phenothiazines which were developed from the antihistamine promethazine hydrochloride are readily absorbed and quickly metabolized in the liver. In most instances this is a two-stage sequence of hydroxylation (oxidation) and later conjugation with glucuronic acid. Jarvik (28) states that 168 possible metabolites of chlorpromazine have been claimed and that there are probably other metabolic routes taken by the different members of the group. The metabolites are excreted in both urine and feces, but traces of them may still be present in the body 6–18 months later.

CASE REPORT 9–2

Mrs. Fairly aged 70, was admitted to the continuing care hospital for assessment in March 1977, with a history of falling and seizures. She was an arteriopath with bilateral carotid bruits. On March 15th she returned home on weekend leave, had a seizure, broke her tibia and fibula, and was admitted to the hospital for orthopedic attention. She returned to the continuing care hospital within 2–3 days.

Mrs. Fairly was a heavily built woman who was prone to complain, but she patiently accepted the need for prolonged rest. Her leg was encased from metatarsophalangeal joints to the junction of middle and upper thirds of her thigh with 20° flexion at the knee. She was thus faced with spending 10 weeks in bed or in a chair with very limited mobility.

All went well until almost the end of the 10 weeks. Then, quite suddenly, she went absolutely berserk and announced that she was not going to stay in the hospital a day longer, a statement which she shrieked out repeatedly, disturbing the whole ward. After seeing her and talking to her on two or three occasions, during which time she continued to shout, the geriatrician decided to give her 50 mg chlorpromazine intramuscularly. On this she calmed down a little, but required a further 25 mg by the same route 2 hours later before she settled down and slept during the night. She was back to her normal self the next morning. No further phenothiazine was required or was given.

This is an illustration of one way in which antipsychotic drugs may be used. Another situation, in which nursing staff or relatives may appeal for help, arises in caring for demented individuals with behavioral disorders. These range from a mild wanderlust, resulting in visits to other people's rooms and lockers, to rising from bed at night and causing a disturbance. In either a hospital or a domestic environment, these activities cause considerable emotional upsets. In these situations an excellent drug is thioridazine hydrochloride, a phenothiazine which is best given in a single dose each night. Given at bedtime with a warm drink, 50 mg initially has sedative as well as antipsychotic effects and may well make specific hypnotics unnecessary. It now seems likely that there is no need for multiple doses of phenothiazines and that a regular nocturnal dose or at most a 12-hour regimen is the most effective method of using them. It should be stressed, however, that the object is to attain a steady level of the drug in the body which will help the individual to maintain a more rational attitude toward what is going on around them.

Haloperidol has actions which are very similar to those of the piperazine phenothiazines such as trifluoperazine hydrochloride or perphenazine, but this drug is a butyrophenone. A potent antipsychotic, it commonly causes parkinsonian features to develop and has to be used with caution in the elderly.

Benzodiazepines

Among the most commonly prescribed drugs in the world today is diazepam, which is the prototype benzodiazepine. It is probably the most commonly used drug in the Western World (19). Classed pharmacologically as a tranquilizer, its potency falls between that of chlorpromazine and meprobamate. One pharmacologic attribute of diazepam is important for the older patient. Klotz *et al.* (30) demonstrated that the half-life of diazepam in the body increased from 20 hours at age 20 to 90 hours at age 80. They studied 33 normal individuals aged 15–82 who were given either an intravenous bolus of 0.1 mg/kg or an oral dose of 10 mg diazepam (Fig. 9–10).

Benzodiazepines have a well-recognized potential for accumulation apart from this striking age effect (19). Thus clinical effects not obvious after 1 or 2 days of treatment may develop after 5–10 days; the corollary is that after the drug is discontinued there may be persisting action for a further 5–10 days. The fact that 99% of diazepam is bound to albumin (32) may account for the slow biotransformation and long half-life. An equilibrium between the drug and the body takes a few days to establish but thereafter is reasonably maintained.

The other members of the group, which are chlordiazepoxide (Librium), ox-

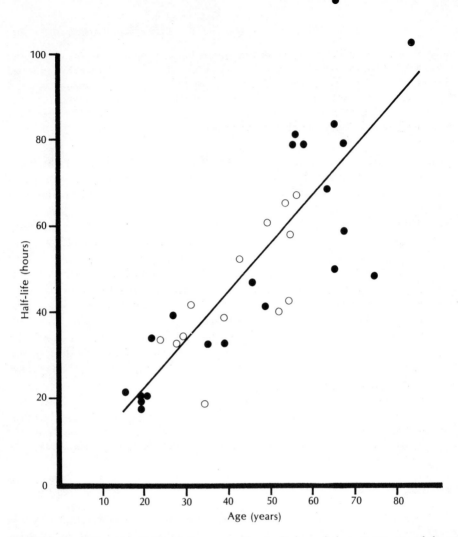

Fig. 9–10. Correlation of half-life of diazepam with age. Each symbol represents one of the 33 normal individuals •. nonsmokers. ○ smokers (more than 20 cigarettes/day). (Klotz V *et al.:* J Clin Invest 55:347–359, 1975)

azepam, flurazepam hydrochloride, nitrazepam, and clorazepate dipotassium, all have similar properties to diazepam. Oxazepam is excreted more quickly than the others, and its half-life in healthy subjects ranges 3–21 hours, which is appreciably less than its colleagues.

The adverse effects of benzodiazepines include fatigue, drowsiness, muscle weakness, confusion, nystagmus, ataxia, and dysarthria. The first are relatively common, and because they are prominent features of illness in the elderly, it is difficult to decide whether they are attributable to disease or to the drug. As a consequence of increased lethargy, patients may not eat or drink as much as they otherwise would, and mild states of dehydration may develop to increase the weakening effect of the drug. This effect may be enhanced by the property of benzodiazepines which causes muscle relaxation. Another adverse effect which has been reported is the occurrence of nightmares with self-destructive features (20, 44).

CASE REPORT 9–3

Mr. Andrews, aged 72, suffered from a severe degree of parkinsonism which was controlled by levodopa plus carbidopa. During one spell in a continuing care hospital, he was making excellent progress but became extremely depressed by the recurrence of a vivid dream which ended with his being "chopped up" by enemies. At this time he was taking 5 mg diazepam (Valium) each night. When the Valium was discontinued and replaced by thioridazine hydrochloride, 50 mg, these nightmares disappeared completely and did not recur.

Benzodiazepines are frequently used to treat elderly patients. They have a reputation for safety because they seldom threaten life. On the other hand, pharmacologists have pointed out that they should be "used with caution in elderly patients who may become confused [28]." Central nervous system manifestations such as drowsiness, somnolence, and muscle weakness are "more likely to occur in elderly persons [19]." If the drugs offered significant benefits over others which claim to achieve the same effect, a case could be made for benzodiazepines in geriatric medicine. No one has made such a case, and in the author's view, benzodiazepines should seldom be used for the elderly because of their debilitating effects.

If a benzodiazepine is used in spite of the possibility of adverse reactions, there is little doubt that oxazepam is the one preferred. There is good evidence (19) that the half-life of this drug is less than the others. It is itself a metabolite of diazepam and is rapidly glucuronidated to achieve its biotransformation in the liver.

ANTIDEPRESSANTS

Depressive states commonly occur in elderly patients. Many of these are a reaction to the restricting nature of disability at this time of life; others are precipitated by bereavement. Helpful advice and discussion of problems must always be the first concern of the physician who encounters such situations, but occasionally support by appropriate drug treatment may be necessary.

The monoamine inhibitors should be discarded completely. The potential for a disastrous reaction is great with such drugs because of the known unreliability of the old person's drug-taking compliance and the well-documented fact that a great many old people are consuming a great many drugs. The author believes there is no place for them in the pharmacopeia for the elderly.

Tricyclic antidepressants have, on the other hand, a useful role to play in geriatric medicine. Developed and introduced in 1958, imipramine hydrochloride was the first in the field but was followed quickly by amitriptyline hydrochloride. The former drug has little if any calming capability, while the latter does have a modest sedation effect. In other respects they and their analogs have similar actions. The most common adverse effects in old people are anticholinergic, postural hypotensive, and cardiac rhythm upsets. Dry mouth, constipation, dizziness, tachycardia, palpitations, blurred vision, and urinary retention may all occur (28). To counter these giving the daily dose as an evening medication has been widely advocated. This has proved satisfactory in most cases in the author's experience and avoids the worst of the side-effects. Beware, however, of the old man with an enlarging prostate who may develop urinary retention or the old lady who is used to rising to pass urine at least once each night and falls because of a postural drop in blood pressure.

Particular care has to be exercised with patients who may already be taking digoxin or another antiarrhythmic drug because of arteriosclerotic heart disease with unstable rhythms. For them it is wise to avoid the tricyclics altogether.

SEDATIVES

There is a widely held belief that old people sleep badly. De Beauvoir (2) points out that a 1959 study in French institutions showed that old people sleep for more than 7 hours a night. Custom has it that we go to bed at night to sleep, and if we don't, we feel that there must be something wrong. There is no physiologic or pathologic reason why we should believe this, but with the human race the pressure to conform is great and this includes sleeping! Many old people doze happily for hours during the day but are upset if they find themselves lying awake at night. "Doctor, please, some more of these" is the cry.

Davison (11) has developed a more sensible way of approaching insomnia (Table 9-6). The essence of his management is to attack the underlying stress or problem that may be keeping the subject awake. If one can determine that there is no specific stress or problem causing the insomnia, reassurance and encouragement to read, get up and have a warm drink, or play records is of much greater benefit than reaching for the prescription pad.

There are, however, patients who need help to sleep, and for them there is only one rule. The experience of most physicians who have practiced geriatric medicine is that barbiturate hypnotics should be avoided in elderly patients. There are two reasons for this view; the first is that delirious reactions may occur, and the second is that these drugs may accumulate and cause a syndrome which is suggestive of dementia, with intellectual impairment, slowing of speech, and an unsteady gait.

Irvine et al. (27) demonstrated how a single oral dose of amobarbital sodium, which is regarded as a quick-acting barbiturate, tends to linger much longer in the bloodstream of old people compared with younger ones (Fig. 9-5). In addition, therefore, to causing nocturnal restlessness and delirium in some cases, hangover effects may produce confusion and ataxia. Continuing use of any hypnotic is undesirable, and Davison (11) points out that Kales and Kales in their sleep laboratory evaluation of psychoactive drugs reported that "patients on long continued drugs for insomnia slept as poorly as insomniacs not taking any medication."

TABLE 9-6. Management of Insomnia

Underlying cause	Treatment
Anxiety	Relieve social stress Tranquilizer Hypnotic
Depression	Relieve social stress (especially isolation) Antidepressants ECT (Electroconvulsive Therapy)—rarely

Bodily discomfort	Relieve somatic pain, distended
	  bowel, bladder, or pruritus
	Treat associated anxiety and/or
	  depression

Acute confusional state	Treat underlying organic disease Look for depression and dementia
Organic dementia	Relieve bodily discomfort Tranquilizer

(Davison W: Br J Hosp Med 5: 83–95, 1971)

As with all iatrogenic conditions the important diagnostic key is awareness of the two-edged nature of all drugs. While barbiturates invite trouble for the octogenarian, other hypnotics such as chloral hydrate or dichloralphenazone are effective. They are quickly removed from the body, and their only adverse effect is gastric upset in a small proportion of subjects. Nitrazepam in Europe and flurazepam hydrochloride in North America each work well; provided that no medication is taken one or two nights a week to avoid accumulation, they should cause no problems. Oxazepam is perhaps to be preferred, but its sedative action may not be quite as quick.

The sleep laboratory experience suggests that continuous use of hypnotics is of little value. Sleep is a habit, and a person who gets out of that habit may need help to revert. To reestablish the pattern 1–1.5 g chloral hydrate or 30–45 mg oxazepam can be given. Then the dosage should be reduced, and after 2–3 weeks the medication should be discontinued. This achieves the best results and causes the fewest iatrogenic complications.

ANTICONVULSANTS

Epilepsy is not uncommon in the very old. It occurs most often in those who have previously had a cerebrovascular accident, but it may also occur without apparent cause. The situation should be carefully assessed to exclude meningiomas or other neurologic conditions which might be surgically treated. In all such cases, consultation with a neurologist is advisable.

On occasion the situation calls for the use of anticonvulsant medication, and the drug which is most popular for this purpose is diphenylhydantoin. Phenobarbital is better avoided (see Sedatives) although in the author's experience it is better tolerated as an anticonvulsant than are its fellows as hypnotics.

CASE REPORT 9–4

During the early part of 1975 Mrs. West, aged 75, experienced a series of blackouts. Her family physician believed that these were due to epileptic attacks and commenced treatment with 100 mg diphenylhydantoin t.i.d. The attacks were not adequately controlled, however, and an appointment was made with a neurologist. As luck would have it, in the neurologist's office the patient had a blackout, and the observant specialist noted that it involved a period of asystole. The lady was admitted to the cardiac intensive care unit of the hospital. During the following 2 weeks, Mrs. West had a very rough passage. Her rhythm proved to be very unstable, and a heart block was suspected. She was treated with a variety of antiarrhythmic drugs, digoxin, procainamide hydrochloride (Pronestyl), and propranolol. A pacemaker was inserted and later removed. She had several episodes of ventricular fibrillation and cardiac arrests and was promptly resuscitated from each. By the end of the 2 weeks, however, the heart rhythm had finally settled. Throughout this time diphenylhydantoin was continued.

Four weeks later the geriatrician was asked to see her. It was now impossible to communicate with her, and she lay, inert but comfortable, flat on her back in bed with a nasogastric tube in position. The family were attentive and described how Mrs. West had been intelligent and alert. Since the dramatic 2 weeks, she had been quiet and apathetic and had said nothing for 10 days. It seemed clear that the unfortunate lady had sustained severe brain damage through the recurring anoxic crises of the 2 weeks described. A grave prognosis was given.

Concurrently the resident had asked for a serum diphenylhydantoin level (Fig. 9–11). The toxic level of 50 ng/ml was reduced in 2–3 days, and the patient revived immediately. Three weeks later she walked out of hospital and was well and at home 1 year later. The final twist in the story came when 2 weeks after discontinuing the diphenylhydantoin

Fig. 9–11. Case Report 9–4. Clinical course of Mrs. W. **DPH.** Diphenylhydantoin. **SVT.** Supraventricular tachycardia; **VT.** Ventricular tachycardia; **EPI.** Epileptic

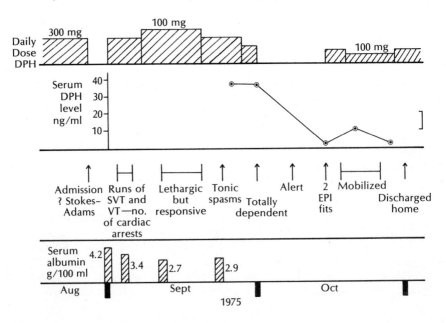

she had a grand mal seizure. She resumed her anticonvulsant at a more modest dosage and all was well.

Diphenylhydantoin is largely bound to protein. In one study (24), 9.9% was unbound at age 17, but the percentage increased steadily to 12.7% unbound at age 53. Others (22) have shown a relationship between binding and albumin levels, both of which are reduced with age. Care with dosage is essential when the patient is old and the serum albumin level is reduced. Brief tabulated details are given of one old man with a low protein level who quickly reached a toxic serum level of diphenylhydantoin.

CASE REPORT 9–5

Male, Manic–Depressive

Age 78

History of CVA with Right Hemiplegia

Sept.	1975:	Drug induced jaundice
Dec.	1975:	Total protein 5.6 g/100 ml
Jan. 19,	1976:	Epileptic convulsion: Diphenylhydantoin commenced 100 mg, t.i.d.
Jan. 29,	1976:	Serum diphenylhydantoin, 31 μg/ml
Feb. 12,	1976:	Serum diphenylhydantoin, 50 μg/ml
Feb. 16,	1976:	Dose reduced to 100 mg daily
Feb. 18,	1976:	Serum diphenylhydantoin, 31 μg/ml
Feb. 23,	1976:	Diphenylhydantoin D/C
Feb. 25,	1976:	Serum diphenylhydantoin, 7 μg/ml

Toxic manifestation: writhing mouth movements

ANTIPARKINSONIAN DRUGS

There are a number of syndromes involving increased muscular rigidity, facial fixation, and bradykinesia which are encountered in elderly patients. These include idiopathic paralysis agitans, Alzheimer's disease with concomitant fixed akinetic rigidity, postencephalitic parkinsonism, and rarer entities such as olivopontocerebellar degeneration and progressive supranuclear palsy.

Parkinson's disease is a unique illness with clear-cut physical signs (39). The combination of flexed posture, cogwheel rigidity, akinesia, and rhythmic limb tremor when at rest are easily recognizable. The immobile staring eyes, complete lack of gesture, speaking in a monotone with a small voice, and small writing complete the picture. The festinating or retropulsive gait or walking in a series of small shuffling steps which may speed up prior to a pitch forward on the subject's face are common to all such syndromes. Phenothiazine and butyrophenone drugs block dopamine receptors, producing extrapyramidal signs and increasing the frequency of parkinsonian-like disease.

Most or all of these features may be related to loss of pigmented cells which manufacture dopamine and norepinephrine, the two catecholamine neurotransmitters. Levodopa was introduced in 1967 (9) and has improved the prospects for sufferers from Parkinson's disease. It is more effective in moderating brady-kinesia and rigidity than in reducing tremor and is of no value in the treatment of arteriosclerotic Parkinson's syndrome or extrapyramidal signs caused by phenothiazines. To complicate an already confused picture levodopa plus car-bidopa can cause involuntary movements similar to the dyskinesias caused by phenothiazines (see Phenothiazines). Not only that, but an increasing number of patients are developing the distressing features of a tardive dyskinesia with perpetual movements usually of the mouth and face but occasionally of limbs and trunk.

Kobayaski (31) states that dyskinesias are found in 3%–6% of a mixed popu-lation of psychiatric patients and 40% of elderly institutionalized patients with-out drug inducement. There is little doubt, therefore, that this condition is common in elderly cerebrally disabled subjects. Although dyskinesias do occur spontaneously, the majority of cases are drug induced.

CASE REPORT 9–6

Mrs. Lean, aged 73, was admitted to Victoria Hospital, London, Ontario on March 28th, 1976 with a peptic ulcer and a history of falling in the nursing home in which she lived. The reason for admission was abdominal distention and fever. She was taking 50 mg chlorpromazine, 100 mg desipramine hydrochloride, 20 mg diazepam, and 2 mg benztro-pine maxylate (Cogentin) daily.

She was a thin cachectic female who responded only to pain. She was dehydrated with two decubitus ulcers, marked general rigidity, neck stiffness, and hypernatremia (Na= 163 mg/100 ml). After rehydration a more careful assessment of the neurologic picture suggested damage in frontal lobes and basal ganglia. All medications were discontinued. First attempts to relieve her symptom with levodopa plus carbidopa were unsuccessful. She was seen by the geriatrician in May, 1976 and transferred to the continuing care hospital on May 28th. She still had a nasogastric tube and an indwelling catheter *in situ*.

A further course of levodopa plus carbidopa was given, and the tubes were removed. Within 2 weeks there was a striking transformation in her physical state; she was eating well, talking, and beginning to help herself. This improvement was well maintained, and she continued to help herself until 18 months later. During this period it proved possible to reduce and eventually discontinue levodopa plus carbidopa—but experience revealed a need for continuing antidepressant therapy.

Her final diagnoses were senile dementia of the Alzheimer type and considerable brain damage resulting in the rigidity and a depressive state. She remains marooned in her own world but is physically in fair shape, although not well enough to leave the hospital.

How does one introduce rational therapy into such a confused clinical situa-tion? Dopaminergic and cholinergic systems are normally in balance. In Parkin-son's disease there is loss of dopaminergic neurons which results in rigidity and tremor. In addition to blocking dopamine receptors, phenothiazines and butyrophenones may also create a state of denervation hypersensitivity. The dyskinesia is thought to be related to this hypersensitive state, which explains why discontinuing an antipsychotic drug may make the dyskinesia worse; it releases dopamine to act on the sensitive receptors. Indeed, the condition may appear for the first time after the blocker is stopped. Dyskinesias may similarly be caused by the administration of levodopa (see Case Report 9–6).

There is one further clue to possible treatment. Dopamine receptors are of two types: 1) inhibitory receptors which are found mostly in the caudate nucleus and 2) excitatory which are in the minority (12). The suggestion has been made that imbalance between the two may be responsible for the different kinds of dyskinesia which may occur in levodopa treated patients.

Faced with an elderly patient suffering from parkinsonism, the physician's first objective must be to clarify the cause as far as possible. In cases of idiopathic paralysis agitans with no dementia and no drug element, treatment depends on the major clinical features. In cases where rigidity and bradykinesia are the major problems levodopa is much the best drug and should be used with a decarboxylase inhibitor such as carbidopa. The combination should be introduced slowly and patiently, beginning with 125 mg twice daily, preferably given with meals. The anorexic and dyspeptic complications are least when it is given in this way. Over a period of a month it is possible to increase this dosage to 250 mg three or four times daily. That is the upper limit for anyone over 70.

Where the results are disappointing, introduction of amantidine or one of the anticholinergic agents such as trihexyphenidyl hydrochloride, orphenadrine, or benztropine mesylate may be helpful. If tremor is the more prominent feature, these drugs are often to be preferred to levodopa because they are more effective against this disturbance.

In conditions of akinetic rigidity, levodopa is worth a trial on an empirical basis. A careful watch for side-effects is necessary, however, in particular the ominous appearance of orofacial dyskinesia. If this does appear, levodopa must be withdrawn, which may cure the dyskinesia. If not, the most effective measure at present is to use thiopropazate hydrochloride. This is a phenothiazine dopamine blocker and has proved useful in this situation.

The treatment of parkinsonism caused by phenothiazine or butyrophenone consists of withdrawal of the medication. This is the most important step, since neither levodopa nor the anticholinergics have proved of much value. For tardive dyskinesia, thiopropazate hydrochloride is still the best available. Recent work suggests that there may be merit in a combination of apomorphine with levodopa, but this claim has yet to be substantiated.

Other drugs which have been tried with varying success include deanol acetamidobenzoate which was beneficial in 7 out of 23 cases and physostigmine, 1 mg of which eliminated dyskinesia in 2, helped 1, but had little effect in 5 others (33). The greatest hope must be, however, that students of neurotransmission in the brain and of cerebral metabolism will be able to produce more knowledge of the fundamentals of function in the central nervous system.

ANTIDIABETIC ORAL AGENTS

Carbohydrate metabolism alters with age, and there is an appreciable incidence of mature onset diabetes in the later decades (see Ch. 2, Physical Aspects of Aging). The majority of these are associated with obesity, and a suitable diet is all that is required. There are, however, a small number of active antidiabetic preparations such as tolbutamide, chlorpropamide, glyburide, phenformin hydrochloride, and metformin. It is tempting to prescribe such drugs as an insurance that the elderly patient with a highish blood sugar (200–300 mg/100 ml), will not develop diabetic complications.

The major danger in this situation is that blood sugar levels will drop too low. Chlorpropamide, in particular, can cause serious hypoglycemic turns. What is more difficult to recognize, it may cause periodic mild hypoglycemic periods which over a span of weeks may do considerable permanent damage to the brain. For this reason it is wise never to introduce these drugs without arranging for a careful screening of the patient's carbohydrate metabolism. Some endocrinologists now claim that there is no place for these drugs. While this author is not in agreement with such a total rejection of their use, the need for extreme care is urged. The danger for the elderly diabetic lies in overtreatment.

ANTICOAGULANT DRUGS

Agents to prevent blood clotting are also likely to cause serious iatrogenic problems. Many years ago in successive weeks two patients died from hemorrhage caused by these drugs. The first was a fit old man who fractured his femur at the age of 84 and was put on routine anticoagulation in the orthopedic ward. One week later with no warning he had a massive gastric bleed from an ulcer and died within minutes. The second was an old lady who was given an anticoagulant at the age of 81 for phlebothrombosis in one leg. Three days later she went into shock and collapsed with a large fluctuant pelvic mass due to hemorrhage. She, too, died shortly afterwards.

This may have happened because of persistently hyperelevated prothrombin times resulting from a greater quantity of free warfarin in the blood, consequent upon two drugs competing for binding space (see Table 9–1). The second reason is the possible lack of vitamin K (23).

PREVENTION OF IATROGENIC DISORDERS

The price of freedom from iatrogenic disease is eternal vigilance. The following are this author's personal rules:

1. If the need for a drug is questionable, do not prescribe it.
2. Never hesitate to stop all drugs if need demands.
3. Review treatment frequently.
4. Encourage patients to bring bottles of drugs; remove and destroy all superfluous drugs.
5. Simplify dosage schedules.
6. Do not prescribe more than five drugs.
7. Avoid barbiturates.
8. Use extreme care with antihypertensives.

REFERENCES

1. Baylis EM, Hall MS, Lewis G, Marks V: Effects of renal function on plasma digoxin levels in elderly ambulant patients in domiciliary practice. Br Med J I:338–341, 1972
2. Beavoir S de: Old Age. Great Britain, André Deutsch Ltd and George Wiedenfeld and Nicholson Ltd, 1972, p 28
3. Bender AD: Pharmacodynamic consequences of aging and their implications in the treatment of the elderly patient. Med Ann DC 36:267–271, 1967
4. Bennett WM, Singer I, Golper T, Feig P, Coggins CH: Guidelines for drug therapy in renal failure. Ann Intern Med 86:754–783, 1977
5. Borda I, Jick H, Slone D, Divan B, Gilman B, Chalmers TC: Studies of drug usage in five Boston hospitals. JAMA 202:506–510, 1967
6. Cape RDT, Shorrock C, Tree R, Pablo R, Campbell AJ, Seymour DC: Square pegs in round holes. Can Med Assoc 117:1284–1287, 1977
7. Castleden CM, Kaye CM, Parsons RL: The effect of age on plasma levels of propranolol and practolol in man. Br J Clin Pharmacol 2:303–306, 1972
8. Chan K, Kendall MJ, Mitchard N, Wells WDE: The effect of ageing on plasma pethidine concentration. Br J Clin Pharmacol 2:297–302, 1975
9. Corzias GC, Van Noert MH, Schiffer LM: Aromatic amino acids and modification of parkinsonism. N Engl J Med 276:374– , 1967
10. Crooks J, Shepherd AMM, Stevenson IH: Drugs and the elderly—The nature of the problem. Health Bull (Edinb) 33:222–227, 1975
11. Davison W: Drug hazards in the elderly. Br J Hosp Med 5:83–95, 1971
12. (Editorial): After Dopa. Lancet I:786, 1976
13. Evered DC, Chapman C: Plasma digoxin concentrations and digoxin toxicity in hospital patients. Br Heart H 33:540–545, 1971
14. Ewy GH, Kapadia GG, Yao L, Lullin M, March FI: Digoxin metabolism in the elderly. Circulation 39:449–453, 1969
15. Fish DG, MacDonnell JA: Utilizations of Medications by the Elderly. Paper presented to the Canadian Association of Gerontology, Toronto, 1975
16. Fottrell E, Sheikh M, Kothari R, Sayed I: Long-stay patients with long-stay drugs. Lancet I:81–82, 1976
17. Gibson IJM, O'Hare MM: Prescription of drugs for old people at home. Gerontol Clin 10:-271–280, 1968
18. Gorrod JW: Absorption, metabolism and excretion of drugs in geriatric subjects. Gerontol Clin 16:30–42, 1974
19. Greenblatt DJ, Shader RI: Drug therapy benzodiazepines. N Engl J Med 291:1011–1015; 1239–1243, 1974
20. Hall RCW, Joffe JR: Aberrant response to diazepam: a new syndrome. Am J Psychiatry 129:738–742, 1972
21. Hansen JM, Kampmann J, Laursen H: Renal excretion of drugs in the elderly. Lancet I:1170, 1970
22. Hayes MJ, Langman MJS, Short AH: Changes in drug metabolism with increasing age—Phenytoin clearance and protein binding. Br J Clin Pharmacol 2:73–79, 1975
23. Hewick D, Moreland T, Shepherd AMM, Stevenson IH: The effect of age on sensitivity to and handling of warfarin sodium (abstr). Clin Sci Mol Med 49(3):13P, 1975
24. Hooper WD, Bochner F, Eadie MJ, Tyrer JH: Plasma protein binding of diphenylhydantoin. Clin Pharmacol Ther 15:276–282, 1974
25. Hurwitz N: Predisposing factors in adverse reactions to drugs. Br Med J I:536–539, 1969
26. Hurwitz N, Wade OL: Intensive hospital monitoring of adverse reactions to drugs. Br Med J I:531–536, 1969
27. Irvine RE, Grove J, Toseland PA, Trounce JR: The effect of age on the hydroxylation of amylobarbitone sodium in man. Br J Clin Pharmacol I:41–43, 1974
28. Jarvik ME: Drugs used in the treatment of psychiatric disorders. In Goodman LS, Gillman A (eds): The Pharmacological Basis of Therapeutics. New York, MacMillan, 1970, pp 151–202

29. Jori A, DiSalle E, Quadri A: Rate of aminopyrine disappearance from plasma in young and aged humans. Pharmacology 8:273–279, 1972

30. Klotz V, Avant GR, Hoyumpa A, Schenker S, Wilkinson GR: The effects of age and liver disease on the disposition and elimination of diazepam in adult Man. J Clin Invest 55:347–359, 1975

31. Kobayaski RM: Drug therapy of tardive dyskinesia. N Engl J Med 296:257–259, 1977

32. Koch-Weser J, Sellers EM: Drug therapy. Binding of drugs to serum albumin. N Engl J Med 294:311–316; 426–531, 1976

33. Kristensen OL, Weismann K, Huttens L: Renal function and the rate of disappearance of methotrexate from serum. Eur J Pharmacol 8:439, 1975

34. Learoyd BM: Psychotropic drugs and the elderly patient. Med J Aust I:1131–1133, 1972

35. Matthews VL, Feather J: Utilization of health services in western Canada: basic Canadian data from the World Health Organization/International Collaborative Study of Medical Care Utilization. Can Med Assoc J 114:309–312, 1976

36. Miller RR: Overzichtsartikelen. Comprehensive prospective drug surveillance—A report from the Boston Collaborative Drug Surveillance Program. Pharm Weekblad 109:461–481, 1974

37. Ogilvie IR, Ruedy J: Adverse drug reactions during hospitalization. Can Med Assoc J 97: 1450–1457, 1967

38. O'Malley K, Crooks J, Duke E, Stevenson IH: Effect of age and sex on human drug metabolism. Br Med J 3:607–609, 1971

39. Parkes JD, Marsden CD: The treatment of Parkinson's disease. Br J Hosp Med 7:284–294, 1973

40. Petersen DM, Thomas CW: Acute drug reactions among the elderly. J Gerontol 30:552–556, 1975

41. Rawlins MD: Variability of response to drugs in man. Br J Hosp Med 8:803–811, 1974

42. Roberts MA, Caird FI: Steady-state kinetics of digoxin in the elderly. Age Ageing 5:214–223, 1976

43. Ruedy J: Choice of drugs in the elderly patient. Ontario Med Rev 44:281–288, 1977

44. Ryan HF, Merrill FB, Scott GE: Increase in suicidal thoughts and tendencies: association with diazepam therapy. JAMA 203:1137–1139, 1968

45. Shapiro S, Slone D, Lewis GB, Jick H: The epidemiology of digoxin. J Chronic Dis 22:361–371, 1969

46. Spence JD, Sibbald W, Cape RDT: Pseudohypertension in the elderly. (Unpublished data)

47. Triggs EJ, Nation RL, Long A, Ashley JJ: Pharmacokinetics in the elderly. Eur J Clin Pharmacol 8:55–62, 1975

48. Trounce JR: Drugs in the elderly. Br J Clin Pharmacol 2:289–291, 1975

49. United States Department of Health, Education and Welfare, Task Force on Prescription Drugs: The Drug Users. Washington DC, US Government Printing Office, 1968

Chapter 10

THE PHILOSOPHY OF CONTINUING CARE

Geriatrics Ward

Tonight I find myself
In a crowd where everybody's nearing sixty.
I'm cornered by a gerontologist with a whisky sour;
We get into deep discussion about aging.

"Keep the snails off those sweet peas daily.
Mind the grandchildren whenever you must.
Finish the novel's final chapters;
Revise them endlessly. Then plan
A long trip to England to make stonerubbings
In all the minor hidden churches.
Classify these rubbings by time,
Locale, and subject, with cross-indexes.
Now get the whole thing published.
Start a yo–yo quilt.
Pull up the sweet peas; plant tomatoes,
Italian green beans, bell peppers.
Compost wet garbage. Listen
To all the Donizetti operas
(Many are on underground recordings
Or on private tapes. Write letters
All around the country to locate these.)
At ninety-five, and going strong,
No EKG for twenty years, take a brisk
Run around the block each day at dawn."

Now we're joined by Lois, with a bourbon and water.
"I used to work with old people," she says.
"I used to line them up, four in a row,
And feed them strawberry shortcake,
Whether they liked it or not."

Judith Clarence

CASE REPORT 10–1

Born in 1902 in Scotland, Mrs. Ellis emigrated to Canada at an early age. She lived most of her life and raised her family in New Brunswick. She never lost her characteristic Scottish accent or her independence of spirit. Her husband was 7 years her senior, and when Mrs. Ellis had a myocardial infarct in 1970 they decided to leave New Brunswick and move to Ontario, where they established themselves next door to their daughter. For several years all went well, but in September 1974, Mrs. Ellis had a brief cerebrovascular accident with left hemiparesis which cleared quickly.

One year later she began the last stage of her life, during which her now severely damaged myocardium greatly limited her activity. During this period of 22 months she spent a total of 181 days in the hospital and 448 at home (Fig. 10–1). Mrs. Ellis spent 68 days in the hospital between September 22nd, 1975 and March 3rd, 1976; she was admitted four times (Table 10–1). By the end of this period it was clearly established that the myocardium was seriously damaged from her previous infarction and there was a suggestion of an aneurysmal dilatation of the left ventricle. There was evidence of paralysis of the left phrenic nerve with permanent elevation of the left side of the diaphragm. Renal function was chronically impaired with creatinine clearance of 20–30 ml/min. As a result, digoxin dosage was adequate at 0.125 mg/day. Because of relative lack of activity, bowel function was unsatisfactory without aid, and constipation precipitated pulmonary edema because of increased exertion on more than one occasion. Diabetes mellitus, from which she had suffered since 1965, presented few problems. Neurologic features were transient leg weakness in September 1975 and weakness of left arm and face in December of the same year. Drug treatment included digoxin, furosemide, spironolactone (Aldactone), and isosorbide dinitrate (Isordil). To build more stability into the situation and create a plan for continuing care that would allow Mrs. Ellis to spend as much time at home as possible, she was transferred to the continuing care hospital.

Between March 3rd, 1976 and June 30th, 1976 Mrs. Ellis remained a patient of this hospital, but towards the end of this period she spent increasing amounts of time at home. In June 1976 she was able to attend the wedding of her granddaughter. Apart from one critical period early in her stay when acute pulmonary edema developed following straining at stool, her progress was largely uneventful with a slow building of confidence and strength.

The final year of her life extended from July 1st, 1976 until June 26th, 1977. During this period she spent only 34 days in the hospital and was able to travel to New Brunswick to celebrate her golden wedding in August of 1976. She continued to have recurrent minor crises with her bowels, with pulmonary edema, and with recurrence of left monoplegia, but these were soon controlled. In April 1977 during a 2-week period in the hospital, the second episode of digoxin toxicity occurred (see Case Report 9–1).

On June 24th, 1977 she again developed acute shortness of breath and was seen in the emergency department. The diuretic was increased, and within a few hours she felt better and returned home. The following day, according to her daughter, she was well and in excellent spirits. She died in her sleep during the night of June 25th, in her own bed, as she had wished.

As a postscript to this report one should add that her 82-year-old husband, who had remained reasonably well throughout these 22 months died 10 days after his wife.

This case illustrates the successful management of serious disability in an elderly patient. By using hospitals and continuing care institutions to provide support to the family, it was possible for Mrs. Ellis to spend the last 2 years of her life in her own home and to achieve her personal ambition. One major support was her devoted daughter, who spent a lot of her time supervising and managing the care of her mother.

Fig. 10–1. Case Report 10–1. Course of Mrs. E's illness, indicating proportion of her last 22 months spent at home. A. September, 1975 through August, 1976. B. September, 1976 through June, 1977.

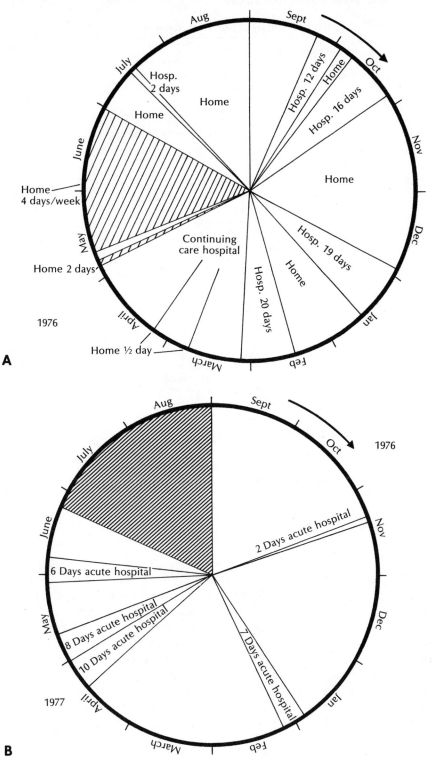

TABLE 10-1. History of Mrs. E's Hospital Admissions

Admission	Symptom
First	Weakness of legs Fall (trying to walk) Immobility Obtundity Absent leg reflexes Diminished air entry L.L. Lobe Jugular venous congestion Edema to midcalf Diabetes mellitus Gallop rhythm

Second	Increasing fatigue
	Trifasicular block
	Arteriosclerotic heart disease
	    fluid retention
	    ? Cardiomyopathy
	Mild uremia
	Incontinence of urine
	Anemia
	Periods of confusion

Third	Short of breath—Orthopneic Edema to midthigh Bilateral basal rales Bundle branch block Diabetes Need for oxygen Confusional episode Nausea and vomiting
Fourth	Chest pain Shortness of breath Nausea and vomiting Jugular venous congestion Anemia Weakness of left arm and left leg

February 16th, 1976 "Prognosis now very poor, very confused"

February 19th, 1976 Cheyne-Stokes respiration, incontinent of urine

February 28th, 1976 Brighter—eating ?Parkwood

From September 1975 until her death in June 1977, this lady was always on the verge of serious cardiac decompensation, and she almost died on three occasions. She required skilled care from time to time in addition to continuing supervision. She exemplified problems of iatrogenic disorder, twice being seriously ill with digoxin overdosage. On the first occasion this was recognized when she came into the hospital, but the second occurred as a result of an inadvertent overdosage in the hospital.

Many patients of her age and with her degree of disability are admitted to continuing care hospitals on a permanent basis. The success of Mrs. Ellis' last year was that nine-tenths of it was spent at home.

GOALS OF GERIATRIC MEDICINE

"Life is short, but the art is long, the opportunity fleeting, the experiment perilous, the judgement difficult." This aphorism, attributed to Hippocrates, might well describe geriatrics, which is from a practical standpoint one of the most difficult types of medicine to practice. Expectations of cure or even partial recovery are much less than in younger people. In the eighth and ninth decades, most people anticipate the end of life; whether they do so philosophically or with anxiety depends on their natures. The idea that physicians should be actively holding back the final step is one which does not appeal to many people. It would be unrealistic, therefore, to argue that the goal of medicine at this age is the same as it is for the child, the young adult, or even the individual in mature middle age.

What the elderly patient seeks, almost more than cure, is independence. The goal, therefore, of the physician practicing geriatric medicine is to maintain the independence of his or her patients and help them to live out their lives in their own homes. This goal will and should affect judgments which are made not only in treatment but in investigation of some of the more complex clinical situations that one encounters.

ACHIEVING THE GOAL

In order to make a valuable contribution toward preserving the patient's independence, the physician must have as clearsighted a view of the nature of the patient's clinical situation as possible. For the family physician, this may mean a consultation with a geriatrician/internist, a psychiatrist, a physiatrist, or other specialist. Having used their skills, the family physician knows the clinical possibilities of the situation. At this point there may well be two or three possible lines of management. Before deciding which line to follow, the physician should discuss the situation with the patient and involved relatives. It is important to remember that each individual must be fully involved in the decision making concerning his or her own future. The fundamental principle of management of illness in an elderly person is to combine clinical expertise, which uses all the skills of advanced scientific medicine, with careful, kindly consideration of the individual and his or her personality.

INFLUENCE OF TIME

One of the most common misapprehensions of physicians is that time is of relatively little importance to the elderly, chronically ill individual. After all, it may be said, if the illness is going to continue, it matters not whether suitable steps are taken today or tomorrow. What can be put off until tomorrow should never be done today in some people's view. This is a dangerous attitude.

To understand the importance of time one has to examine the reaction of the elderly to disability. They have a low expectation of their own prospects. To them advancing years means increasing disability, and many of the more insidious disabilities which become obvious to them as the years go by are accepted without complaint and without consulting their physicians. This was demonstrated by Williamson and his colleagues (7) in Edinburgh in 1964.

CONCEALED DISABILITY

The particular conditions that were unknown to the practitioner were the more chronic and more embarrassing problems, namely, dementing illness and urinary troubles, frequency and incontinence (see Fig. 5–2). Yet time may be of considerable importance if physicians are to intervene with any success in these situations.

In 1977, it is not possible to cure or significantly alter a dementing illness by drugs. Recognition of it at an early stage can, however, make future management easier. Physician and family can cooperate in a program of care based on sensory stimulation and reality orientation. Steps can be taken in good time to seek appropriate institutional help, including day hospital support.

The longer urinary incontinence is allowed to continue unrecognized, the greater the difficulty in assisting the individual to regain control. Much help can be offered if mechanisms can be explained at the onset of the problem. To the person unversed in medical matters with little understanding of the body's functioning it may seem unlikely that anything can be done. Careful explanations of urgency and precipitancy, leading to episodes of incontinence, can help to prevent urinary incontinence from becoming established, however (see Ch. 7, Incontinence).

POSSIBLE PREVENTION

The rationale for establishing preventive clinics was described by Anderson and Cowan (1) at Rutherglen in Glasgow in 1955. In this pioneering effort the subjects who were screened were aged 55 and over. This was an extension of the practice, common in North America, of individuals having an annual checkup. It is arguable that, while it is theoretically sound to begin preventive geriatric medicine at this age, it is likely to prove expensive and offer only modest benefits. The critical age comes later, and the difficult years are those between 70 and 80. During this time, many enter the final phase of life, while those destined to live into very old age continue to lead active lives. Any preventive program, therefore, is likely to be most effective if it concentrates on this decade. This is the time when increasing numbers may experience difficulties with memory and bladder control. For the family physician anxious to provide more than a disease treatment service for patients, the possibility of organizing regular screening of patients in their 70s can be recommended.

CRISIS SITUATIONS

No statistics are available, but many illnesses in the elderly are treated in emergency departments. Most elderly patients are treated in the same way as they would have been at a younger age. The patients are returned home as quickly as possible, with little thought of the social or medical background. Experience suggests that an appreciable number of such elderly patients never regain their previous level of health but tend to slip into increasing disability and dependence, which may persist for many months before it is recognized. Here again, time is important. One acute illness frequently unveils a number of preexisting but unrecognized troubles.

It is understandable that the surgeon dealing with a fractured neck of femur or an intestinal obstruction may not wish to become involved with coexisting medical disabilities. It is arguable, however, that the management of elderly patients in such a situation should include a thorough check by an internist or family physician who should take stock of the whole person. By doing this, documenting the pathologic conditions present, and examining the whole lifestyle of the individual, it should be possible to construct a plan for that person's future. The general philosophy of letting sleeping dogs lie is fine if you know what the sleeping dogs are! What so often happens is that no attempt is made to uncover hidden illnesses and they are allowed to develop to a stage in which they are very difficult to manage.

Careful consideration of time in the clinical situation of any ill old person makes it obvious that a plan for the continuing care of these individuals is needed. Invariably there are a number of pathologic processes developing and a sensible combination of communication and treatment can greatly improve the patient's ability to preserve independence.

PHYSICAL AND EMOTIONAL SUPPORT

The British Geriatric Society's definition of geriatric medicine is "that it is concerned with the clinical, preventive, remedial and social aspects of illness in the elderly." The main task of the physician must be to learn more about the nature and management of disease at this age. There are many trained social workers with great enthusiasm for helping the elderly, and it is better for physicians to advise and guide the social workers about particular patients, whenever this is relevant, rather than attempt to perform social work themselves. In planning clinical management, however, it is important to recognize the need for adequate support, particularly for individuals living in their own homes.

The physician who knows and understands the disability from which the individual suffers is the appropriate person to recommend the nature of support. Such support ranges from a simple handle placed at a strategic point in the house to the need for someone to provide household help (Table 10–2). Having decided what type of support is necessary, the physician's task is then to inform the

TABLE 10-2. Check List of Supports

Type	Options
Adaptations to structure of home	Handles, bath rails, bed fittings, alterations to step, ramps, safety devices on cooking equipment, repositioning of power points and light switches
Equipment	Canes, walkers, wheelchairs, raised lavatory seats or chairs, rehabilitation exercise equipment
Personal help	Homemaker, friendly visitor, nurse, therapist

appropriate services so that they can arrange to provide it. These physical arrangements may be difficult to make, but there is seldom any problem in deciding what is necessary.

There is another type of support, however, which is crucial in a number of situations. These situations are not particularly common but may be extremely awkward when they do occur. The following two cases illustrate a severe aspect of what, for lack of a better expression, one might call a crisis of confidence.

CASE REPORT 10–2

In January 1977, Mrs. Foster aged 81, spent a short time in the hospital because of edema of the legs. This was easily controlled with a modest dose of diuretic, and she returned to her senior citizen's apartment, where she lived alone. In April 1977, she developed severe pains in the back about the level of the 5th and 6th dorsal vertebrae. There was no associated shortness of breath, no cough, nor any relationship between breathing and the pain. A diagnosis of polymyalgia rheumatica was considered, and a trial with steroid therapy was given.

ESR proved to be only 25 mm/hour, and the therapy was ineffective; on May 4th the old lady was admitted to the hospital. X-ray of the spine and ribs revealed a modest degree of osteoporotic change with some disk degeneration, but this hardly seemed to account for the severity of the symptoms. With regular analgesia, however, she improved sufficiently to allow her to return home on May 20th.

Her improvement did not last, and she was back in the hospital within 3 weeks. A slow program to rebuild her confidence in herself began, but 2 months went by before there were signs that she was recovering her independent spirit. After several short periods at home, she was able to resume her life in her own apartment with her self-confidence restored.

CASE REPORT 10–3

A 74-year-old widow who lived alone in her own apartment, Mrs. Steel was shocked to learn that her older sister had cancer. Following receipt of the news she had a trivial accident in which she injured her back when she dropped awkwardly into a chair. She developed severe backache which persisted, and she was admitted to a general hospital where she was seen by the geriatrician in November 1976. X-rays revealed disk degenerations, old compression fractures, and significant osteoporosis.

Later, transferred to a continuing care hospital and equipped with a corset, she improved to the point where she was virtually independent. In February 1977 a home visit was suggested. Within 1 week the back was worse than ever and the visit was abandoned. After a further few months of rehabilitation she again was able to manage all her own self-care, but at the suggestion of a home visit protested volubly that she couldn't entertain such an idea. It seems very unlikely that she will now leave the institution in which she has made her home.

These two ladies, each in their own way, were capable of dressing, washing, and going to and from the washroom. They demanded little help from the nursing staff. There was no obvious reason why they should not have returned to their own homes, although both lived alone. For reasons which are difficult to explain they became very dependent on the institution in which they were accommodated, feeling secure only in the sheltered environment of a hospital. Ultimately, one recovered and the other did not.

CASE REPORT 10–4

Mrs. Stone, aged 86, enjoyed good health until the age of 80. She then had a severe attack of herpes zoster which affected the ophthalmic division of the right trigeminal nerve. As a result, she developed severe, persistent postherpetic neuralgia and ectropion which required stitching of the lateral portion of her eyelids together. Mrs. Stone lived alone in a small house which had been a standard prefabricated one put up during World War II. Although intended to last only 10 years, this little house was still in existence 30 years later. She kept it scrupulously clean and was very proud of it. She attended the day hospital at Selly-Oak in Birmingham, England 2 days a week. During that time she undertook a variety of occupational therapy tasks, using her hands to crochet or knit. Every 2 months, she would see the geriatrician at his day hospital clinic. Invariably, she would complain long and bitterly about her neuralgia, headaches, and general misery. Over a period of many months a number of drug alterations were tried to improve this situation. Nothing, however, changed the general picture she presented on her regular consultations, which invariably involved tears but ended with a brave smile.

The family physician also saw Mrs. Stone regularly, and between the two physicians and the social and rehabilitative efforts of the day hospital she maintained her sturdy independence to the end.

The case of Mrs. Stone illustrates the effectiveness of kindly supervision and a willingness to listen. This, added to her spirit, kept her in her own home where she wanted to be. The strength of this psychologic support is difficult to measure, but such support is a force of considerable importance in geriatric medicine. Physicians who understand the problems of their elderly patients contribute a great deal to them by regular contact, listening, and discussing.

Keller (2) expressed this well when he said,

with technical and medical knowledge alone little will be achieved. The elderly must never be given the impression by doctors and nursing staff that those caring for them are chronically short of time. Everyone concerned with the elderly patient must in fact be willing to listen to him and try to understand his language.

To this one should add that technical medical knowledge is of considerable importance; without it, earnest humane efforts are much less effective. The physician in geriatric medicine should combine the technical knowledge and skills of the good internist with the understanding and humanity which Keller describes.

GENERAL ADVICE FOR ELDERLY PATIENTS

Physicians are approached by old people or their relatives for advice on a wide variety of topics related to the lifestyle of the old person. Should my mother make another trip to Europe? Is it safe to leave my father on his own while I go on vacation? Is there anything particularly important that my parents should be eating? There are one or two general principles to bear in mind when answering these or similar questions.

There is no way that an old person can be completely protected from the possibility of accident or illness. Reducing activity tends to encourage rather than prevent such episodes. The old live dangerously, and a certain level of stress is beneficial to them. An old person can be talked into becoming dependent by overanxious relatives, friends, or even physicians. There are five rules for living in the eighth and subsequent decades.

REGULAR EXERCISE

Walking is as good as jogging. One should walk as far as one can, comfortably, and repeat the activity two or three times daily. The old should be encouraged to use a cane or even a walker, if necessary to continue this activity safely. Maintaining strength and independence is much more important than being seen to use a cane.

DIET

Everyone should be encouraged to eat a well-rounded diet without fads, including a reasonable amount of bulk. This holds true for any age, but particularly for old people. They normally do not wish to eat so much, and families should be warned about this. If not, they worry that grandmother is not eating enough. Bran and bran muffins can be of great value in helping to maintain regular bowel function. A steady weight level is a reasonable goal for the older person. There is no need for added vitamin supplements to complement the diet, provided that it is of a good mixed nature. Calcium is important (see Ch. 6, Falling), milk and cheese being the richest sources of it.

MENTAL STIMULATION

The mind needs as much activity as the body. With radio, television, clubs, and other social outlets there are few people who cannot maintain their interest in life if they are willing to make a conscious effort to do so. The old person must learn that interest does not spring up spontaneously but must be actively pursued. Those who are housebound and live alone need extra help in this direction, and visiting services can play an important role. At times, elderly persons insist that they do not wish to meet others; while every consideration should be given to individual preferences, there is little doubt that attempts should be made to persuade them to join in some of the activities going on around them.

DECLARATION OF SYMPTOMS

A major educational effort is needed to persuade the old to consult a physician about unpleasant or embarrassing symptoms which indicate some failure of the body to perform normally. The practice of medicine remains largely disease-oriented although the need for prevention of illness is becoming increasingly realized. Our diagnostic skills, including accumulation of a data base and formulation of problem lists, still depend heavily on the subject reporting his or her symptoms. This underlines the need for the patient to bring his clinical complaints to the physician as soon as possible.

DANGERS OF MEDICATION

One cannot overemphasize to the elderly that every medication is a potential poison. For this reason it is important that they consume the minimum. Physicians should make it a point to find out the numbers of pills elderly patients are taking and to explain the dangers of drug interactions. It should be stressed that even those drugs that can be bought over the drug store counter can interact with prescribed medicines and become dangerous.

HOME OR INSTITUTION?

In Canada it has become accepted over the past 30 years that a proportion of old people with medical problems will be admitted to an institution for care during their last months or years. There are three levels of care. The first is for the individual who no longer wants to cope with the problems of daily living, such as shopping, moving from one place to another, cooking, cleaning, or washing. Individuals may be able to do all of these things with a little difficulty, but are reaching a stage in which it is pleasant to have meals provided and to have fewer chores to perform. Such individuals are candidates for admission to a home for the aged.

The second level is for the individual who, in addition to being generally frail and needing a little support, has a disability which makes some nursing care desirable. This is usually provided by nursing homes which allow a level of nursing up to about 2 hours daily. Finally, there are those who require a considerable amount of nursing care and who cannot be managed in an environment other than a hospital with full nursing and rehabilitation facilities available. These are usually accommodated in continuing care hospitals.

Although it is obvious to a clinician that people will move from one to another of these different levels, it has been the accepted plan of the politicians to develop these facilities in separate institutions. The result has been a rather rigid system of institutional care. Institutions should be, however, a means of support for old people to help them to remain in their own homes.

REHABILITATION

Rehabilitation is the fourth stage in the clinical management of an illness, the first three being investigation, diagnosis, and treatment. Even after a disease is cured, an old person requires an appreciable period of rehabilitation to recover full vigor. If the patient lives alone and is not feeling well, there is little stimulus to put maximum effort into the rehabilitation process, which then becomes more difficult. General hospitals, where the majority of acute illnesses are treated, are not organized to provide the tranquil atmosphere and gentle, persuasive insistence on rehabilitation that is essential for the elderly patient. There is, therefore, considerable value in having beds in a continuing care hospital which are set aside for short-stay purposes such as convalescence for this type of person. There are a number of old people who continue to live in their own homes during convalescence, aided by relatives, friends, or homemakers. When their support system breaks down, they need immediate admission to an institution on a short-term basis. If a daughter is ill, wishes a holiday, or wants to attend a grandchild's wedding in a far-flung corner of the globe, it should be possible to arrange for temporary care for the grandmother in the type of institution appropriate for her.

SHORT-STAY ADMISSIONS

The concept of short-stay admissions to institutions, which have traditionally been associated with long-term care only, is an important new principle that should become rapidly established throughout North America. All of these institutions should be organized on a basis of 95% bed occupancy. If economic considerations compel operating on a 100% basis, there will never be any beds available in the institutions for such short-stay purposes. Such institutions can be among the most valuable of all supports for old people living in their own homes because an instant response is available in times of crisis. Institutions should be regarded as supports which not only accomodate severely disabled old people during the last years of their lives but also provide transient accomodation for the wide variety of situations which occur in life.

MIXING YOUNG AND OLD

A distressing feature of the North American institutional system is its failure to recognize the special needs of a small but highly significant group of severely disabled individuals—the young. These patients have sustained their disability either through accidents, neurologic disease ranging from the occasional case of poliomyelitis to paraplegias from a variety of causes, multiple sclerosis, motor neuron disease, rheumatoid arthritis, or ankylosing spondylitis. Individuals who have suffered severe disability in early life look forward to living for many years. The practice of including them in institutions full of elderly people is unfair to both groups.

Although this book is concerned with the clinical consequences of old age, it is pertinent to comment on the mixing of young and old. There are two reasons which compel examination of the problem. The first is that younger individuals inevitably feel that they have been put on a shelf or swept out of sight along with the elderly; the second is that the rehabilitation staff of the continuing care institutions, for perfectly good humane reasons, devote a disproportionate amount of their time working with the younger individuals. In Great Britain during the past 10 years, special units for the younger disabled have been established. These have followed the lead of Group Captain Cheshire V.C. who founded the Cheshire homes at the end of World War II to care for severely disabled younger people in as normal and homelike an atmosphere as possible. There is no doubt that North America will follow this lead, as such institutions mean the opportunity for a fuller and more natural life for the young person. His older fellow sufferers in continuing care geriatric institutions will then have the certainty that all available rehabilitation facilities will be used for their benefit.

TERMINAL CARE

Old age can be referred to as the penultimate stage of life, the final one being the process of terminal illness and death. "Men fear death as children fear to go in the dark," and because of this death is seldom mentioned. This attitude is curious in an era when control of the process is firmer than ever before. From the biologist's viewpoint, death is an essential part of life which encourages the species to evolve and improve. Philosophically, there is little doubt that most elderly people do not regard death with the same degree of fear and terror as the young person or the individual in his prime. Thanks to Saunders (5) and Kubler–Ross (3) more dignity, humanity, and understanding has been introduced into care of dying patients.

Terminal care involves communication and relief of distress, and physicians have a reputation for being bad communicators. This criticism is understandable because it is only recently, comparatively, that the profession has had sufficient knowledge of disease to be able to communicate clearly about an individual's clinical state. Fifty years ago there were no antibiotics, no steroids, no understanding of stress or the complexities of immunology. At that time, confidence in the physician was all-important. Experience helped the physician to forecast likely outcomes in a variety of clinical situations, although he was powerless to intervene in many of them. To bolster this confidence and sustain his patients, he developed a bedside manner which combined authoritative statement with kindly paternalism. With these inadequate weapons he achieved a great deal for his patients. The modern physician does not have as much time to study patients as people because knowledge is increasing daily and so many new facts have to be learned. Today the need is to resuscitate communication and combine it with modern scientific knowledge.

As scientific knowledge has increased, so also has the layman's knowledge of medicine. For the first time, professional and layman can speak on equal terms and understand each other. The patient with an incurable illness should be informed about it, if that is his or her wish. By the same token knowledge of mortal illness should not be inflicted on the dying if it is not sought by them. The response to direct questions on this subject should always be clear and unequivocal, if that is possible. It is important to know that one's time on earth is limited, because everyone should have the opportunity to make arrangements if they wish it and are capable of doing so.

To provide comfort in the terminal stages of fatal disease physicians must try and understand the problems of the dying patient. They need the opportunity to express themselves and give vent to any particular private anxiety that they may have about the process of death. The physician's function may be to encourage the individual to discuss such problems with others who may have more to offer in terms of philosophic help. The religious person, for example, derives considerable comfort from the pastor, priest, or other representative of his faith.

One of the oldest and most effective remedies of the medical professional is the narcotic drug. Morphine and its associated analogs relieve pain and suffering in any situation. In modern times, its combination with a phenothiazine creates a mixture which has considerable potency in relieving the suffering of terminal illness. Not all deaths are painful, but one should remember that the process may be distressing even if it does not actually involve physical pain. The cocktail of morphine with chlorpromazine may greatly ease the general distress of a dying person. The need for medication can be recognized more by the anxious appearance of the individual than by any specific complaint of pain. There is no terminal illness in which administration of such medication cannot be justified, and there is no reason for withholding it or using inadequate dosage.

The contributions of Saunders and Kubler–Ross have been invaluable. Rather than special units for terminal care, however, perhaps what is needed is for every physician to provide the same standard of personal care for dying patients as that advocated by the two pioneers in this field.

CONTINUING CARE

CASE REPORT 10–5

Mrs. Ziegler, whose age was unknown, had been a nursing home resident for 5 years when she was admitted to a hospital because of unspecified illness. After being accustomed to an environment of little privacy, unattractive food, dubious cleanliness and minimal medical care, she suddenly received "a lot of attention and [was] treated like a relatively important person." Her nursing home bed had been filled by the time she was discharged, so she was sent to a facility in an unfamiliar part of town. Knowing no one and unable to do other than acquiesce in the arrangement, she was forced to adjust to a new routine with strangers. "The feeling is one of hopelessness and despair. She is not physically able to take care of herself. Her Social Security check comes directly to the nursing facility. She has no place else to 'live.' She is a prisoner. [6]"

It is a sad comment on us all that such tales can be told. Ironically, one suspects that the attention given her in the hospital was aimed at swift evaluation, treatment, and discharge. Many hospital administrators make it clear to the geriatrician that elderly nursing home patients should not be allowed to block beds. This is true to an even greater extent in those hospitals which are used for clinical teaching, even though 30%–40% of the patients in general hospitals are likely to be in the upper age groups. Continuing care is time-consuming, difficult to define, and almost impossible to teach didactically. In spite of this, there are certain general principles around which the student and young physician may develop his or her own methods (Table 10–3).

SYMPTOMATIC AID

Attention to detail is of considerable importance. If the chronically disabled person achieves a relatively stable state, the physician may rely on it and see no need for personal intervention. Any symptom that arises will be attributable to the main disability, be it neurologic, locomotor, or cardiorespiratory. The good physician, however, appreciates that stresses occur even in the apparently stable situation, and the more promptly these are faced and resolved, the better. For this reason regular visits can be beneficial.

Most physicians practice from offices and avoid house calls. The elderly invalid who can manage a regular visit to the office should be encouraged to do so. Minor problems can be stored up and brought forth on these occasions, and the extra effort and drama of the visit adds to its benefits. For those who are unable to visit the office without severe physical, emotional, or even financial hardship, regular house calls should be made.

There is no adequate alternative to the direct contact of physician and patient; the telephone should never be used to discuss symptoms, provide reassurance, or order new medication. It is true the patient on many occasions requires only

TABLE 10-3. Principles of Continuing Care

Frequent careful appraisal of problems.

Provision of demonstrable support to patient and family.

Readiness to intervene at a moment's notice.

Goal to maintain independence in community.

Encouragement to participate in and contribute to normal daily living.

reassurance and interest, but the physician must not be miserly with either. There is no offense which is worse than failing to see and examine a patient who calls for help. Unfortunately, when patients are in a continuing care institution with nursing help available, whether skilled or not, this golden rule is often ignored.

In a significant number of cases, minor adjustments to drug dosage and attention to little details of diet, micturition, or bowel function can be of value. Examples would be drinking an extra pint or more of fluid in very hot weather and have an occasional salt tablet or taking diuretic tablets at the time which proves most suitable to avoid being disturbed at night. Frequent contact assists the observant physician to spot the need for such small but useful contributions to patient care.

ORGANIZATION OF SUPPORT

In summarizing the features of a good continuing care method it is appropriate to emphasize the physician's key advisory role regarding any type of support necessary (Table 10–2). For the patient in a continuing care institution many details can be left to the nursing and rehabilitation staff. In the patient's own home, however, support depends on looking for the crucial aids that could convert an impossible situation into a feasible one. The question which should constantly be in the physician's mind is what can be done to help Mrs. X stay in her own home? Is there any form of aid, any device or gadget that would enable Mr. Y to remain in the house which he paid off only a few years ago?

Some aids are readily available but others are not. There is a temptation to say that is not possible when there may be difficulties in obtaining a particular item. The possibility of difficulties should not, however, prevent any efforts being made to obtain it. The way to create confidence in patients is simple; demonstrate an unequivocal interest in their problems and be willing to try to solve them. If the physician can add relief from a persistent discomfort, a profitable relationship which will greatly encourage the patient can be established. All that is needed is interest and time, although neither is readily available.

RESPONSE TO CRISES

The most stable continuing care problem will be punctuated by a series of fortuitous incidents. Prompt attention to such crises is a crucial part of continuing care. Some patients repeatedly cry wolf, while others stoically remain silent with no complaints; others describe as minor symptoms those which require more than a casual thought. The family physician with knowledge and understanding of the patient can play a major role in preventing unnecessary admissions to the hospital. Although this is a reasonable goal in many instances, the physician must not hesitate to call on the hospital for help when a genuine need arises.

CASE REPORT 10–6

Mrs. Cox, aged 81, lived with her bachelor son who was devoted to her and provided excellent care. Mrs. Cox suffered from lipedema (4). She had enormously fat legs which regularly filled with edema fluid and became inflamed and red periodically. In the fall of 1975 she was admitted to the hospital because of a severe bout of cellulitis affecting the right leg. It became obvious that she was moderately demented and easily prone to tears because of a benign depressive condition. She was also incontinent at times. The prospect of a return home seemed remote, and she was transferred to the continuing care hospital. Patient rehabilitation over a period of 2 months resulted in her being able to walk short distances with a walker and becoming continent most of the time. Her son, who was in his late 50s, decided to retire and stay at home to look after his mother. This arrangement has worked very well. Mrs. Cox pays regular weekly visits to the follow-up program at the continuing care hospital. Her condition fluctuates but remains stable within its own limits.

On three occasions crises have arisen. The first two occurred when the son had to have some relief and went on a 2-week holiday. On each occasion the old lady was brought into the hospital immediately, once to a general hospital and once to the continuing care hospital. On the third occasion she quite suddenly went off her legs, was found to have a reddened and inflamed right leg, and was admitted for antibiotic therapy. On each admission extra diuretic and postural treatment was given to minimize her edema. Thanks to this type of hospital support, however, an old lady who seemed destined for permanent hospitalization still lives where she wants to be, at home with her devoted son.

Perhaps, in a sentence, that sums up the whole function of the physician for his elderly patients. Abraham Cowley has expressed it more attractively:

This I know without being told
Tis time to live as I grow old
Tis time short pleasure now to take
Of little life the best to make
And manage nicely the last stake.

REFERENCES

1. Anderson WF, Cowan NR: Consultative health centre for older people. Lancet II:239, 1955
2. Keller W: Care and treatment of the aged and chronically ill. In von Hahn HP (ed): Practical Geriatrics. Basel, S Karger, 1975, pp 42–54
3. Kübler-Ross E: On Death and Dying. New York, MacMillan, 1969
4. Kundu S, Irving ER, Whittingham GE, Paley RG: Lipoedema. Gerontol Clin 9:40–46, 1967
5. Saunders C: The care of the dying. Gerontol Clin 9:385–390, 1967
6. Sniadach R: Care of the elderly. N Engl J Med 296:1070, 1977
7. Williamson J, Stokoe IH, Gray S, Fisher M, Smith A, McGee A, Stevenson E: Old people at home, their unreported needs. Lancet I:1117–1121, 1964

INDEX